# PETER KAY'S
# Diary

# PETER KAY'S Diary

## THE MONTHLY MEMOIR OF
## A BOY FROM BOLTON

HarperCollins*Publishers*

HarperCollins*Publishers*
1 London Bridge Street
London SE1 9GF

www.harpercollins.co.uk

HarperCollins*Publishers*
Macken House, 39/40 Mayor Street Upper
Dublin 1, D01 C9W8, Ireland

First published by HarperCollins*Publishers* 2025

1 3 5 7 9 10 8 6 4 2

A catalogue record of this book is
available from the British Library

HB ISBN 978-0-00-862336-4
PB ISBN 978-0-00-862337-1

Printed and bound in the UK using 100%
renewable electricity at CPI Group (UK) Ltd

This book contains FSC™ certified paper and other controlled
sources to ensure responsible forest management.

For more information visit: www.harpercollins.co.uk/green

For Susan,
Deirdre and R Julie

# Contents

Introduction 1

January 3

February 27

March 51

April 75

May 99

June 123

July 147

August 173

September 197

October 221

November 245

December 271

# Introduction

The idea for this memoir first struck me shortly after I finished writing my last book, *TV – Big Adventures on the Small Screen* (still available in all respectable charity shops. I also sell signed copies in person, every Sunday at a car boot on Fletcher Street in Bolton, alongside a selection of Duracell batteries, Mach 3 blades, and four-litre bottles of suspiciously cheap bleach).

Most people measure life in years, but I thought I'd try something different – why not map my story through the months of the year? A diary of sorts, with each chapter in this book representing a different month, offering a snapshot of my life at that time, filled with dodgy decisions, bizarre plot twists and more than a few laugh-out-loud moments. It's a twelve-month subscription to my memories – cancel any time, no refunds.

My suggestion? Read the book in chronological order. If you've received this as a Christmas gift, maybe hold off until

# INTRODUCTION

January. Or you could take the scenic route – read one chapter each month, letting it keep you company through the year ahead. Think of the excitement (really, Peter?).

You could binge all twelve chapters in one sitting (that'd be too much for me. It took me an entire summer to finish *Ferris Bueller's Day Off*). Maybe you could go completely rogue and read each chapter out of sequence. But why would you do that? That's just weird.

And, of course, there's always the option to read this intro in the shop, then quietly put the book back and buy something else instead. No hard feelings. The choice is yours.

Unlike my previous books, this time I've been given the freedom to abandon strict chronology and follow the unpredictable thread of my memory. It's been a complete joy to write, and hopefully it'll be just as much fun to read.

So, settle in, relax and join me on a leisurely stroll through the seasons of my mind as I celebrate the twelve-month journey of my life.

# January

The month of January is like the Monday morning of the full year ahead!

A big blank sheet of paper ready to be filled. I start a new diary every new year. Only to find it a few months later, shoved in a drawer with less than a week's worth of entries. That just sums up the month. I start with the best intentions but gradually become disinterested. January's the month of broken resolutions and harsh realities, as the softness of Christmas quickly fades and we get back to the old routine. (Cheers Pete, if we didn't have the new year blues, we have now.)

I always find some Christmas decorations get missed. A single piece of Blu Tack or a wisp of tinsel hung in the corner of a wall. I'll get it. It might be up there until April but I'll get it. There's been half a reindeer dangling in my doctor's surgery since before Covid. I've mentioned it to the receptionists twice, but they're clearly not arsed. I tried to reach it once. Stood on a chair in the waiting room, but my arms weren't long enough. I think the other patients thought I'd dropped an E. I'll take a step ladder with me the next time.

January is tranquil after the circus of December festivities. A week earlier I was dancing the Macarena and wolfing down trifle. Now I'm stood in front of a full-length bedroom mirror with tears in my eyes. Why are we so hard on ourselves? It's hardly surprising really with the media lecturing us. Every night there's a new programme on TV advising us of healthy lifestyle changes, comparing diets, basically telling us we're useless and where we're going so terribly wrong. Then they cut to a commercial break featuring mouth-watering close-ups of 'devil' food that can be delivered to your front door in no time at all. What chance do we stand? My mantra is 'throw the towel in Friday and start again Monday' for the next fifty-two weeks.

There's always some new faddy diet (sorry, eating plan). I've a friend who falls for them all. Keto, Dukan, Juice Cleanse, you name it, she'll be on it. Going a full day on two TUC crackers and a cup of beetroot. One year I bumped into her in Debenhams grazing from a bag of raw meat. Stupidly she even buys diet pills online. Lord knows what's in them, but she farts like a mule. She got suspended from Boot Camp for pumping in front of the sergeant.

I can't keep up with her different fitness classes, she goes to so many. Body pump, Boxercise, Hot Yoga, Twerk It! It'd be cheaper for her to see a clinical psychologist.

4

I've had weight issues since childhood. I detested P.E. I wasn't too bad vaulting the horse box in the school gym but I was crap at climbing the ropes. Our ropes were concealed within a tall wooden frame that would cleverly fold out from the wall in the gym/dining hall. Everybody loved climbing the ropes. I never could. I'd just swing on them like a dead weight. Pretending to be Tarzan. That was far more exciting than walking the length of an upturned gym bench. How I was meant to keep fit doing that I'll never know.

Football was always tough. I was always last to get picked. The teams used to argue over who was having me. 'Oh come on! We had him last week, he's shit.' Then they'd always shove me in goal because they said I was fat and nothing could get past me. The irony was I wasn't fat, and everything did get past me because I was shit in goal.

The other team would come screaming towards me chasing the ball, but I'd be too distracted to notice. Playing off-ground tag with Glenn Coombs or trying to chase a stray Alsatian off the pitch. We used to go to the local park for outdoor P.E. lessons as our school never had any outdoor sports facilities.

Over the years I've tried all kinds of fitness regimes. Running, walking, I've had Fitbits, I've downloaded apps. Couch to 5K, though that really should have been rechristened 'Couch', as that's as far as I ever got.

I even tried Hi-Energy aerobics on Monday nights at a Leisure Centre in Bolton. Me and sixty women all rushing to grab a mat from the back of the room as they played 'High Energy' – Evelyn Thomas. Echoing through the sports hall.

Most of the women would leg it straight to the front so they could be close to the male instructors, who I'm convinced were shagging half the class. I'd find myself a space right at the back. God help you if you stood in somebody else's 'spot'. They'd be glaring at you all through the workout. Throwing daggers while you're trying to do burpees.

Whatever the two instructors did we copied, and I mean EVERYTHING, which tickled me no end. If one of the instructors lost his balance and staggered the whole class did it too. As a few thick people couldn't distinguish between aerobic exercises and reality.

Usually, I'd be about thirty seconds behind everybody else. Panting for breath, desperately trying to keep up. Occasionally taking swigs from a two-litre bottle of Tizer (not the healthiest of energy drinks I grant you). Then as soon as the class was over, I'd head straight over the road to Zorba's Chippy for a fishcake and peas. No chips though. I was on a fitness regime after all.

Gym memberships always start in January and I've had my fair share of those too. Each one a spectacular failure. Well, a failure in as much as I stopped going. Always feeling self-conscious, and I've never looked good in Lycra. I joined the David Lloyd Club when it opened in Bolton. Somehow believing that paying for a membership would force commitment. Fat chance (if you'll forgive the pun).

I was given an instructor, Bret. He put me through my paces. Barking clichéd quotes like 'train harder, live longer', 'strong body, strong mind' and 'come on, push through the pain'. The only thing I wanted to push was Bret under a bus. Being 'Peter Kay' didn't help. Being recognised made things worse. People nodding and pointing. Or maybe that's because I had Bret in a headlock.

I went regularly to the David Lloyd at first but after a few months my dedication slowly waned, and I noticed I was spending more time in the David Lloyd café than the gym. It was hard to resist, especially as I had to walk through the café to leave. Plus, they did a reasonably priced buffet-style breakfast where I could help myself to beans. No contest.

They also had a decent indoor pool which I preferred to the fitness machines. I'd swim lengths. Breaststroke (if she'd let me ... sorry, I suddenly found myself in a *Carry On* film there for a second). I'd swim back and forth in the pool. Passing other swimmers. The same faces every time. We'd catch each other's eye and nod, a polite smile. Then I'd pass them again on the next length and I'd find myself fake staring at the ceiling.

Pushing myself, I went a few times a week. More lengths and the same familiar faces. One swimmer got a bit too over familiar. He went from a nod and a polite smile to 'Hello'. Swiftly followed by asking me if I could lend him some money. I shit you not. He swam up to me in the shallow end and said 'You must have a bit of coin, could you lend me ten grand?' Jesus! That was awkward. I didn't know what to say. I mumbled something about being able to smell the buffet-style breakfast and legged it out of the pool. I never went back after that, and I still had six months on my membership left. I couldn't face seeing that cheeky twat again! As if you'd ask that.

Another reason I didn't go back was men chatting to me in the changing room when they were drying themselves. Stark naked. One foot up on a bench, shaking talcum powder around their genitals. 'So, are you up to much, Pete?' 'Well, right now I'm drying my balls if you don't mind.' I mean I'm all for being social but there's a time and place. The talcum powder would blow everywhere. My hair looked like Pip Schofield's by the time I was dressed.

The final straw was when blokes brought their kids into the changing rooms. Incredibly disconcerting. I'd be in the showers washing Vosene out my eyes and see some five-year-old girl staring up at me. Now I appreciate the dad might have had childcare issues, but I felt like a right paedo.

Working and keeping fit is tough. I know I feel better afterwards but despite that, it's hard to stay motivated. When I do a workout session, I can't wait for it to be over.

Trying to act focused and interested but secretly I'm counting the time. Thinking 'surely we've got to be near the end please God'.

My mum used to have a Rosemary Conley Workout video, so I decided to give it a whirl when the house was empty. Rosemary offered two choices, you could follow her, or you could follow Barbara in the corner of the screen who'd had a hysterectomy. I stuck with Barbara. Ten minutes later I was rolling around on the floor in the back room. Pissed through in sweat. Red in the face. Then Rosemary said, 'Now we've warmed up …'. I thought 'WARMED UP?!' I was already frigged.

Years later I tried Davina McCall's workout DVDs. She'd bring one out every Christmas. Though it'd be an insult to give somebody one of those as a present.

Again, I followed Davina's instructions. Contorted on the floor. Using tins of beans as weights. I rolled over too quickly and smacked my head on the nest of tables. I was out cold until British Gas rang my bell.

The last time I went to a gym I stupidly decided to go seriously hardcore. A mate recommended an old-school gym under some derelict arches in Manchester. What a dump. It was like working out in a crack den. The sessions were one on one, and the lad teaching me was ex-Territorial Army. He was only four foot, but Christ he loved to screech and wail at me. I think he thought I was deaf. I knew I was in trouble when he put on the soundtrack to *Rocky IV* at the start of the class. He had me pulling a fucking truck tyre at one point. It was HELL! I was almost in tears. I'm surprised he didn't have me chasing chickens up the backstreet. I HATED it. I used to tell him I needed the toilet, just so I could hide in the bogs sobbing. I lasted two sessions.

Paddy (McGuinness) worked at a leisure centre in Bolton and set me up a fitness programme in the gym. This was a few years ago before we made *Phoenix Nights*. He used to let me in backwards through the fire door, so I didn't have to pay. The workouts were mainly for local pensioners. So, there was no pressure, and we'd have a laugh with the OAPs. After a session,

Paddy and me would go in the steam room with some of the old blokes. One bloke, Stan, loved his food. He was always recommending places to eat, and he'd describe them with such passion, managing to make a mixed grill sound like a banquet.

'It was manna from heaven. I had steak (he motioned how thick with the width of his fingers), pork, liver, kidney, sausages, liver, chicken (pronounced sh'icken), lamb, liver (I didn't have the heart to mention he'd already said liver twice). A tureen of chips this high (motioned with his hands again) – £6.50 the lot. I tell you I've never seen food like it in my life. Connie couldn't finish hers. It's a smashin' little place, facing the prison in Preston.'

By the way, if you're a fan of *Max & Paddy's Road to Nowhere*, sections of that conversation with Stan will be familiar. Paddy and myself wrote it into a scene where Paddy is describing a mixed grill to Max. It's just before they knock down and kill a cow with their motorhome.

One evening after we'd finished at the gym, I went to get my car and noticed a huge dent on my front wing. Orange paint scraped right across it. I knew straight away who the culprit was. It had to be the Ring 'n' Ride reversing in my street. If you're not familiar with Ring 'n' Ride it was a mobile brothel service in Bolton. I jest, it's a transport service for the elderly. Ferrying them wherever they need to go, like bingo or the crem. But that's usually just one way.

Anyway, the Ring 'n' Ride bus would often pick up Mary Rock who lived across the road. Ring 'n' Rides were painted orange, so I didn't have to be Hercule fecking Poirot to work out who'd done the damage. I was furious. This was my first car, that I've saved up for years to buy.

Paddy was parked outside the leisure centre in his car. I wanted to show him the dent. He'd definitely know somebody who could get it knocked out.

'Have you got a minute? I want to show you something,' I said, pulling alongside his car.

'Yeah, no bother, just pull up in front, I'm just nipping back in, I've forgotten my wallet.'

Paddy opened his car door. So I drove forward, clipped his driver's side door and ripped it off.

Well, his door didn't immediately fall off. It kind of folded back on itself then it just hung in mid-air.

There was then a long silence while we both tried to process what had happened.

Slowly we got out of our cars. Well, Paddy didn't really have a door, so he just easily stepped out of his.

We stared at the carnage. The scraping and crunching sound still ringing in my ears.

Paddy said, 'So what did you want to show me?'

'Erm … I wanted to show you this dent in the side of my car.'

THEN Paddy's car door fell off.

You couldn't have timed it better. Now Paddy and I are good friends. We have been all our lives so fortunately tempers weren't raised. In fact, completely the opposite; we both started to laugh. There was no disputing the culprit was myself, and Paddy would have to claim off my insurance. Which I'd only had in place a few months.

I already had a few prangs and bumps (I wasn't a very good driver, it'd taken six years, four instructors and five tests to pass). I'd crushed my tow bar reversing into a breeze block behind the butchers. I'd also had the dent in my wing from the Ring 'n' Ride bus reversing. Paddy suggested I stick all the damage on the same insurance claim and get them all fixed. That didn't seem like a bad idea. So, I rang my insurance company. They told me to head down to a local car showroom where a bloke would film the damage on my car as part of the claim. Paddy came with me. The fella came out, camcorder in his hand, and started to film. Then Paddy piped up (love that expression), 'Hey, there's some more back here, bud.' The man walked round to the back of my car and Paddy pointed at the tow bar. Suspiciously the fella said, 'Same crash?' Paddy nudged me and I nodded 'Yes'.

'But it's rusted,' he said, a tad suspiciously.

He did have a point.

'There's another bang here, mate,' said Paddy, showing him the Ring 'n' Ride bang.

'Same crash??' he said again, even more suspiciously.

Sheepishly I nodded.

Well, that's when my worry started to build. That night I was talking to a mate who happened to work for an insurance company. He told me to be 'very careful. You can get fucked for lying about stuff like that.' Now I was on my arse. Finally, after all these years I'd got my own car and now I was about to get banned for life.

Fuelled with anxiety I drove back to the leisure centre. I needed to draw a diagram of the accident on my insurance claim form. But how could I convince them that all this damage had happened at the same time? I was in a right panic trying to suss things out. Maybe I could have done an erratic three-point turn and somehow reversed into the wall, thus crushing my tow bar. Then perhaps I could have pulled forward and caught my front wing on an adjacent bollard that happened to be outside the gym – that might explain the Ring 'n' Ride dent.

Fretting, I decided to try out my hypothetical theory. Reversing my car up onto the pavement. Over-revving as I mounted the kerb. People looking around puzzled by the noise, which only made me even more self-conscious.

With my car parked halfway up the pavement, I sketched out my 'alleged' theory with a pencil on the claim form on my bonnet. 'Could this work?' By now I was hyperventilating with fear. 'Surely if I'd hit the bollard when I reversed, I would have damaged my other front wing.' So, in a complete frenzy I began kicking in my other front wing. Booting it with my foot right outside the leisure centre. Boom, boom, boom. People looking around as I pounded my car with my foot. Who was this maniac?

Then I stopped mid-kick. 'Shit!' I suddenly remembered that bloke had already filmed the damage on my car that morning with his camcorder. What a dick. So now I'd made a bigger mess of my car, which was eventually written off as the damage was that bad.

Paddy, on the other hand, got a brand-new car and gave his old one to his dad who used it when he set up his own private detective business. I'm not joking. 'Joe McGuinness Private Eye'. He even took an advert out in the yellow pages. 'Missing Persons? Lost Pets? Husband having an affair? Call Joe Mac, discreet and professional.' He had a pair of binoculars and a torch.

Years ago, when I was on one of my 'many' diet regimes, I went to watch *The Green Mile* at the cinema. It's a long film and halfway through I started to get hunger pangs for a hot dog. I've no idea why or how hot dogs are synonymous with cinemas, but I crave one every time I go. It's the smell that wafts through the foyer.

Hurrying to get back to the film, I stuffed a chunk of hot dog in my mouth. I was hasty for two reasons. Firstly, I'd told Susan I was only nipping to the toilet (Susan knows I never shit in a public toilet, so it had to be a wee). And secondly, because anybody who struggles with food guilt knows the faster you eat the less remorse you have. It's like an out-of-body experience: 'What? *I* ate a hot dog?' Unfortunately, over the years I've become an expert in food guilt. Disposing of all evidence. Hiding chocolate bar wrappers down at the bottom of the bin so nobody can see it.

My mum literally used to hide the biscuits from me. She'd put them in the strangest places. It was like a game. 'Find the

Biscuits'. But as we lived in a terraced house, they were always easy to find. Friends would call, and I'd make them a brew. Then casually reach inside the tumble dryer for a packet of custard creams, like it was normal. The smartest place she ever hid them was the bloody biscuit barrel. I couldn't find them for days.

Anyway, so I was in the cinema shovelling down this hot dog when I happened to catch a glimpse of my reflection in the glass frame of a film poster (I think it was *Babe: Pig in The City* – appropriate). I felt thoroughly ashamed. Staring at myself with half a jumbo hot dog hanging out my mouth. My face smeared in tomato sauce. 'What are you doing, Peter? What have you become? You're better than this.' Immediately I pulled the hot dog from my mouth and threw it in the nearest bin. Then just as it was about to hit the bin-liner I caught it and shoved the remains down my throat. Well, it cost a fortune. I'd make a fresh start on Monday.

I sprinted back into *The Green Mile*. We were sat right at the back; it was a Saturday night and it was packed. Up the steps, two at a time, head bowed allowing maximum viewing for my fellow cinema-goers. Settling back in my seat I leaned over to Susan and whispered, 'What have I missed?' Instantly she replied, 'You've had a hot dog.' 'WHAT?! I have not,' I whispered incredulously.

'I can smell it on your breath,' she said.

My brain went into overdrive. 'Well, that's where you're wrong. If you must know I bumped into a mate of mine in the foyer, Jason Glazier, he had a hot dog and he let me have a bite, so there.' Like I was six.

Jason Glazier. Where in God's name had I plucked that name from? I hadn't seen him since he got suspended for shooting a pigeon with an air rifle and left it on the steps of the convent. In a moment of fight or flight, my brain spat Jason Glazier out of my memory banks and suddenly he was offering me a bite of his hot dog in Cineworld. I'm sure Jason would have wished that to be true, but he was still serving four years for GBH. He was an ex-altar boy too. They're the worst.

I've always relished food as far back as I can remember. It encompasses happiness. My mum used to wheel me around Bolton town centre with a meat pie on my knee and said I was completely happy (I just wished she'd had a pram instead of a wheelbarrow). Those meat pies were gorgeous. They sold them in the Market Hall at a shop coincidentally called Kay's Pies. I wish we *had* been related because I'd still be eating them now. With discount.

The pleasure didn't stop there. When I was at primary school my mum used to drop off a pie and cake with the canteen staff so I could have it for my dinner. I'm not kidding. She knew some of the dinner ladies, so they'd keep it warm for me. You should have seen the other kids' faces. They were struggling to eat turkey twizzlers and semolina. While I was gorging steak pie and a chocolate éclair.

It's not as though I didn't like school dinners either. I didn't mind them. Especially the desserts. It always seemed to be something with custard. In infants, we used to have servers.

Usually, a prefect from the top class would bring our dinners as we were too young.

I'll never forget sitting around a circular table with some other children and as usual trying to entertain. Banging my fists on the table, singing 'Why are we waiting' when our server, Rachel Fox, put down my dessert bowl. My fist caught the edge of the bowl which sent it flipping up in the air, straight onto her school jumper. Splattering it with jam roly-poly and custard. Rachel, if you're reading this I know you'll remember this moment. Once again, please accept my apologies. It was an accident, but I appreciate that if I hadn't been acting the clown it would never have happened. Saying that, I was just following my vocation.

> *'School dinners, concrete chips*
> *Soggy semolina, Soggy semolina*
> *I feel sick, toilet quick*
> *It's too late, I done it on my plate'*
> William Shakespeare, 1598

There was the occasional school dinner I wasn't partial to. Cold haddock springs to mind. Sago and Tapioca pudding, blurrgh, but overall (and thanks to my mum's weekly pie shop delivery) I never suffered from empty plate syndrome. That and the fact that you were never allowed to throw away any food at our primary school.

The head nun had a very short temper and always stunk of booze, which is why we nicknamed her 'Ale Mary'. She'd loiter at the front of the canteen, stood behind two huge plastic slop bins. This formidable tiny woman, always in black and white, would inspect everybody's plate as they skulked towards her. If she saw even the tiniest morsel of food she'd shoo you back to your table with her bony finger. Which was completely barbaric. She'd mumble something about 'the starving children of Biafra' (incidentally Biafra later changed to Ethiopia. And apparently, it's High Wycombe these days. A shocking state of affairs). So thanks to Ale Mary there was a permanent queue of children sobbing and retching in our school canteen.

Dinners went up a gear when I went to my secondary school – Mount St Joseph (which the nuns often did). Now we finally had some choice. It was weird having to pay for my dinners. In primary school, we'd all bring our dinner money in on Monday and give it to Mrs Quinn who'd scoot around the classrooms and collect the cash in her Quality Street tin. Now at secondary school, I had to get used to carrying cash. The average school meal would cost about 50p (which seems really cheap now). That's mains, pudding, and a drink too.

Being entrepreneurial (and a pig) I devised a cunning plan. I'd buy a meal, eat it, then tell the nice Irish lady on the tills that I'd given her a pound, but she'd only given me change from 50p. She'd apologise, give me another 50p in change and I'd go and get another dinner. I feel great shame just confessing this. But I'm trying to convey to you my love of food. It's the highlight of my day. Especially when I was at school. Food stopped me from going insane with boredom. As I said, I didn't mind school dinners. Which basically consisted of everything with chips. Chicken and chips. Pie and chips. Pizza and chips. On Fridays, it was fish and chips. It's just a shame Jamie Oliver stuck his nose in and ruined everything.

Sometimes I'd take a packed lunch and STILL have a cooked dinner. My mum would pack a lunch of chicken paste butties, a peach melba yoghurt (Blurrgh!) and a Blue Riband chocolate bar, all snugly packed into my Karate Kid lunch box. Other kids preferred a tuck shop dinner. Which was usually a Wham Bar or Highland Toffee and a bag of cheesy corn puffs. Washed down with a carton of pop. Which for some bizarre reason kids seemed to enjoy drinking upside down, biting a hole through the bottom of the carton. No wonder half of the lads I went to school with ended up in prison. They'd down all that, and be smacked off their tits all afternoon. Swinging off the light fittings like chimps.

As I got older, I started to venture 'home' for my dinner as I only lived ten minutes down the road. Some of my mates would join me and we'd frequent Grease's, a chippy local to school. We christened it Grease's on account of the amount of their greasy food, but that never bothered me. I'd get a 'mix'. Half a fish, half chips and half a portion of peas for 75p. Bloody bargain.

You could take away or eat in. When I say eat in, please don't be picturing a diner or anything that sophisticated. Eating in at Grease's involved parting some coloured beads that hung from a doorway behind the counter. Then entering the back room of a terraced house come chip shop. Where basically, you'd sit at the family table eating your 'mix' while the telly was on. It felt weird and intrusive, so I didn't do it. Much.

As Grease's was *my* local chip shop my dad used to send me for our Friday chippy tea and force me to take a bowl (or a basin). Which embarrassed the hell out of me in my cool teenage years, but my dad insisted as it meant he'd get some extra gravy.

He wasn't wrong. I would undoubtedly get more than if I got the same meal in a styrofoam tray. There was a method to his madness.

My dad was a steak and kidney pudding man. Which is now a dwindling northern delicacy. Often referred to locally as 'a babby's yed' as it's supposed to resemble a baby's head. A bit macabre in my opinion but who am I to quibble with parochial semantics?

I was always reluctant to take a basin. I felt like a right nelly. Standing in the queue holding a smoky-coloured Pyrex bowl (the same one for years). Fortunately, Eileen who served in the chip shop would wail down the queue 'Anybody need their basins warming?' My humiliation accentuated as I blushingly handed her my bowl. Then Eileen would stash it in the heated glass cabinet alongside the cooked fish, pies, sausages and scallops. (I'm salivating just writing this.)

I've just realised that a lot of this rhetoric about peas and gravy probably won't mean much to any southern readers. As many a chip shop 'darn sarth' rarely sells anything moist. Such a shame. If you're ever up in Lancashire you must try a steak and kidney pudding with gravy but think on, you are not allowed to take a bowl (or basin) any more as that quintessential custom has sadly fallen foul of health and safety bods.

Even more embarrassing was when my dad made me take our old newspapers as 'the chip shop will be glad of them'. I didn't mind that too much as Grease's were grateful for them and would often reward me with an extra portion of chips.

Chips served in newspaper seems alien now. It would be common practice years ago and also handy as you could eat your chips and read the news. Albeit from a few weeks ago. Sometimes you'd slop gravy over some dolly-bird's knockers on page 3. (Did I just write that?!)

Hang on! They don't still do topless women on page 3, do they? Just wait while I google it … (SLIGHT PAUSE FOR T'INTERNET SEARCH) … No, they stopped it a few years ago. Still too late in my opinion. Turning to page 3 in a newspaper could be very embarrassing, especially if you were reading a story on page 3 and somebody saw you. 'Oh, aye, you dirty perv!'

I'm not woke in any way, shape or form but there was a time in British society when opening a newspaper and seeing a topless woman would set you up for the day. I remember my dad used to scribble round her breasts with a biro and draw a pair of glasses on her. Either that or black a few of her teeth out. Defacing a newspaper was one of the joys of childhood. I've lost count of how many times I drew a tash on Margaret Thatcher.

Where was I? Oh, yes, I was stood in the chippy queue. Which could be very long on a Friday night. Fish on Friday again. It's still the case today. Funny that we used to do a family big shop every Friday (it's the law) and then go to the chippy for tea. I never understood that. We'd spend our weekly budget on food, then we'd go to the chippy. Not that I complained, ever.

Eileen served. Cecil stoked. And neither crossed over. Folk could be queuing out the door and Cecil would never serve. He wouldn't even turn around. He'd just make small talk via his reflection in the mirror as he stoked the fryer when Eileen had nipped in the back for a wee or a quick fag – or both.

Cecil would reassure the customers, 'She won't be long now.' Everybody would wait, then Cecil would shout 'EILEEN SHOP'.

Awkwardly time would pass. More customers would gather in the queue. 'EILEEN SHOP' Cecil would wail as tensions rose. But there was still no sign of Eileen. Now folk were queuing back to Greta's wool shop three doors down.

Cecil wore crisp white overalls. Embroidered with the letters 'FFF' on his breast pocket. Fish Friars Federation. That's why he didn't give a toss about serving any customers. He was well above that. In his mind, he couldn't turn around and look them in the eye, even if he wanted to. 'EILEEN SHOP, NOW! FOR THE LOVE OF CHRIST ...' I saw the veins pop on Cecil's neck.

Also, Grease's ONLY served BRITISH food. Reinforced visually by the Union Jack Cecil had painted into the shop sign. God help a customer if they unwittingly asked him for a spring roll or some sweet and sour chicken. Cecil would blow a gasket. 'We only serve British food. None of that foreign muck.' Gesturing to his Union Jack sign.

He once commented to a regular when I was stood in the queue '… you're telling me those Chinese chippies make ALL their money just through fish and chips? Bollocks. There's something else going on, I'm telling you.'

'Like what?'

'It'll be a front for Triads.'

The reason our local Chinese chip shop made more money than Grease's was because it opened six days a week from noon to 10pm. Cecil and Eileen only opened three dinner-times and on a Friday night; they were shut bank holidays. Took Christmas off. And had a fortnight in Fuengirola twice a year.

'EILEEN SHOP! SUFFERING JESUS WOMAN HAVE YOU FALLEN DOWN THAT TOILET?'

With that Eileen came bursting through the full-length beads. Straightening her hair net and stinking of B&H. 'Right, cock, what you 'avin'?'

Our local Chinese chip shop was called The Wing-Wah, but we got banned from calling in during our school dinner because Simon Loftus kept hiding things. He leaned over the counter, lifted the vinegar bottle, and balanced it on top of the shop door frame. Then he asked Mrs Wah if he could have 'plenty of vinegar' but she couldn't find it. Flummoxed, she searched around the counter. Even shouted to her husband in Chinese, but the vinegar was missing. Then she spotted it on top of the door frame and lost her mind. Wailing in her mother tongue as she chased us out of the shop. Then she stuck her Closed sign up … and her middle finger.

Inevitably we'd always be late back to school and get told off.

'Oh, nice of you to join us, Mr Kay and co. Why are you late?'

A good way of getting out of a bollocking was to give a long-winded excuse. I was really good at those. 'Well, Sister, what happened was, I go home for my dinner as you know and this morning my mum said she was going to leave a pie in the oven for me but when I got home I realised that I didn't have my key and my mum had gone to work. I was locked out and the pie was in the oven so I had no choice but to go down to the supermarket where my mum works so I could borrow her key, so I could go back home and get the pie out before it burned the house down. So, I got back home and …'

'Oh, just sit down, Kay,' she'd say, losing the will to live. It never failed.

Another trick we used to use was to fart. They'd be harping on about rules, giving you a tongue-lashing that lasted ages, so I came up with the idea of us all farting. The more of you the better. So, as she chunnered on we'd all be red in the face trying to break 'group' wind. Eventually, we'd let rip and the smell would reach her sanctimonious nostrils. Then with tears in her eyes, she'd abruptly end her lecture and let us all go.

Hey, I may have been crap academically, but I was clever at these kinds of strategies. The farting trick never failed. Except for the time Shaun Lever pushed too hard and followed through. 'Who's dropped their back?' winced Sister Matic. We all pointed at Shaun. 'My God, boy, you need raking out.' We were all swiftly bundled out of the classroom and off to our next lesson. I can still taste that smell to this day.

# February

Half-arsed birds can be heard at dawn, struggling to chirp. They're not ready yet for any full operettas. Each morning the light stretches a fraction further but we're still a far cry from deepest summer and a 5am sunrise.

The older I've become the more oppressed I feel by winter. I realise I could go and live in Australia or somewhere similar, but ironically, I'd then miss the winter. I'd never miss snow. That pisses me right off. Though not as much as how the British media reacts to it. Each year you'd think it was the first time snow had EVER fallen. How can snow STILL be headline news? Telling us that everything has ground to a halt. It's February FFS. What did we expect?

My nan used to say, 'How do they go on in Russia? It snows all the time over there and they never shut shop.' Mind you, she did slip when she was gritting her path and broke her wrist. She rang me in a right panic. I told her to quickly put some ice on it until I got there.

'My path?'

'No, your wrist.'

'I've not got any ice, Peter.'

'Have you got any frozen peas?'

'Hold on,' she said. I could hear her shuffling things around in her kitchen.

She came back to the phone.

'No, I've only got tinned peas.'

It certainly doesn't snow like it used to. I remember it being thick and heavy. Lasting for weeks. Those big dirty grey icebergs gathered by the side of the main roads. They looked surreal. Pedestrians walking past them like they were normal.

Children love snow. Two reasons mainly. First, it's giddy to dash outside and play in it. However, they're back inside after twenty minutes. Their gloves soaking wet, their hands freezing. I always have a nice bath ready to warm them up. Second, they're praying the schools might shut. That rarely ever happens, especially in Bolton. Snow just doesn't seem to stick these days. Probably climate change. I bought two boxes of inflatable sledges in a Black Friday sale. That was seven years ago, and they've still never been blown up.

I've lost the joy of snow. A factor of age no doubt. I think the only saving grace when it snows is everything looks beautiful. You could have a right dump of a garden but when it snows it suddenly looks like a scene from Narnia. I filmed in the snow once, when I made a Christmas music video for a character I once played called Geraldine McQueen. But that was fake snow, supplied by a company called Snow Business – with their tagline 'There's no business like …' written down the side of their van.

I've filmed in real snow and I've also filmed in February in snow. Well, I travelled to filming in the snow for a cameo for the series *Inside No. 9* with Steve Pemberton and Reece Shearsmith. I've known Reece for many years, and he's played a few characters in projects I've made. So, when he asked me if I'd make a brief appearance, I couldn't really say no. Though with hindsight I wish I had.

The episode was filmed in London, as I said it was snowing heavily, and my train was delayed for a few hours because snow had disrupted travel. 'I don't know how they go in Russia,' I said to the train inspector. London was frozen. Fortunately, the scene I was filming was inside, well I say fortunately but it was so bloody cold we may as well have been filming outside. It was a derelict building doubling as an art installation where a series of gruesome murders was about to take place. In the story, you understand, not in real life.

My part was an assistant carer, who was escorting a patient on opening night. I was approached by a mysterious figure, who the viewers couldn't see. Then as I was conversing the mysterious figure pushed me backwards onto one of the exhibits. It was a throne-like chair with sharp spikes in the seat of it. I was fatally impaled, and my paper plate of canapes fell to the floor while I ad-libbed the line 'Oh, I've dropped my Ritz.' In a slightly camp voice. Roll the opening credits. Job done, back on the next train home … or so I thought.

I started to say my goodbyes and take off my costume but was told there was more to film. Apparently, my character's dead body would be seen lying on the floor for the rest of the scene. 'Bloody hell, can you not use somebody else?' Unfortunately not, as there could be an issue with 'continuity'.

So not only did I have to stay, I also had to lie in a pool of prop blood. This horrible dark red sticky stuff made from a syrup-like substance. It took the rest of the day to film, the rest of the cast performing their lines as I lay freezing in this vile liquid that slowly soaked through my costume and into my underpants.

Occasionally I moaned. Glancing up at Reece.

'You said a brief cameo on the phone. I'd be straight in and out, you said.'

If lying in that red gunk wasn't bad enough, Felicity Kendal, who was also in the episode playing a blind woman, kept whacking me with her white stick every time she said a line. I was starting to lose it. 'If she hits me one more time with that stick, I'll shove it up her arse. Sideways.'

Finally, the scene was complete, but time had run over so much that I was now in a rush for my last train. Quickly I asked a lady in the make-up department where I could get a shower. 'Shower?' she said awkwardly, 'We've no showers … er … I've got wet wipes.' Bloody wet wipes!!

With little choice, I had to pull my clothes on over this sticky goo which had now congealed across my body. The production company had booked me a taxi bike (which is basically a motorbike that gives you a backy). They're popular in London because of the traffic. Cold and sticky from the fake blood, I held on to this rider for dear life as he sped me through the bitterly cold snow to Euston station. I was in a filthy mood as I ambled down the platform looking like I'd shit my pants. I had to throw my clothes in the bin when I got home, they were all stained red and ruined and my legs were pink for a week.

Speaking of red and pink, February is the month of love (see what I did?) when we celebrate Valentine's Day. We also commemorate pancake Tuesday (and I love a pancake). Even typing the word pancake has sent my hunger pangs into overdrive. Hold on, I'm going to go and make some. I won't be long ...

*Fifteen-minute gap, twenty with the washing up.*

Now they were a treat, and I've still got some batter left over for more later. No Nutella though so I had to melt down a Twirl I found in the back of the cupboard.

My mum used to make a few sneaky pancakes on Sunday afternoons with left-over batter from the Yorkshire pudding mix. They were gorgeous. I'd look forward to her shouting me when they were ready. I always seemed to be watching *Space: 1999* for some reason (funny that 1999 came and went. And there was never a spaceship in sight).

We used to visit the Dutch Pancake House in Manchester. They served enormous pancakes. You could have savoury with ham or cheese or sweet ones with strawberries, ice cream and chocolate. Sadly, it's shut down now. Though I do think it only really did well in February.

In my early days doing stand-up, I got a bizarre booking hosting a pancake race for Asda staff. All I had to do was commentate on the races. It was in the reception area of their head office in Leeds and was just supposed to be a bit of fun over lunchtime, but they were all really competitive. Two duty managers crashed into one another running with their frying pans. They both ended up in A&E when they tumbled over the finish line and went arse first through a fire door. Anyway, I got £250 and ate my own body weight in pancakes.

Regarding Valentine's Day, it's a right old swizz. But the pressure's on to show your affection, otherwise you can look like a right heartless pig. Just a little something, flowers (but they always shoot up in price. Why not procure your flowers from a roadside tribute like I do? Though I much prefer a headstone down the cemetery, as you don't have to stop on a busy main road with your hazards on … I'm joking of course).

Susan and I usually have those M&S dine-in for two meals. We know how to push the boat out. They did camembert for starters (sadly no seashells this year). Salmon en croute for mains with green veg and a couple of love heart macaroons for dessert. We could go out for a meal, but it's Valentine's Day, it'll be packed everywhere and feels like a rip-off.

I remember the first time we ever went for a Valentine's meal at some fancy restaurant in Manchester. That baffled me. A waiter stood behind me as I tried to turn the page in the menu, but couldn't, as it was just one single page, so not much choice. I treated myself to steak, but when it arrived I couldn't find it on my plate. It turned out to be hidden under some leaves. I'd never seen anything like it. I thought the chef had left the back door open and they must have blown in. The waiter assured me it was garnish, but I wasn't convinced. We had the tiniest portions. I'm sure Nouvelle Cuisine is French for 'fuck all'.

The next year we plumbed for a takeout from the Chinese and went to the video shop (I knew how to spoil a lady). We always struggled to agree on what film to get. Susan always wanted a rom-com, while I wanted some action (and a video). We were ages in Blockbuster and our chicken in black bean was lukewarm by the time we got back to my mum's.

The thought of going to a video shop seems archaic, now that we can stream hundreds of films from our homes, or our phones even. To think we used to have to return video tapes by 7pm the next day or you'd get fined. If you forgot to rewind it, you'd get another fine. Ridiculous.

Once I returned one of our blank video tapes by mistake. The girl from the video shop rang to say I'd dropped off a tape labelled 'Mum's Video – Do Not Use'. When it should have been *Speed 2*.

My local video shop was the centre of my universe growing up. I'd spend hours in there bothering Asif, the owner, about the latest videos coming out and could I bagsy any old film posters. I would spend hours hanging them in my tiny, terraced bedroom. Other kids had posters of football and pop music. I had *The Cannonball Run 2* and *Highlander* (now that's a double bill to die for).

I also lived for pirating. And I don't mean running around with a sword and an eye patch. I mean pirating videos. I just hope I don't get prosecuted all these years later. It's like that anti-video piracy advert you'd often see before the film started. The voiceover used to say, 'Would you steal a car?' Well, no I wouldn't, but I would pirate copies of *Crocodile Dundee 1 & 2* onto a four-hour tape.

I'd ask Kathleen over the road if I could borrow her video recorder for a few hours (a few days, more like). Then I'd set about trying to copy everything my pocket money would allow. I was a member of a few video shops around Bolton, so I'd cycle across town hiring videos for pirating.

Select-a-video (dreadful title), Global Video, Variety Video, Rentertainment (another bad one). I'd have the two video recorders copying through the night. I'd even set my alarm, stagger downstairs, and dozily change tapes so I could record another couple of films. I know it was illegal, but it felt joyous, and I was hardly masterminding an organised crime ring. I never hired any of them out. They were all for my own collection. Your honour.

I was never in Jackie Chatterjee's league. She had a massive collection of pirate videos. My mum worked with Jackie down at our local supermarket. You wouldn't think to look at her but this unremarkable lady, in her mid-sixties, was the Pablo Escobar of pirating in our neighbourhood. She even carried a typewritten list in her handbag of all the videos you could hire for 75p a week. Holy Moly! Well, I was ringing Jackie's doorbell morning, noon and night. Blowing my pocket money on some of the weirdest double bills I've ever come across. *Carrie* and *The Goonies*, *My Left Foot* and *Beetlejuice* and how could I forget my all-time favourite, *Honey, I Shrunk the Kids* and *Schindler's List*. What the hell was Jackie thinking?

Over the years I built up quite a collection and I was extremely proud of it too. I'd spend hours making bespoke labels for the video tapes. Painstakingly drawing each and every letter in felt tip. Sometimes I'd cut individual letters out of my mum's magazines before she'd even had a chance to read them. She'd go to the toilet and shout, 'Peter, will you stop cutting holes in my *My Weekly*.' I've always thought I'd be a dab hand at ransom notes.

Please note that all the above took place before I discovered my penis.

As you've probably gathered, videos were a big obsession of mine. Every Thursday night I'd listen to a film show on my local radio station Piccadilly 261. It was hosted by Jim 'the video funster' Murray. I'm sure he christened himself that.

He'd review the latest video releases and host a weekly film quiz where you could also win videos. I used to ring in every week but was never successful. Then one week I managed to get through to the switchboard and somebody answered the phone. I actually got on the air and spoke to Jim 'the video funster' Murray (I was very nervous). Answering correctly, I won a copy of the film *Mask* (though not the hit Jim Carrey comedy, that other film called *Mask* starring Cher and the elephant man on a motorbike). Now I know why I'd got through to the switchboard so easily. Nobody else wanted to win that film.

I'd never won anything before (though I'd have preferred the previous week's prize, a copy of *Beverly Hills Cop*). Speaking to Jim 'the video funster' Murray was a thrill. Off the air, he asked if I'd like to come into the station the following week and review a new video release. Would I? Oh my God yes, yes, and yes again. Plus, it'd be pre-recorded in the afternoon, so I'd get to miss a bit of school too. Wow! I'd definitely hit the big time.

Not only did my mum and dad let me have the afternoon off, but they also came with me to Manchester. Well, I say they came with me, they escorted me on the bus as I was only thirteen. Going to Piccadilly Radio was a huge deal. I'd grown up listening to the station. I even had a 261-radio station sticker proudly displayed in my bedroom window. I listened to all the DJs on the station and was surprised to see giant black-and-white images of them paraded on the outside of the station building. It was quite a shock, as none of the DJs looked anything like they sounded.

Jim 'the funster' Murray met us in reception. He also looked nothing like he sounded. Well-fed, sporting a peroxide perm and glasses (each frame a different colour). He was the essence of the word funster and proved to be a real live-wire. I think they call it ADHD now. He never stopped talking. I'm sure if he was hooked up to a turbine, he could easily have powered a small village in Shropshire.

He escorted the three of us through to an office room with a TV and video on a stand. The lights were dimmed and we sat through a new film called *Oxford Blues* (no, I'd never heard of it either). It was supposedly a comedy about the Oxford boat race with Rob Lowe and Ally Sheedy from the Brat Pack films (it's got 5.4 on IMDb, I've just looked it up).

I say 'we' watched it because Jim 'the funster' Murray asked my mum and dad if they'd like to stay and watch it too. I was a bit gutted as I wanted to watch it on my own. Mind you, my mum and dad weren't so chuffed either as they'd fancied a mooch around the shops and my dad around the pubs. But I think they felt obliged when they were put on the spot.

*Oxford Blues* turned out to be 'a right load of old shit' (well that's what my dad said on the train home). He wasn't wrong. When the credits rolled, Jim 'the funster' Murray shoved a microphone in front of my mouth and asked what I thought of the film. All I could think to say was 'It was kind of good how they made boat racing interesting.' I was no Barry Norman. I just wished it could've been something good, like *Rambo* or *A Nightmare on Elm Street*. (Well, probably because I wouldn't have been old enough to watch them.)

Struggling for a decent vox pop, Jim 'the funster' shoved his mic in my mum's direction. Surprised, she coyly spoke in her soft northern Irish accent, 'Oh, it wasn't my cup of tea.' Well, Jim must have liked that soundbite as he edited it into his show. Excited, we all gathered around the radio in the back room. My Bolton accent sounded really broad and then when my mum's one-line review made it into the show we all laughed a lot. She was mortified but we played that recording to everyone who called around for the rest of the year.

Even though *Oxford Blues* turned out to be crap, the whole experience was brilliant. The only thing that ruined it was getting a bollocking the next day at school. In my giddiness, I thought it'd be funny to write my reason for absence as 'bomb-scare' in the school signing-out book. Our headmistress Sister Sledge wasn't amused. No sense of humour. Nun

Along with flowers, chocolates are always a stereotypical winner when it comes to Valentine's gifts (sorry, I drifted off my earlier point). My wife Susan likes Lindt, and now hopefully I'll get a shitload sent to me when they read this. Mind you, I think their adverts are a bit of a lie. They show a chocolatier, delicately piping individual chocolates, sporting a chef's white hat. I mean, as if. They'd never have enough if he was making them at that speed. They should show what really goes on, a conveyor belt endlessly churning out millions of Lindt. Ah well, there goes my free Lindt chocolates. If I worked at the Lindt factory, I'd be stuffing my face all day. I wonder if the staff get freebies. They must have odd-shaped balls. The chocolate, not the staff. (That wasn't very funny at all.)

When I worked at Franny Lee's factory packing toilet rolls, I used to get freebies every fortnight. The staff would be given a pack filled with products the company made. Toilet rolls, kitchen rolls, cling film and foil. My mum was well chuffed, and we had enough foil and cling film to sink a ship. The management offered the free pack in an effort to stop staff from stealing but it never worked, and I'd still occasionally see women shoving toilet rolls down their knickers as they headed home at the end of a shift.

When I worked down the cash and carry, lads would take boxes of 'rubbish' around the back and tip them in a skip. But hidden underneath the 'rubbish' was contraband. A box of Mars bars, a pack of Gillette razors, a Sara Lee Black Forest gateau. They'd finish work, then later at night when it was quiet, they'd cycle back to the cash and carry and retrieve the contraband out of the skip. I'll never forget wading through rotting fruit and veg for a pack of Scotch video tapes.

Where was I? Valentine's. You know I never got a single Valentine's card when I was growing up. Aw, I hear you cry. I made a few for my mum at primary school (alright Oedipus) but that was more of an exercise in craft. Involving red tissue paper, glitter and lots of pink crayoning. My mum acted all surprised. They wouldn't even stand up on the mantelpiece.

The first Valentine's card I ever bought was for a girl in the first year of secondary school (that's year seven for anyone born after the fall of the Berlin Wall). I walked for miles to a card shop where nobody might see me buy it. I snuck the card up to my bedroom, sitting for ages, contemplating what verse to compose:

# FEBRUARY

*'Will you be my valentine? Think about it.*
*If you will that's great, if not, who gives a shit.'*

I'm kidding, I never wrote that. I do remember what I did write but I'm far too embarrassed to tell you. What I also remember is accidentally putting the card in the wrong desk at school so she never bloody got it. Fortunately, I signed my name with a question mark, as the girl who got my card was Theresa Crankfist, who had a penchant for blowing snot bubbles out of her nose, but she was a genius at maths so it kind of balanced things out.

The only other Valentine's cards I ever saw were the ones we used to buy for the nuns each year and post through the convent door, forging Jesus's signature.

*'Roses are red, violets are blue, sugar is sweet,*
*I died for you.'*

Believe it or not, I once fell in love on Valentine's Day. It was at a time in my life when I was lost. All my friends were going off to Uni each year and I felt disillusioned. Working five days a week at the cash and carry. Jaded, I decided to apply for a university course in Art and Drama.

Feeling equipped with my BTEC in Performing Arts and my one GCSE in Art I headed off to an interview/open day at a Uni in Crewe. I was asked to bring some of my GCSE artwork. The problem was I didn't really have any. You see my art teacher at school, Mr Bannon, was a great man and a really good friend. He still is, in fact I've just been around his house fitting a dodgy fire stick (shush).

When it came time for Mr Bannon to predict my GCSE grade, I asked him if he wouldn't mind putting me down for a B. He said he felt he couldn't, so we settled on a C (this was the eighties, a completely different era when a teacher-pupil friendship could be exploited for a fairly decent grade).

Mr Bannon was truly inspirational. Not only in art but also in music. He never taught music, but he made me a lot of mix tapes, which introduced me to songs and artists I still listen to today. He also put me in charge of the school video camera and gave me a key to a storeroom where I set up an edit suite. Well, I say edit suite, it was two video recorders wired together. I'd spend hours in there editing events for the school archive (and doing some sneaky pirating too). One of the school events I edited was highlights from the Caring Church Week we had in 1987 which had been organised by the nuns. That's when we had the whole week off timetable so we could pray, sing hymns and attend loads of masses. A gaggle of priests descended on the school. The nuns were like lovestruck teenagers. Swooning around the priests like Brosettes.

I bet half of those priests are in prison now. There were a few rumours floating around that week. Sightings of priests down The Dancing Bare, Bolton's one and only lap dancing club, but I'm not one for gossip.

One of the funniest moments during the Caring Church Week was when Father Ralph, a Geordie priest, called us all into the library for a slide show 'highlighting the plight in

Ethiopia'. Lights were dimmed, blinds closed, and then we heard the opening bars of a familiar song. 'He Ain't Heavy, He's My Brother' by The Hollies. We were then forced to watch images of people starving on a projector screen.

I don't want to sound callous, but it was one of those awkward moments where you completely know you shouldn't laugh but somehow having to suppress your laughter seems to make it all the more hard not to laugh. I was sat with some friends, and we were really struggling to keep straight faces. Tears streaming down our cheeks. I was even nipping my own leg as a painful distraction because I knew how badly we'd get bollocked. It was so inappropriate.

Then just when I thought we were going to make it, the song reached the lyric 'he ain't heavy, he's my brother' and we discovered that Father Ralph had purposefully timed the image of a child being weighed on some scales.

This was too much, and we erupted. Howling with laughter. Sister Sledge swooped over like a big black bat, 'YOU FIVE, GET TO MY OFFICE NOW.' It was a fair cop, and we did, quite rightfully, receive a mighty bollocking.

Anyway, I've drifted again, like Robert Maxwell (topical). Oh, that was it, I was off for an open day for a college in Crewe and I needed some artwork. So, I asked my old art teacher Mr Bannon if he'd kindly let me borrow some artwork. Highly unorthodox but needs must. He let me sift through that current year's GSCE artwork and picked the best ones, obviously rubbing off any that had signatures at the bottom, that would have completely given the game away. Mr

Bannon gave me strict instructions to take great care of the artwork and get it back to him the day after the interview. Don't worry, I returned them all, this isn't leading up to the farcical moment of me losing everything or accidentally dropping it into a river.

So, on a bright, frosty Valentine's morning, I boarded a train for Crewe. My dad had offered to come with me, I was glad of the company. I think he enjoyed having a purpose as he'd recently been made redundant. And he'd started trainspotting again.

Just a side note to tell you I'm writing this while listening to *Sunday Love Songs* Valentine's special. So, the backdrop couldn't be more appropriate. I really miss Steve Wright. He was bloody brilliant.

We caught the train to Crewe from Manchester Piccadilly and settling into my seat I noticed a girl sat across from me further down the carriage. We exchanged glances, a slight smile. Maybe it was my imagination.

Arriving at Crewe, my dad said he was off to explore the local sights (pubs) and would see me back at the station later. I had to catch a bus to the Uni campus. The rain had lifted and the day was getting brighter. And continued when I stepped onto the bus to discover the only other passenger on board was the girl I'd seen earlier on the train. It was good to see a familiar face. We acknowledged each other and she motioned for me to sit next to her. My heart flipped.

Fionnuala (or Finn as she preferred) was a ball of fire. Filled to the brim with exuberance, wit and a strong Bradford accent which I adored. She had a pretty, understated beauty with expressive blue eyes that made me feel at ease. We talked like we'd known each other for years. Finn was applying for art and drama too, and she was no shrinking violet. Laughing, singing, quoting lines from films, she genuinely made me laugh a lot. Which was hugely attractive. I'd never met a girl like this before that made me feel so comfortable. Our rapport was effortless and for most of the day we were inseparable. So much so, I forgot why I was there.

By the time I met back up with my dad at the station I was becoming increasingly melancholy as I knew my time with Finn would soon be coming to an end.

We sat next to each other on the journey back to Manchester, both facing my dad.

Our fingers gently touching under the table. Oh my God, I hadn't misread the signs.

Now I knew my feelings were reciprocated I suddenly became shy and struggled to make eye contact with Finn. Funny how the dynamic can change. My heart weighed heavy as we pulled into Manchester Piccadilly. We said our goodbyes and it was like a scene from *Brief Encounter*, only in colour and not as dramatic as my dad was stood beside the both of us. I thought the penny might have dropped and he would have wandered off to WHSmith's for a browse. Not a chance.

Welling up, I watched Finn wave from the window of her train as it pulled out of the station. I turned reluctantly and headed home. Clutching a scrap of paper with her address and phone number. Lordy, I'm enjoying writing this. I've never written about affairs of the heart before. I think I could give Mills & Boon a run for their money.

My stomach was churning like a washing machine. I'd never felt like this. It physically ached and I was completely consumed with Finn. As soon as I got home, I called her (I bet she thought I was a right stalker). Fortunately, nothing appeared to have faded in the three hours since we parted. We chatted for ages. The annoying thing was I kept hearing clicking on the line. Somebody kept picking up another phone extension at her end and listening to us. Finn would shout 'Put it down I'm on the phone.' She was on her home phone, no mobiles in those days. Otherwise, I'd have been texting her as soon as she got on her train. Finn explained that it was her cousin who was staying at her house with her while her parents were away on holiday. I thought nothing of it. Eventually, we said goodnight and promised to keep in touch. What a day!

Did I sleep? Well, if I did Finn certainly had a starring role in my dreams. I woke for college the next morning, my stomach felt like it'd been kicked by a small horse. I made a completely spontaneous decision. In a fit of romantic passion, I decided to bunk off college for the day and head over to Bradford to see Finn. She would be surprised. Carpe diem.

Before you could sing the chorus to 'Truly Madly Deeply' by Savage Garden (and, let's be honest, who can?) I was back on 'our' platform at Manchester Piccadilly, about to board a train to Bradford. A tad nervous as I'd never travelled that far on my own.

When I arrived in Bradford, I rang Finn's number from a payphone. Frustratingly it was engaged. I tried several times. Undeterred I flagged down a taxi and told the driver the address. He said, 'High town or low town?'

Shit, I didn't know. I took a guess at high town and off we went.

After a few minutes of silence in the taxi I found myself compelled to say 'So have you been busy? What time are you on till?' I just couldn't resist.

We arrived in a quiet street, with rows of smart terraced houses, the left side drenched in sunlight. I spotted the house number and got out. Uneasy, I knocked on the front door and waited. Please God this is the right house. I saw the shape of a person through frosted glass moving inside. I knocked again. The figure returned, then retreated. What were they doing? I felt too embarrassed to knock a third time as clearly they'd seen me. I started to panic. What the hell was I doing here?

Then a man appeared at the bay window beside the front door. Tall, mid-twenties, with wild and untamed hair. He looked like he'd just got up. He might have for all I knew but he looked sane enough. I asked if Finn was in. He said she was out. I thought thank the Lord. At least I'd got the right house. But what to do? It turned out he was her cousin, visiting while her parents were away on holiday. So he was the clown who'd been listening in on our call the night before?

'She's gone out and took the front door key, so I'm locked in.'

So that's why he'd come to the window and not the door.

I thought, locked *in*? Well, that's a first.

'Finn's taken the phone off the hook in her bedroom so I can't call her.'

Ahh, that's why the phone had been constantly engaged.

But why had she done that with the home phone? Strange.

There was an awkward silence as we both looked at each other.

'You can come in if you like?' he said.

'How?'

Then he gestured to the front room bay window between us.

'I can't climb through that?'

'Up to you. I've no idea when she'll be back.'

This situation was getting crazier by the minute, but I was bursting for a wee.

Two minutes later I was stood on a wheelie bin hoisting myself up through the front room window. The lad (I still didn't know his name) had his arms outstretched attempting to lift me in. Thank God it was a quiet street. If anybody had seen me, I'd have ended up on *Crimewatch*.

I don't know how but somehow I managed to get through that window. Romance can be a great motivator. I fell into his arms and we both tumbled onto the sofa like gay lovers. It was like a scene from a sitcom.

'I'm Col,' he said, and we shook hands. I went for a wee, while Col made a brew, and then we both watched *This Morning*. Awkwardly we commented on the weather and Fred

Talbot on his weather map. What was I doing here? How had I ended up in Bradford with a stranger listening to Chris Steele's advice on vaginal dryness? And where the hell was Finn? I mean, fair enough she'd no idea I was even coming, let alone that I was sat in her front room.

Time was running out. I'd bunked off college for the day, but I had to be back in Bolton for five as I was working an evening shift at the cash and carry. I hadn't envisaged the day's events unfolding like this.

Finally, with about half an hour left before I'd have to climb back out of the front room window, I heard a key in the front door. Finn had returned and what a shock she got when she saw me sat on the couch, drinking my fourth cup of Yorkshire tea. She couldn't believe I was there, then she was incredibly apologetic for not being home. Obviously, she'd no idea I was a stalker. Sadly, we only had time for a quick hug, then she gave me a lift back to the station in her Nissan Micra.

She explained she'd taken the phone off the hook in her bedroom because her cousin Col kept ringing his girlfriend, long distance (hence the clicking during our conversations the previous night), so that was her way of keeping the phone costs down.

We arrived at the station in no time at all. I yearned for more time with Finn and could tell my impromptu visit had completely overwhelmed her. On reflection, it must have come across as full-on (story of my love life). I mean, imagine turning up at somebody's house after just meeting her the day before. Outrageous.

Then Finn uttered those painfully familiar words that have shattered countless hearts since time began, 'Let's just be friends.' I was gutted. The times I'd heard that. 'I think you're lovely, funny, kind, thoughtful, but let's just be friends,' because they'd rather waste their time fancying some arsehole who treats them like crap.

Impulsiveness had definitely been my downfall. I tried to convince myself of other reasons on the journey home, 'It wouldn't have worked; we lived too far apart,' but whatever way I worked it, I was crushed. My stomach still aching, now with heartbreak (well, that's what I thought but it actually turned out to be a stomach bug and I threw up in my hands at the cash and carry. Only I could mistake love for a stomach bug.)

Finn and I kept in touch, writing to each other, but sadly we drifted. Then by absolute chance, we met up again, twenty-five years later. Finn was now a stage manager working on a touring production of *Mamma Mia*, which arrived in Manchester. I went to the show with some friends. Finn found out I was in the audience. Well, Peter Kay was in the audience, surely not the same stalker who'd broken into her parents' house all those years before. I got a message in the interval from Finn and my heart leapt. Would I like to go backstage and see her after the show? The cast sang 'Slipping Through My Fingers' and we reminisced about our Valentine's Day in Crewe all those years before. I had a lump in my throat or maybe it was a wine gum?

*Mamma Mia* was joyous. It left me feeling jubilant, so much so that when I went backstage and met some of the cast I made a complete cock of myself. You've probably seen *Mamma Mia* (it's on ITV2 every week) and if you haven't I'm about to ruin it (come on, it's hardly *The Sixth Sense*). At the end, Sophie elopes with her fiancé Sky. They sail away towards a beautiful moon while everybody sings 'I Have a Dream'. I'm welling up just thinking about it now. So when I saw the girl who played Sophie in the show, I gave her a big hug and said 'congratulations'.

'For what?' she said slightly taken aback.

'For ending up with Sky, falling in love?' The end of that sentence wilted as the realisation hit me. It's a show, Peter, it's not real.

How embarrassing.

I turned to see Finn laughing in the wings behind me. We hugged. It was so good to see her again. I never confessed to her that my feelings turned out to be a stomach bug. Well, maybe they weren't.

Incidentally, I never did get on the course at Crewe College. Lord knows why. As I had some of the best artwork from a whole GSCE year. I still can't believe those pupils let me down.

# March

1989, I'm stood on the deck of a ferry sailing into Belfast. We've travelled overnight from Stranraer in Scotland. As the ferry glides smoothly through the calm waters, the shape of distant hills emerges gradually. I can see the iconic Harland & Wolff cranes silhouetting against the pastel-blue sky. The morning sunrise is glorious. Casting a golden glow across the horizon. The city of Belfast straight ahead. Its skyline reflecting in the tranquil waters. I'm listening to 'Belfast Child' on my Walkman. I appreciate it's schmalzty but Simple Minds have just had their first number one in the charts and it's framing the moment perfectly.

I'm sixteen, and accompanying my mum as we visit her family for a fortnight. Our dates mean we'll be in Ireland for St Patrick's Day, something I'd never experienced before. I imagined a non-stop raucous party of revelry over a three-day period but was surprised at how tame the celebrations were.

My mum's family had taken the pledge, which was a total abstinence on alcohol, so there certainly wasn't any drink for kick-off. Not that it bothered me. I've always been teetotal. Well, apart from the occasional Baileys. I've never liked any alcohol I've tried. What I do know is if beer tasted like Vimto or Tizer I'd be a full-on piss head.

Maybe the St Patrick's Day festivities were low-key because we were in the north of Ireland. There was still a lot of suspicion and paranoia at the time, the Troubles were still rife and people had a preference for keeping their heads down. I've always found Irish people celebrate St Patrick's Day far more elsewhere around the world. In fact, the further away the Irish are from Ireland the more misty-eyed they appear to become for the old home country.

What never fails to amaze me is no matter where you go on this planet, whatever far-flung arsehole end of nowhere you find yourself, there'll always be an Irish bar. I've always found it strange that the British celebrate St Patrick more than St George. Maybe it's because commemorating St George doesn't entail going on a three-day bender wearing a ginger wig and a green top hat.

We'd also be in Ireland for Mother's Day too, which would be nice for my mum. Being able to be with her mother for the first time in ages. My granny used to visit us in Bolton occasionally. She caught the train to Bolton once, where we were waiting to meet her at the station, but she never arrived. Her train came and went, no granny. We waited around then reluctantly we went home confused and hoped she'd call with an explanation.

Sure enough, she did. My granny was catching a train from Blackpool to Bolton and the first stop on the line was Poulton-le-Fylde which apparently the train announcer shortened to Poulton. My granny thought he said 'Bolton' and got off the train. While we waited forty-five miles away. It was a simple mistake. She eventually got to our house at midnight.

That reminds me of the bloke going to Cheltenham who fell asleep on the train. He woke up when the train pulled into a station. Hazily misreading a sign saying Gentleman and got off. He was only in Droitwich, the dopey sod.

One of my granny's most treasured memories was dancing with Donald Campbell, the legendary water speed racer. It was the 1950s and my granny was working as a waitress in a hotel in the Lake District, Newby Bridge. Donald Campbell held many British racing records but sadly died in 1967 when his renowned jet craft *Bluebird* flipped over on Lake Coniston at 300mph, killing him instantly. They never found his body until it came out of a tap in Oldham in 1982, so that solved that mystery. Sorry, that was a joke too far. They actually recovered his body in 2001.

Going to Ireland also meant I got to spend time with my cousins, which I used to really enjoy, especially as I didn't have any cousins in Bolton. My dad was an only child, but my mum's side of the family certainly made up for it. She had seven siblings in total. Five sisters and two brothers who all had plenty of children which meant plenty of cousins to spend time with. It was so lovely to have some real family as opposed to those 'Aunties and Uncles' growing up who usually just worked with my parents. It was very confusing.

We only ever visited Ireland every two or three years, because it was so expensive to fly. Travelling by plane was still an upper-class sport at the time (excluding Freddie Laker's Skytrain, where you could fly to New York for a ridiculous £32). Going on the ferry was long and convoluted but it was cheap, which is why we travelled by boat in March 89. Our financial situation was abstemious (we were brassic).

Northern Ireland was at the very height of the Troubles when I was growing up, so there wasn't any healthy price competition on flights to a war zone. British Airways had a monopoly and they were expensive. The journey only took thirty minutes from Manchester. No sooner had you stowed away your tray tables than you were making your descent. We were so thrilled to fly. Feeling the exhilaration of take-off. Eager to look out of the window at the patchwork quilt fields below. Even saving the mini cans of Coca-Cola we drank on board as souvenirs. I had two of them proudly displayed on my bedroom shelf for years. Showing them to whoever came round. (Nobody ever came round.)

My dad never came to Ireland with us. He said he felt uneasy about being a Brit in Northern Ireland at that time and if he opened his mouth he feared reprisals. I missed him and remembered sobbing one night when my mum put me to bed and the radio was playing 'When I Need You' – Leo Sayer, I was nineteen. I'm joking, I would have been about four.

# MARCH

We'd stop at my granny and grandad's house in Coalisland which was always overflowing with religious memorabilia. It was like a shrine. They also had a real coal fire in the front room that I loved to throw things on when I was left alone. I was a right little arsonist. The fascination of watching stuff burn. Sometimes I'd get caught and told off, especially if I chucked anything plastic on the fire as it would stink the house out. Plus I had a picture of the sacred heart of Jesus gazing down at me. I'm sure I once saw him frown.

My grandad always reminded me of Alastair Burnet, the ITN newsreader. With a big shock of white hair. He was a quiet, serious man who rarely smiled unless he was watching Sgt Bilko or Mr Magoo, then his face would light up and he'd laugh so fiercely the flames on the fire would flicker.

He'd sit in his upright armchair and granny would bring him his meals (by the way I'm talking about my grandad now, not Alastair Burnet). My granny would eat on her own in the kitchen. When he'd finished my grandad would place the empty crockery on the floor and my granny would collect it. Even at a young age, I thought this was a bit chauvinistic (well tight) but that was the way things were with that generation. If I put my plate on the floor for Susan to collect, she'd probably smash the plate over my head.

Years later I discovered that my grandad was a bona fide hero. In fact, he received a special commendation award for bravery for saving another man's life in 1965. He worked as a linesman, installing and maintaining electricity cables when a fellow worker accidentally came into contact with two live conductors. My grandad pulled him down off the live lines. Receiving a shock himself in the process. Then administered first aid until an ambulance arrived. The certificate stated that my grandad's 'prompt action undoubtedly saved the linesman from further serious injury or even death'.

This incident was all but forgotten until the commendation certificate was discovered among my grandad's personal effects after he died. He hadn't even bothered to get it framed. It was alongside an article from the local paper, with a photo of him receiving his award. He was standing with the guy whose life he saved (with his hair still stood on end) and the president of the electricity company. I've had them both framed since.

When we went to Ireland we'd stay at my grandparents' house. Most days me and my mum would walk down to the town or take a bus to Dungannon or Cookstown, two slightly bigger towns nearby. We'd wander around the shops, everybody seemed oblivious to the bombed-out buildings that lay in ruins or the RAF helicopters that regularly flew overhead. People had just got used to it over the years and now it was just the norm. But for me it was both frightening and surreal.

Sometimes my mum would treat me to something from the shops. A matchbox car or some felt tips and a drawing pad. Hours of fun back at my granny's, especially if I 'accidentally' drew something crap, then I'd have to rip it up and throw it on the fire. Woo-hoo!

Coalisland was the same as many other towns coping with the Troubles in Northern Ireland. Right in the centre of the town was an enormous army barracks where British soldiers were stationed. Over fifty feet high, it was an impenetrable corrugated steel fortress with a multitude of CCTV and towered communications mast. Well, I say it was impenetrable but somebody made the stupid decision to build the barracks at the bottom of a hill. This meant members or IRA sympathisers could run down the hill, through back gardens with fresh washing hung out and lob petrol bombs or grenades into the compound. That design flaw certainly kept the Brits on their toes.

Again, like it or not everybody had to accept the barracks' existence as well as the British soldiers living among them. On Sundays, we'd go to mass and then we'd call at Sullivan's, a big newsagent on the main High Street that was popular for its whippy ice creams. It was a family-owned shop. Kind of an early version of a Nisa local.

Once I walked out of Sullivan's with a 99 and bumped into a soldier carrying a semi-automatic rifle. That was scary. He laughed and said 'Give us a lick' in a cockney accent. I wasn't laughing, I was agog staring at his rifle and he certainly wasn't getting his tongue around my flake.

Another thing that used to fascinate me was the military murals I'd see on the gable end of buildings or random walls. These were painted tributes to victims of the conflict in Northern Ireland. I find some of them disturbing. Images of men in balaclavas pointing machine guns in the air. With dates and words, sometimes in Gaelic. I'd also find some of these murals disturbing because they were such bad portraits. No doubt because they were frantically painted at four in the morning by a greengrocer with an O-Level in art.

I think they should have a series called *Irish Mural Portrait Artist of the Year*. Where highbrow art critics retrospectively analyse murals from the conflict in Northern Ireland.

'Where's the expression and form? Such a garish mix of colours with little or no perspective.'

'Oh, I agree, such a shockingly flat technique leading to impecunious compositional flaws.'

I'd definitely watch it. Another common theme I noticed within these murals was that the subjects often had different-sized eyes or crooked mouths. They weren't great. I saw one of the hunger striker Bobby Sands and he looked like Janet Street-Porter.

We were on 'holiday' at my granny's in 1981 when Bobby Sands tragically succumbed to his hunger strike. Everybody in the neighbourhood was required to hang a black flag on the outside of their house. My grandad made a makeshift flag from a black bin bag. I shudder to think what might have happened if he'd refused.

As I said, it was still a time of paranoia and suspicion from all sides. People living on their nerves. Auntie Bernie came to visit us in Bolton and said she found it strange to be around parked cars and not have any fear of them suddenly exploding. I hadn't even contemplated that or how common that feeling must have been until she pointed it out.

If me and my mum weren't out shopping then we'd be visiting relatives around Coalisland. My mum would spend hours drinking tea, eating biscuits and putting the world to rights with her sisters while I'd be stuck outside in a field throwing stones at cows.

Some of my cousins were talented musicians and played in many competitions across Ireland. Kids love musical instruments and I was no exception. I'll never forget the unbridled joy of fiddling with my cousin Malachy's banjo. It was stunning. I didn't know what I was doing. Just plucking away at the strings. Then he got out a bodhran and I was drumming away like a child possessed. The family also had a gorgeous deep red-coloured accordion which I struggled to even lift, it was so heavy. My cousin strapped it around my neck and it weighed me forward as I sat on the edge of the bunk bed. Trying desperately to pump air through the bellows and push away at the keys, nothing.

My cousins also had a shed in the garden where they gathered each night to go on their CB radio. Which was all the rage at the time thanks to the song and film *Convoy*. Their handles made me laugh. My cousin Fergus had the handle Joe 90 (he looked a bit like him). Pat was Kindly Light. Mine was Brit Scum. I'm joking. I never had one.

It was such a weird thrill sitting in that shed listening to radio static. Chatting to strangers about all kinds of crap for hours. I grappled to understand the CB lingo. All this 'ten four good buddy' and 'eyeball, eyeball'. Then we kept picking up the British soldiers at the barracks down the town with their massive antenna. They told us to 'get off this frequency' in a gruff cockney accent. My cousins sang a rebel song down the mic. Changing the lyrics to 'Swords of a Thousand Men' – Tenpole Tudor. 'Hoorah, hoorah, hoorah yeah, shoot Maggie Thatcher with the guns of the IRA'.

Inevitably some of my cousins' heads were seriously turned by the Troubles. I suppose it was hard not to be caught up in the excitement which was around them all the time. They loved telling me tales and showing me sights. I found the macabre of it all fascinating. One cousin drove me up to Belfast where we cruised the Falls Road as he played 'Murder Incorporated' by Bruce Springsteen on his car stereo. He was entranced by the Troubles. He even shoved a load of IRA magazines in my suitcase just before we left. My mum found them and lost her mind – throwing them on granny's fire. 'If they'd found those at the airport we'd have been strip-searched.' She wasn't wrong.

However, my mum failed to notice the VHS tape my cousin had stashed beneath my drawing pad at the bottom of the case. When I got back to Bolton I anxiously slid the video in the recorder and pressed play. My mum was out. The first thing I saw was the opening headlines of the BBC's *Nine O'clock News* reporting an incident that had taken place in Coalisland. Members of the IRA had driven into the centre of the town and fired at the British Army barracks with a machine gun mounted on the back of a lorry. This had disconnected the barracks communications (and no doubt my cousin's CB frivolities in his shed).

The IRA attackers then drove off at speed, without any apparent pursuit from the security forces. (I've copied all this off Wikipedia by the way.) While making their escape they drove past the home of Tony Doris, an IRA man who had been killed by the British Army the previous year, where they stopped to fire into the air, shouting: 'Up the 'RA, that's for Tony Doris!' (Nothing like a bit of discretion, lads.)

Witnesses also reported the IRA men waving Irish Tricolours from the back of the lorry (you'd just keep your head down wouldn't you?). They then drove into the car park of St Patrick's Roman Catholic Church in the village of Clonoe (I went to my cousin's wedding there and the priest made a reprehensible remark about one parishioner's baby being Down Syndrome – it was so bad I can't even repeat it).

The IRA were in the process of abandoning their attack vehicles when they were ambushed by a British Army detachment that had been lying in wait for them, primarily composed of soldiers from the Special Air Service, who engaged sustained automatic fire with them. Four IRA members between the ages of nineteen and twenty-three were fatally wounded.

Then the video I was watching cut from Peter Sissons reading the BBC news to a shot of an open-top coffin and the body of one of the youngest IRA members laid out in a front room. The camcorder then slowly panned around his corpse. I was nearly sick with shock. It then cut to shots of a funeral. Hundreds of mourners gathered in Coalisland including Martin McGuinness and Gerry Adams who walked behind the coffins (I showed it to my friend who saw Gerry Adams and was puzzled why George Lucas was there).

After the funeral procession, there was about an hour of IRA training footage in the countryside somewhere with various rebel songs dubbed over the top. Then the recording ended. Flickering sash ran up the screen and then there was the last half hour of an episode of *Treasure Hunt* that somebody must have recorded on the VHS. I was speechless. And never found out if Anneka Rice got her final clue.

Years later I told my mum about the tape. She shook her head in disgust. I'd since thrown it in the bin. It was disturbing viewing. The only good thing to come out of that whole horrible incident was that my cousin said it forced him 'to wise up and turn his back on such mindlessness'.

Years later when I was back in Coalisland and met a fella, I'll call him Milo Hanrahan because that was his name. He coached the local under-elevens football club. He was asking all about Bolton Wanderers, but I haven't got a bloody clue about football. So I just nodded and repeated the last word of everything he said so it appeared I understood.

He was a pleasant fella, a bit boisterous, but what my auntie told me about him I'd never have guessed in a million years. She said he'd not long been out of prison. Released as part of the Good Friday peace agreement. He was inside for shooting three British soldiers. It's all very dark.

He was allegedly waiting in a ditch for them to go past on patrol. He was there for hours and his wife had even made him a packed lunch. That got me – his wife making him some sandwiches and putting him a flask up, 'Here, wrap up warm, Milo,' putting a scarf around his neck – 'You'll catch your death. I've warmed a tin of mulligatawny for you.' Anyway, he was halfway through eating an apple when he saw the soldiers approach. So he tossed the apple into the field, took aim and shot them. Horrible. Well, and here's the twist, the apple he was eating was later discovered in the field. Then forensics took a plaster of Paris mould of the teeth indentations and that's how they caught him. Madly enough I watched it in an episode of a BBC series about forensic investigations. Apparently, this was the first ever case in the world where the perpetrator was caught using this technique. And now he was teaching under-elevens football.

The peace agreement was essential to draw a line under years of unimaginable loss, tragedy and pain. But for many, it was the bitterest pill to swallow in order to move towards the bigger picture of a peaceful future. I've seen Northern Ireland prosper in the past three decades. You wouldn't recognise Belfast any more, it's a stunning place with a beautiful waterfront, the Titanic Quarter, it's a massive haven for tourists.

During the years of conflict, time had stood still in Northern Ireland. Nobody wanted to invest money in a war zone. Since the peace agreement, I've seen whole areas dramatically flourish. New housing, shopping centres, multiplex cinemas. The current generation doesn't want a return to the past and sacrifice what they have now. The generation of idealistic, angry freedom fighters now have children and grandchildren and they don't want to see anything happen to them. Love heals.

While watching a fascinating doc about the conflict in Northern Ireland an ex-soldier said a line which completely summed up the change in attitude:

'When I was seventeen I was in charge of guns. I have a granddaughter now who's seventeen and I could not imagine handing her a gun. In fact, I could not imagine handing her anything other than a strawberry fucking milkshake.'

Mum continued to go 'back home' as the years passed. Mainly to pitch in with her siblings looking after my granny who still lived in the very same house they'd all grown up in. My granny passed in 2014; coincidentally I was over in Ireland when my mum told me the sad news. I was in southern Ireland but decided to drive up north for the funeral. I'd no funeral attire as we were on a family holiday, but I stopped at Tesco's en route and managed to pick up a full black suit, shirt and shoes for fifty-four euros. Every little helps.

Nobody knew I was coming, not even my mum, and it was lovely to see her face when I turned up at my granny's house. It was also great to see all my cousins again, some I hadn't seen for years. Family members took turns carrying granny's coffin and I got the opportunity which meant a lot to me. We all walked behind the hearse, down the hill into town, past Sullivan's the newsagents and where the barracks used to be. It was now shut down, dismantled in 2006. Then we walked up to the chapel where my grandad was buried.

We stood by the side of the grave. The coffin was being lowered when I saw a man and a woman in matching shell suits glaring at me from behind a tree. Big beaming smiles on the pair of them as they caught my eye. Occasionally I glanced over and they'd both give me the thumbs up. It was a bit inappropriate for a funeral, and I certainly didn't recognise either of them.

After the burial, they came bounding over. On closer inspection, I discovered it was a mother and grown-up son (in his fifties).

'Jeez, Peter, we can't believe it's you, we're both big fans, we just wanted to say hello ...'

Then his mum chirped up: 'Can we ask you, Peter, why have you never played Elvis? Because you're the image of him.'

I was struggling to process what she'd said. Then her son chipped in again.

'... and you're the image of your mummy too.'

'So, my mum also looks like Elvis.'

I just smiled politely and backed off. Nuts. My mum doesn't look like Elvis by the way, and do I? Maybe a bit, just before he died, from a distance and if you squint.

I love my mum very much and like most children I've spent most of my life trying to make her happy. As many of you know I called one of my stand-up tours 'Mum Wants a Bungalow' because she did and she eventually got one. She's been settled in there for over twenty years and the only issue she has now is that she suffers from bungalow legs. It's an actual condition. She struggles to climb the stairs when she comes to our house. She just points at them and stares, at the stairs.

It was on my Mum Wants a Bungalow Tour when I played Belfast and my mum came backstage after the show. She said, 'You look tired, son. I saw you up on that stage tonight and you seemed knackered. Are you looking after yourself?' I reassured her as best I could then she said, 'Would you mind saying hello to some family?' Then she opened a door and I swear about thirty people piled in. If they were family I'd never clapped eyes on them. Well, I recognised one or two. My mum led me around each and every one, signing autographs and taking selfies. I didn't mind, I just thought it was hilarious, one minute she's concerned about me being knackered then she's whoring me out to all and sundry. If I wasn't knackered before, I certainly was an hour later.

Speed walking through Euston station as fast as my legs could carry me. With the world and his wife charging behind me. All frantically heading for my train. My diligence paid off and I managed to bagsy a single seat. Little victories. I plugged my phone on charge and bit into a chicken royale as we rolled out of the station, heading north.

I'd taken this journey many times over the years. The duration may have got quicker and the trains tarted up a bit, but basically, nothing's changed except for a sticker with a QR code which apparently meant I could place an order at the buffet car via my phone and have it delivered to my seat. Great, if only the train's Wi-Fi was working but as usual it wasn't.

Travelling by train can be soothing. It doesn't take long before the gentle rocking motion causes my eyes to sporadically open and close. Catching glimpses from my window of the predictable urban sprawl. Sainsbury's, Home Bargains,

# MARCH

KFC, Halfords, Greggs, Screwfix, Aldi and Kwik Fit, all nestled among smaller, more familiar sights found on the British high street. Boarded-up pubs, halal kebabs, tattooists, charity shops, pound shops and of course vape shops.

As we head into the countryside I'm always overwhelmed by the sheer expanse of greenery. Mile upon mile of endless rolling hills and fields. Though many of the fields are still flooded from recent rains. Patches of foliage speckle pastures divided by blossoming hedgerows and stone walls. Cows and sheep graze, surrounded by daffodils and, oh look, another vape shop. 'Ye Olde Country Vape Escape'. Catchy.

Despite March being seasonally humdrum, sunshine blasted into the carriage and I noticed passengers shedding layers due to the unexpected heat. After my inevitable snooze, I woke to feel an uneasiness in my stomach. I shirked it off for a while, but it wasn't for lifting. I was about twenty minutes from my final destination, but I felt like I needed the toilet immediately. Surely this couldn't be happening. I'd managed to get to this stage in my life without taking a shit on a train and come hell or high water I wasn't about to start now. I ordered my arse to simmer, several times, but when you've got to go, you've got to go and I'm sorry to say I really needed to go.

'Please be vacant' I mumbled as I sidled down the carriage towards the bog. It was like a scene from *Trainspotting*. I didn't want to touch anything. I'd used train toilets many times for a wee but never for a Brad Pitt. My dad used to tell me always that when you flushed it went straight onto the track. Apparently, that's why you should never flush in the station. I believed that for years.

I spent several minutes delicately stacking individual pieces of toilet paper around the seat. Only to have them all blow out of place when the draft from off my arse hit the seat. Never mind, I was down. Hopefully, it'd all be over quickly. I didn't want to miss my stop and end up Christ knows where. The next stop after mine was Penrith.

There was a small queue when I finally opened the door and I felt myself blush as I scurried back to my seat. Thank the Lord for my Covid mask, otherwise I'd have been all over X before we reached Wigan.

Leaving the platform, I doubled back to the kiosk to buy a bottle of water. I needed to keep hydrated. I got out my card to pay contactless (there was a time I'd have frowned on that but Covid changed the world).

'£2.05' said the voice behind the counter.

'How much?'

'£2.05.'

'It's alright, I'll leave it.'

'Train station prices,' he shouted.

I said, 'I know where I am, pal. £2.05 for a small bottle of water!! You should wear a mask and a striped jumper.' I wasn't paying that.

It wasn't even a brand I recognised, bottled Al-Qaeda water brewed in the mountains of Afghanistan. I bobbed into an off-licence over the road and bought a similar-sized bottle for 80p. Then I headed home before my arse erupted a second time.

That was Friday. When Sunday came round my lower right back was throbbing like a bastard. I didn't feel well at all so I did what anybody would do in the situation. I looked up my symptoms with Dr Google. It was looking like a kidney stone. Fast forward twenty-four hours and my suspicions were confirmed via a CT scan at the local hospital. It turned out I had a big stone blocking the exit of my right kidney. I quizzed the urologist. 'When you say a big stone, how big are we talking? Because I'm picturing the opening scene from *Raiders of the Lost Ark* when a giant stone ball chases Indiana Jones.' He reassured me but said I needed emergency surgery to remove the kidney stone which would also involve having a stent fitted up my urethra (Franklin) in order to maintain my kidney functions. Fuck a duck.

My pre-op bloods confirmed his suspicions and apparently 'my kidney functions were deranged', well that's how the nurse delicately put it. As much as I was shocked, I was also relieved and felt vindicated as I actually had something wrong with me and it wasn't just hypochondria. However, kidney stone pain is legendary and I was starting to sob and make the occasional high-pitched whining sound. Like when you fire an air rifle at a dog's testicles. You know …?

A urologist informed me he'd be inserting a small camera fitted with a laser and that they'd be blasting the kidney stone to smithereens. It sounded like a scene from *Armageddon* (I like to relate all of my medical procedures to Hollywood movies).

I asked the doctor if I'd be able to shower and bathe after the procedure.

'Oh, there won't be any incisions or dressings. We go in through your …'

And then he gave a whistle.

'Bellybutton,' I said. I wished.

'No, your …' and he proceeded to whistle again. What's with this whistling? Then the penny dropped with a huge realisation.

Oh my God, he means he's going in through the hole at the end of my penis.

My world collapsed. Red lights flashed in my head. He can't go up there? It's out of bounds, private land. Area 51. A camera won't fit up there, let alone one carrying a laser. Was this guy on glue?

The anaesthetist was loud, a big booming Yorkshire voice. He thrust out his hand. 'BIG FAN, PETER, ANY CHANCE OF A SELFIE'. I mean, talk about inappropriate, I was lying on a table in theatre. But how can you say no to an anaesthetist? This guy is about to put me to sleep. You really don't want to piss them off. One extra flick of the wrist and I could be unconscious for weeks and either way he could still get a selfie.

Anaesthetic was administered. 'AT THIS POINT I USUALLY ASK THE PATIENT WHAT THEY DO FOR A LIVING BUT I KNOW WHAT YOU DO,' he boomed.

Sarcastically I turned to another nurse and said, 'Is it me or are you also struggling to hear him?'

'I DO A LOT OF WORK WITH THE ELDERLY AND THEY STRUGGLE TO HEAR ME.'

'How?' I said, but he didn't hear me.

'RIGHT, I'M GOING TO GIVE YOU THE GOOD STUFF NOW, GET YOU STRAIGHT TO SLEEP.'

'You sound like Bill Cosby.'

Anyway, I don't know what the good stuff was but my arsehole was stinging when I passed out.

I dreamt I was Indiana Jones being chased by that giant stone ball as I fired lasers over my shoulder. Each shot futile.

Waking up in recovery was hazy. The gentle voice of an Irish nurse telling me 'They managed to remove the stone.' 'Hooray,' I said softly, while drifting in and out of consciousness. I hoped she was talking to me and not the person in the next bed. Just like Jesus, they rolled away the stone. This too was a miracle. Well, that's what I thought until my general anaesthetic wore off and the pain kicked in. It felt like I was pissing razor blades as I slumped over a toilet, weeping.

As the urologist said, a stent was fitted to help with swelling caused by the major trauma to my urethra (Franklin). And it felt like major trauma. In fact, if my urethra had a face it would have been 'The Scream' by Edvard Munch. So much discomfort and continual throbbing pain. I asked my urologist how the stent would be removed. He said that one option was to leave a piece of string out of the end of my penis and then pull it out.

'What? Like a party popper? Should I throw a volley of streamers?' He wasn't amused. Ultimately he decided against the string as he said it could snag. On what, a kitchen drawer handle? I'm hardly going to be parading around my house naked, much. He also said, 'It can cause issues if you get an erection.' How? I wondered. Who'd be thinking of having sex with a piece of string hanging out of their penis?

Anyway, suffice to say none of the above was applicable and I returned a 'very long' week later to have my stent extracted, which I was dreading. The urologist said I didn't need any pain relief. He said it'd be a walk in the park. Though I don't know which parks he walks through. 'It's just like having a catheter removed.' I asked him if he'd ever had a catheter removed, and he said 'no'.

Well, what the hell was he on about then?

I lay on the table in a side room from the operating theatre. Three other blokes watched on. I hasten to add they were medical staff and not just three blokes from the canteen. Still, it somehow made things worse having an audience. The urologist advised me to breathe deeply, in and out. Then grabbed my penis like he was grabbing a snake and squeezed it, which caused my eyes to bulge like a cartoon.

Now I was breathing like a panting dog on heat.

'Slow your breathing down.'

Slow it down?! He's just grabbed my cock and swung it like a skipping rope. He was lucky I didn't headbutt him.

Then he hurled a glob of numbing gel down the end of my penis. It dribbled all down my balls and onto my thighs. All cold and gooey. I mean how could he miss?

'Leave that to numb for a minute or two,' he said, then exactly forty seconds later he rammed a small hook right down my pipe to retrieve the stent. I howled and wanted to shout 'THAT WAS NOT A FUCKING MINUTE OR TWO, PAL!' but then suddenly silence. It was over and he'd retrieved the stent. Thank. The. Lord.

He asked if I'd like to see it. I looked at him like he'd two heads. No, I didn't want to see it. I was just glad it was all over. It was painful and unpleasant and a dreadful experience that I never wish to repeat. Ever!

# April

Like December is defined by Christmas, April is predominantly defined by Easter. Today is Good Friday and you can't get more Easter than that. I realise there's more to April than Easter, there's also the Grand National. I once had a dream about the winner of the National, but unfortunately it was the day after.

Sometimes Easter falls in March. In fact, most people don't even realise when Easter is until it's suddenly on their doorstep. This is inevitably followed by the comment 'Easter already? This year's flying.' Rightfully Easter should be slap bang in the middle of April in my opinion.

When we had our Easter holidays at school, we'd return to find spring had sprung. The playground was enveloped in vegetation. Mother Nature had been out with her green felt tips and the trees and bushes were in full throttle. A joy to behold.

Easter signifies religion to me, especially today, Good Friday, where we were always told it was a sin to eat meat. Though I usually remember that halfway through a bacon butty, 'Oh shit, I'm going to burn.' Apparently, the 'no meat on Friday' rule had applied for years in the Catholic Church. Hence fish on Friday. That's why chippy teas were so popular on Fridays. Though perhaps not as much these days, sadly. Maybe we've all become a bit too healthy. There's nothing wrong with an occasional chippy tea. Especially at the end of a working week. It's a real treat and used to be a highlight when I was growing up. The queues outside the local chippies on a Friday teatime would be enormous. And the aroma was intoxicating. I've never understood why it's never been brought out as a perfume. I'm sure Yves Saint Laurent's Chippy Tea or Calvin Klein's Fish Supper would do a bomb. You heard it here first.

Were you aware Good Friday isn't a holy day of obligation? I never knew that until recently. I mean, if there was ever a day, you'd think you'd be obliged to go to church you think it'd be the day Jesus, our Lord and saviour, was crucified. When I was an altar boy Good Friday was a really big deal. Parishioners filed into church at 3pm. The place packed to the hilt (and yet nobody was obliged). The altar laid barren all through Lent without flowers. The priest would be in silence, flanked by altar boys. The service was always sombre and lasted longer than usual. That was because there was an incredibly long gospel, the trial and crucifixion of Jesus. In fact, it was so long it was transcribed into a play within the mass booklet.

Various parishioners took roles. The bloke who did the collection played Pontius Pilate (perfect casting for him as he was a bit of an arrogant arsehole). He relished the part; one year he wore a red robe. Other males from the parish played disciples. I always felt bad for whoever drew the short straw and got lumbered playing Judas – the pantomime baddy of the New Testament. Betraying Jesus for thirty pieces of silver (about £38.50 in today's money). He was so full of remorse that he hung himself. A scene that ITV chose to cut from the film *Jesus Christ Superstar* when they showed it last Easter Sunday. So in that version Judas just did a bunk with his money.

The role of Jesus was of course played by the priest. While the congregation played the part of the crowd. We had to decide who would be crucified. A choice between Jesus or Barabbas (who I've heard was a bit of a rum bugger). Apparently, he incited riots and murdered people. Well, that's what I've just read on Wikipedia – but you can't always trust Wikipedia. I read last week that Paddy McGuinness is playing Frank Spencer in a remake of *Some Mothers Do 'Ave 'Em*. When I messaged him to see if it was true, he replied with the single word 'bollocks'.

Jesus was on trial for proclaiming he was the king of the Jews, but nobody got hurt.

Pontius Pilate had the chance to commute a prisoner's death sentence by asking the crowds who they wanted to be pardoned. 'Who do you choose?' and the crowd respond 'Barabbas'. Which the congregation had to shout. This always bugged me, so I'd always shout 'Jesus' as loud as I could. Then to make matters worse we had to shout 'Crucify him! Crucify him!' I felt like shit. Why put the blame on us?

The story of the crucifixion had been ingrained in me through school. The nuns forced us to sit through *Jesus of Nazareth* every Easter. The annual 'Jesus of Nazareth-athon' we called it. Nine hours. Now don't get me wrong, I think *Jesus of Nazareth* is a monumental piece of work. The definitive story of Jesus, featuring a galaxy of stars from stage and screen. And for my money, you'll never see a finer Jesus than Robert Powell.

Our inciteful knowledge of *Jesus of Nazareth* would come in handy during R.E. lessons when we'd taunt Sister Matic as she read from the bible, and we'd take turns interrupting her.

'The soldiers took Jesus to see Pontius Pilate.'

'You mean Rod Steiger, Sister?'

'Yes, that's right, my child,' nonplussed but flattered we were so interested. She continued 'Meanwhile, Judas ...' – another interruption.

'You mean Lovejoy, Sister, Ian McShane.'

'Yes,' she snapped. Composed herself and continued. 'As Jesus hung from the cross, he shouted to the centurion below.'

'You mean Ernest Borgnine, Sister, from *Airwolf?*' Then she lost it and chucked a wooden board at us.

Another ritual at Good Friday mass was the Veneration of the Cross. When the priest held a weighty effigy depicting the crucifixion and the congregation were invited up to the altar to kiss the feet of Jesus. I'd never really given much thought to this ritual until I was in my teens. It was really bizarre. The bit that bothered me the most was after each person kissed Jesus's feet. The priest would wipe them clean each time with the same piece of cloth. Far from hygienic. The congregation might have had cold sores or herpes or anything. Bugger that! I just used to pretend to kiss it and hover my lips over Jesus's feet.

But the die-hard parishioners couldn't give a monkey's. It was tradition and they were sticking to it. Such rituals helped endorse their ticket into heaven. I used to serve at morning mass every Easter. It was like Groundhog Day. The same parishioners in the same seats every day and woe betide anybody who dared to take their place. They'd be smited with a look that could melt butter.

My family had our regular seat in church. Always at the back, on the left. My dad picked it so he could bunk off after communion and head to the Willows pub around the corner.

My mum always used to let me bring a toy to church so I could play with it quietly during mass. I'd annoy parishioners by racing my car along the back of the wooden bench in front. Adding my own sound effects, like the roaring of an engine and screeching brakes. But then I had to stop when my wife Susan confiscated my car.

I was convinced the parishioners behind hated me too. For some reason, I always had uncontrollable flatulence during mass. Lord knows why. Perhaps I should have asked him. Maybe it was nerves, but I just couldn't stop trumping. Then when it came to making the sign of peace with the congregation

I'd be mortified because I was obliged to turn to the parishioners behind and shake their hands. Sheepishly mumbling 'peace be with you' without eye contact. I bet they were thinking 'stick a cork up it, you dirty pig'.

Not only did Easter signify going to church but also chocolate eggs. Though I've still no clue where chocolate eggs fit into the bible. I used to think Jesus only rose from the dead on Easter Sunday so he could have his Easter eggs. I still do. And now I think I'm going straight to hell for saying that.

There is a joke about Jesus struggling to eat Maltesers on Easter Sunday because they keep slipping through the holes in his hands, but I'd never lower myself to tell a joke like that. Could I also apologise to my mum and mother-in-law who'll be reading this and are both devout Catholics. They have homemade altars on their kitchen windowsills. With statues, rosary beads and tea lights from IKEA. Anyway, I'm hoping the seven years I served as an altar boy will grant me some mercy when I reach the pearly gates. God has to have a sense of humour. Look at a platypus.

Holy Thursday or Maundy Thursday falls the day before Good Friday. This was the night Jesus and his disciples had their last supper. A moment iconically portrayed in a portrait by Leonardo da Vinci and an image I found printed on a bathmat in Knock, County Mayo, Ireland.

Knock is a popular religious shrine and tourist attraction visited by thousands each year. We have family nearby, so always call for a few prayers, a cream tea and a top-up of holy water. Knock has holy water on tap, literally. It's available in the grounds of the shrine so you can fill up any time. I once saw a bloke washing himself with holy water. Shirt off, naked top half, swilling holy water around his face and under his arms. Bold as brass.

My mum uses holy water, so I collected a couple of litre bottles but unbeknown to me one of my receptacles had a hole in it. On the plane home, holy water leaked all over my clothes. Ah well, at least they got blessed.

Knock Shrine is also legendary for its huge assortment of religious merchandise. With several shops on the surrounding streets knocking out every kind of sacred paraphernalia you could imagine. I got the shock of my life when I thought I saw a portrait of Jesus wink at me. It was an apparition; on closer inspection I realised it was a holographic portrait of the sacred heart that projected movement when viewed at certain angles. Phew! What a relief. Still, I bought three of them and a bendy Jesus for my dashboard.

Growing up our house was filled with religious artefacts. It was just the norm.

We had a holy water font stuck to the wall near the front door and my mum always made us dip and bless ourselves as we exited the house. She accidentally mistook white spirit for holy water once so R Julie and me went to school smelling like a couple of painters. We stunk, and you could still smell turps on our school uniforms after three or four washes.

Like many Catholic households, we had a picture of the sacred heart of Jesus on the wall. My mum still has the same picture hanging in her kitchen. It didn't feel odd growing up but years later when my own children saw it they wondered what it was all about. I'd never quite realised how gruesome it was. The image of a man with outstretched palms, bleeding holes in both. And his bloody heart visible on the outside of his body. It is quite disturbing, but it had always been the norm for us. We grew up with some shocking graphic imagery in the Catholic Church. Like the stations of the cross placed around the walls of the church. Each with pretty horrific imagery of Jesus being beaten and tortured. Don't worry, I've not gone all woke. I just find it fascinating. Was all this disturbing imagery part and parcel (I love that expression) of Catholicism's controlling intention? Hence the fear of God. Which leads me back to Jesus's crucifixion. My nephew once said, 'It wasn't a very good Friday for Jesus, was it?' He wasn't wrong.

Holy Communion was also a peculiar ritual that I struggled to understand. We spent months learning all about the sacrament in R.E. with Sister R Doin' it. Telling us how we'd be receiving 'the body of Christ'.

'Receiving it in what way, sister?'

'You swallow it.'

'Eh … I'm not a cannibal.'

Another board duster lobbed at my head. They were nasty bitches. I mean, I wasn't trying to be insolent. I'd just been told I'd have to eat the body of a bearded man. Not that it was the beard that bothered me, it was chomping on the body bit. What a relief when Jesus's body turned out to be a circular piece of rice paper. Then she started also referring to it as the bread of life. But then I was equally disappointed because

# APRIL

I was expecting a warm baguette with the best butter. Don't even get me started on drinking Jesus's blood! You can understand why a child would be baffled.

I was far more interested in the first communion party we'd be having after in the school hall. I heard gossip about bowls of crisps, French Fancies and Viennetta, which was quite posh at the time.

All the above is tame compared to how they celebrate first communions today. Parents throwing extravagant parties. It can cost a family a small fortune. That's after buying the communion outfits. Boys are easy, a suit from M&S, but girls' communion dresses can be expensive and flashy. If you're not careful your daughter can soon look like she's ready for a Big Fat Gypsy Wedding.

Holy Communion involved the congregation queuing and kneeling along the altar rail. The priest would make his way along the rail administering communion. Each recipient would tilt their head back, slightly opening their mouth, and extend their tongue. The priest then placed the body of Christ (the small white piece of rice paper as opposed to a bearded fella's ear or nose or arm) on the outstretched tongue. My job as altar boy was to follow behind the priest holding a circular metal plate which I had to place under each recipient's chin. Just in case they ever missed their mouths. They rarely ever did. Though I did manage to catch a few pairs of false teeth. They'd always bang on my metal plate with a clatter.

What I did have to endure at Holy Communion was a parade of tongues, which was quite traumatic for a child. You can bet if I ever have a nightmare there are tongues in it somewhere.

This constant stream of tongues was quite a surreal sight, and in an effort to process the ordeal, I decided to give the tongues names.

## The Overachiever

This tongue came bounding out like it was auditioning for the lead role in a musical. Fully extended it resembled Gene Simmons' tongue from Kiss. Stretching so far it could have easily licked the recipient's eyebrows.

## The Timid Tongue

My least favourite. It barely poked out past the teeth. I mean, why bother? The priest almost needed a magnifying glass to find it and we both had to lean right in.

## The Lazy Licker

This one wasn't arsed if it got any Holy Communion or not and would just casually flop out like it was on an all-inclusive holiday or drunk at a BBQ. A bit more interested than The Timid Tongue but not by much.

## The Nervous Nellie

Mrs Newns, a loyal parishioner, had one of these. It trembled and shook. As if it couldn't quite cope with Holy Communion. Anxious, like the tongue was thinking, 'What if I fuck this up?' Though Mrs Newns would never swear. She was 106 years old.

## The Lickety-Split

This tongue darted out. Scooped up the body of Christ then popped back in. Like a chameleon snagging a fly. Quick and efficient, blink and you'd miss it.

## The Soloist

This multi-tasking tongue was accompanied by lips still attempting to sing a hymn. Caught by surprise mid-lyric, but it always dutifully delivered when its time came.

## The Big Gob

More of a mouth than a tongue. It would arrive at the altar wide open. The recipient looking like they were ready for dental surgery rather than Communion.

## Eager Beaver

My favourite. This tongue couldn't wait to taste the body of Christ. It was out, ready, waiting at the altar, almost like it was saying, 'Pick me, oh please pick me!'

## The Altar Tease

The tongue always slid out suggestively. And subtly swirled seductively, almost playful. It was a tongue that teased the sacred wafer and managed to combine piety with a touch of sluttiness. It wanted the priest more than the eucharist.

*The Thorn Birds* was a big hit at the time, and it gave some parishioners saucy desires for defrocking their priest. Millions relished watching Richard Chamberlain as Father Ralph de Bricassart torn between the Lord and lust. It said in the *Daily Mirror* that when the last episode of *The Thorn Birds* ended emergency generators had to be activated on the national grid just to cope with all the people brewing up. Apparently, the same thing happened when J.R. was shot on *Dallas*. That was popular to such an extent I wore an 'I Shot J.R.' hat during our holiday to Butlin's.

Where was I? Oh yes, tongues. We had thin tongues, wide tongues, nicotine-stained tongues and deformed tongues (with sections missing). I could see food in between the parishioner's teeth. There was an abundance of bad breath. In fact, I still struggle with PTSD. I think the Catholic Church should set up a careline for ex-altar boys who were subjected to such traumatic tongue practices.

A more preferable option was to receive the eucharist in your hand, then place it in your mouth. Far less disturbing. This was made official practice, well, it was at our church. I can't speak about what still goes on with the missions in Africa or Peru. That's their business.

We would receive an annual visit from a priest serving in the missions. We'd get a different one each year – all of them unintelligible. They'd preach a lengthy sermon then pimp all the cash from our second collection. You know I wouldn't be shocked if church collections offered 'contactless' payment now. Little PDQ machines on the baskets as they go around.

I bet there's a lot of people who wish the priests had been contactless, but I won't navigate those murky waters. Suffice to say that I thankfully never saw or experienced anything untoward during my time as an altar boy. But unfortunately, such abhorrent behaviour destroyed many people's faith and lives.

My mum was extremely proud when I was asked to be an altar boy at school. I just saw it as an excuse to get out of doing P.E. I'd also heard you got money for serving funerals. Fat chance. Our local undertakers McManus (or *McMeanus*) split all their tips with the priest.

The altar boys never saw a penny. I did get a tenner once from a widower who thought I was sobbing when I was actually laughing my head off. I had my back to him so all he could see were my shoulders bobbing up and down. It was his wife's funeral, Grandma Ivy, well, that's what was written in flowers on the lid of the white casket coffin.

Halfway through the service, a pushy aunt nudged the grandchildren to 'get up'. The teenagers sloped out of the benches and reluctantly stood either side of the coffin. The aunt pointed her finger down. Then the grandchildren leant forward and rested their cheeks against the lid of the coffin. Father Michael pressed play on a tape player, and we heard the opening bars of 'There's No One Quite Like Grandma' – St Winifred's school choir. How could I not laugh? Even Father Michael struggled to keep a straight face. The grandchildren had to stand there for the whole song. The best bit was when they lifted their cheeks from the coffin lid. The water-based paint had left a white impression on one side of their faces. They looked like mini-Phantoms of the Opera.

The last funeral I attended was a cremation and it was an embarrassing disaster. A good friend of mine had lost his brother, Frank. Despite not knowing his brother I felt obliged to pay my respects. Unfortunately, Frank was quite young when he passed. So, I knew there'd be a big turnout at the service. I had my concerns. I wouldn't know anybody. Reassuring me, my friend told me to look for his ex-wife Ann and the kids, as he'd be carrying the coffin. It took me an age to find a parking space. Sure enough, when I arrived the place was packed. Mourners had gathered outside the chapel. I saw Ann and the kids and gave them a wave. With tears in her eyes, Ann introduced me to Carol, Frank's widow, who was poleaxed with grief. Immediately she threw her arms around me. We'd never met but I had no choice but to submit as she hugged me and howled into my shoulder. What a shame. We broke our embrace as the funeral procession came towards us. The crowds parted and I saw my friend carrying his brother's coffin. We turned to enter and that's when Carol and Ann both spontaneously linked me. Weeping on either side they led me into the chapel. I was trapped as they walked me down the aisle towards the front bench, traditionally reserved for close family. But I wasn't close family. I hadn't even met the deceased and yet there I was sat on the front row. I could feel the wrath of the other mourners glaring at me. 'Oh, look at Mr TV sat with the widow. Who does he think he is?' Ironically, I could have died myself.

Another memorable funeral I served as an altar boy was when Father Graham fell into a grave. He was a big old Irish priest built like a brick shithouse. One minute we were walking through the cemetery and when I turned around he'd gone. Somebody had forgotten to place boards over the open graves and Father Graham had slipped in the snow and fallen in.

'Father? Father?' I shouted aimlessly. Then I heard a faint cry. Father Graham's distinct Cork accent, 'I'm down here. I'm down this fecking hole. Go and get help, boy.' He was that big he got wedged in the hole. It took four of us to get him out. We had to borrow a mini digger.

Father Graham was a sly old bugger. After he died it transpired he'd been shagging his housekeeper Pat for over twenty years. She even had her own room in the presbytery. When *she* died, they were buried side by side. All men have needs. In my view, the Catholic Church should definitely let priests marry. Maybe if they had there might not have been so much depravity. I knew quite a few priests who went 'over the wall' because they couldn't keep it in their pants or simply fell in love. The 'Thorn Birds' effect.

The Catholic faith is riddled with ambiguities. In fact, we stopped going to church on Sundays when my mum found a loophole in the bible. It states, 'Keep the sabbath day holy,' but it doesn't actually say you have to go to church. So, we'd just have a full breakfast on Sunday morning and watch *The Waltons*.

We didn't just make our first Holy Communion at school, we also had to fulfil other sacraments like confirmation. I didn't really understand that one. All I remember was the bishop laid his hands on me while the holy spirit entered me (make of that what you will). And confession. My least favourite sacrament so far (I'm not looking forward to The Last Rites). The thought of confessing my sins to the priest just didn't make sense. Why would you grass yourself up? It felt immoral. And yet we were encouraged to go behind a closed door in a tiny space and tell our secrets to a man sat behind a curtain. That sounds like a sin in itself.

I was always convinced he'd recognise my voice. I also couldn't think of anything I'd done wrong, so ironically, I had to lie about my sins in order to make a good confession. I mean, I had done some things wrong but there was no way I was ever going to tell the priest.

Serving on the altar did have one benefit. It helped overcome any fear I had about being in front of a large group of people. The church congregation was like an audience and even though I wasn't performing as such I was part of a ceremony which is kind of a performance. Either way, after seven years on the altar I felt confident in front of a crowd, and I think that really helped. I felt like Daniel in *The Karate Kid* and Father Michael was Mr Myagi.

As I said earlier, the church was always chock-full for Good Friday mass and one year there was a huge storm outside. The sky went dark, the wind got up and the heavens opened so loud we could hardly hear the priest. It felt as if the crucifixion was happening all over again. Typical of British weather, two hours later there wasn't a cloud in the sky and the sun was glorious as I rode my sister's bike around the empty streets.

People forget how quiet Good Fridays used to be. It's a bank holiday, and in those days shops didn't open. Sundays were the same. My mum used to send me round to Mrs Dewhurst's back shop to get eggs for the packet Yorkshire pudding mix. Mrs Dewhurst used to live in the back of the dingy little shop and would be so slow getting to the counter the local kids would rob her blind. (And she was partially sighted.) That's if they weren't scared of her ferocious dog that used to leap up and down behind the counter. It terrified me. 'Get down, Sambo,' she'd shout (not the most politically correct name for a dog).

I'd always take advantage of my trips to Mrs Dewhurst's shop by returning any empty pop bottles we might have. 10p back on an empty bottle of Tizer would go a long way. I could get a wealth of goodies from the penny tray. The penny tray will be lost on children today. Mainly because you can buy fuck all for a penny any more. Remember half-pees? It seems absurd now that things used to cost 23½p or 89½p. It feels like such a funny, trivial amount.

Now it costs 40p for a single Fruit Salad or Refresher Chew. A pack of Parma Violets are a quid. Can you believe it? Perhaps it's the government upping the prices to stop children from eating sugar which is now like crack cocaine. I guarantee there'll be an age requirement on sugary treats in a few years. You'll have to crack out some ID just to buy a Twix.

It's got to be a good thing because my generation never stood a chance. I'm surprised we're still here after all the sugar we consumed on penny trays.

Cola bottles, flying saucers, white mice, spangles, shrimps, those necklaces you could eat, dib dabs, love hearts, fried eggs, I could go on. OK, I will: black jacks (they turned your tongue black. Imagine what they did to your insides), candy cigarettes, bazookas, bon-bons, fizzers, flumps, foam bananas, drum-stick lollies, giant strawberries, juicy lips, jelly snakes, pear drops and pineapple cubes, all washed down with a can of Quatro and you'd be off your tits for a month. What chance did we stand? Two words – space dust. I rest my case, your honour. I can remember when a Bounty was one of your five a day.

Food scientists definitely experimented on us. We were consumer guinea pigs. Just look at Pop Tarts, Angel Delight and Arctic Rolls. I once begged my mum to buy a concoction called Ice Magic. It was a chocolate sauce that when poured on your ice cream would set in seconds, forming a hardened shell that you had to crack with your spoon. Lord knows what it was made from. Probably enough e-numbers to kill a small pony.

No doubt our great, great, grandchildren will be regaling legendary tales of us buying a thing called 'Pick 'n' Mix' when we went to the cinema.

'I can't believe it,' they'll say. 'It was actually legal for them to buy sugar in a public place. They'd take these small plastic shovels and fill up paper bags with these Pick 'n' Mix sweets. Then the bag of sweets would get weighed on scales, like drugs, and nobody would stop them?' That's where it's heading, folks.

We still bring our own treats to the cinema. Smuggling them in like drug mules because 'I still won't pay those cinema prices'. It's learnt behaviour. My mum was the same.

# APRIL

Staggering into the Odeon with her anorak bulging with concealed sweets and chocolate. A two-litre bottle of Rola Cola down each sleeve and a packet of Monster Munch in each pocket. You could hear her scrunching a mile away. She looked like one of those homo wrestlers, as my nan used to call them. Then we'd have all the contraband eaten before the trailers were finished. We still do the same now.

I'm a self-confessed chocolate junkie. I experienced one of my darkest moments last Christmas when Susan caught me eating chocolate from the dog's advent calendar.

April is by far worse than Christmas for chocolate temptation. Easter Sunday arrives and an avalanche of chocolate eggs appears on the kitchen sideboard. The temptation is excruciating. I have zero willpower. I swear I can literally hear the chocolate eggs calling me: 'Peter, come and eat us, we're just sitting here.' I can't walk through the kitchen without snapping off some chocolate shell and gorging it (even better when it's chilling in the fridge).

There's nothing lovelier than sitting on the couch with a chocolate egg, a big glass of milk and a biblical epic on the telly. What a treat. Delicately unwrapping the foil around the egg. Gently separating the chocolate shells. Then knocking them together so I could make the sound of a horse's hooves. 'Clippity-clop, clippity-clop' (alright, Peter, we get it).

On Easter Sunday we'd just want to eat our chocolate eggs, but we'd have to go to church again for another long mass with another huge gospel. But I did always enjoy seeing the altar decorated with flowers after the forty days of Lent.

Suddenly it felt alive, bursting with spring: yellows, golds, whites and purples. A carnival of colours celebrating the resurrection. And the aroma from the floral displays scenting the air. I was particularly fond of freesias and, as an altar boy, I'd tilt my head forward when I knelt at the altar so I could subtly inhale their intoxicating scent. I'd also smuggle a couple of cream eggs under my cassock so I could sneakily scoff them during Easter Sunday mass. That's one of the great mysteries of life. Not the resurrection of our Lord Jesus but how and why cream eggs continue to shrink in size while increasing in price.

We'd get overloaded with so many Easter eggs I'd find myself experimenting in the kitchen. Melting their chocolate shells over a saucepan of boiling water in an effort to make my own unique Easter egg or chocolate sculpture. But it always ended in a sticky mess. I was completely inspired by Willy Wonka from *Charlie and the Chocolate Factory* – my favourite all-time book.

Once you'd overdosed on chocolate eggs there wasn't much to do on Easter Sunday. You could sit and watch *Hop* or *Easter Parade* but there are hardly any real Easter films.

The BBC always have a habit of showing *Oliver* on Easter Sunday. It's a classic but the scene where Bill Sykes murders Nancy doesn't sit too well after a lamb roast dinner.

We went away over Easter once, to Ireland, and it snowed in April. (Prince wrote a song about it.) We were watching *Oliver* at Auntie Bernie's house and it was blowing a blizzard outside. God love Auntie Bernie, she used to make the most gorgeous, deep-fried chips. So crispy. (I think I've put a stone on just writing this chapter.) She'd also give us a lift back home to my granny's. Being in a car was a major excitement as we never had one growing up. So, I was made up whenever I got a chance to travel in someone's car. Just beeping the horn was a thrill (I was very easy to please).

Uncle Frank used to take us out in his car sometimes. One Good Friday he took us all out for a drive after mass in his new Ford Capri Ghia. I was well chuffed and spent most of the afternoon with my face pressed up against the front room window waiting for him to arrive. He wasn't even my real uncle. He'd just borrowed my dad's orbital sander. We even went on holiday with him and his family. We stopped in some ropey B&B in Blackpool. I'll never forget it. Uncle Frank's bedroom window fell out in the middle of the night. Crash! What a racket. The glass and whole frame for no obvious reason. The landlord said it was the wind, but it was calm as a coma on the prom. More like shoddy workmanship. The landlord filled the hole with cardboard and gaffer tape. Said he couldn't get any wood till the morning.

Uncle Frank's kids slept through the whole palaver. Then woke up to find the words 'Strawberry Splits' written on cardboard where the window used to be. Anyway, all that happened in September and has no business being in this chapter.

Speaking of B&Bs, the landlord whose window fell out was telling us over breakfast that he'd had a fella stay the previous week who'd committed suicide. Cheery. (He told us this over breakfast which I'll never forget as mine had green mould.) He said he served this fella breakfast and he'd asked for more beans, he obliged but then he asked for more. He said he was a bit reluctant but obliged again, in fact he said, 'He finished off a full tin of beans.' Then he caught a tram to Blackpool Tower, went straight up to the top and threw himself off. The police were called to investigate, and they ended up questioning the landlord back at the B&B. They told him what had happened, and he said he couldn't get his head around why the fella would do such a thing, as he'd been full of beans that morning.

And on that, my friend, I'll head over to the month of May.

# May

Almost unnoticeably we suddenly find ourselves engulfed by lush vegetation. Shades of green that would make a leprechaun blush. Soft pink blossoms pepper side streets as the extended daylight reawakens energy levels we'd forgotten we ever had. And as everything reawakens, I try hard to cherish these days. May is undoubtedly my favourite month. Everything feels so much more achievable, especially when dappled in sunlight. It's a far cry from three months earlier when it was pitch black by 5pm and I was in bed before the end of *Emmerdale*.

Everything feels like a bonus in May because there's less expectation. It doesn't carry the burden of the summer months when we feel entitled to good weather.

As usual, I'm doing the hokey-cokey with our central heating. It's off, it's on. Each day the weather is so interchangeable. Another thing that amuses me is how excited the

British get when we see a bit of sun. We can't wait. Diving straight into holiday clothes when the temperatures really aren't that warm. Girls wandering streets in skimpy bikinis. Sun's out, guns out as people sit freezing in beer gardens and in denial. Frustrated, as the next day we're reaching for coats.

May holds many fond memories. It was the month my wife and I got the keys to our first house. That was nerve-racking. Being confronted with one of the scariest words in the English language – mortgage. I don't know why they don't teach life skills at school. Explaining mortgages and how we pay them. My biggest fear was always getting in over my head and being unable to pay it back. For a long time being a comedian never felt like a proper job. Still doesn't really. Maybe because it never offered much stability. When I was about to make *Phoenix Nights*, I wanted Bernard Manning to play a part in the series. I went round to his house in Manchester to chat and convince him to play a role. As usual, he was sat in an armchair in just his underpants and vest. What a sight. I confided in him my fears regarding signing for a mortgage and he offered me some advice in his own inimitable way.

'Buy the fucking house, you'll be able to afford it, you'll be fine. Do some graft and take a leap of faith because what you need is a good big, solid house with plenty of room. Why don't you take a look around here? There are some lovely houses. Fetch Susan over, I'll put some pants on.'

He was dead right (with his advice, not his pants). We signed for the mortgage and over the next few years we both worked hard to pay as much of it off as we could. We loved that house. The only problem we found was the invasion of privacy that came hand-in-hand with fame.

We'd have people driving past all the time. Looking to see where I lived. They'd slow down and have a good gawp at the house. We'd be sat in the front room. The worst thing was that we lived in a cul-de-sac, so they inevitably had to turn around at the end of the road and have another gander on the way back. I felt like I was living in *The Truman Show* and as the fame increased so did the intrusion.

We once had a woman follow us home from Asda after we'd done our big shop. It was about four miles away. We were getting shopping out of the boot, and she was on her mobile doing a live commentary on us. 'Yeah, he's getting his shopping out with his wife now … nice house.' I thought what a cheeky sod as I lobbed some tomatoes at her head. Tinned.

What attracted us to the house the most was that it didn't need much doing to it. It was well furnished already which was handy for me as I'm crap at DIY. Years later we had a leak on the conservatory roof when it lashed it down. I didn't know where to turn. Then I remembered that the original owner sold conservatories, so I called him to see if he had any advice. 'I'll come round and take a look,' he said. I was grateful but had to fob him off as we'd been in the house six years at that point and still hadn't changed a thing. I was too embarrassed to have him walk back in and see nothing had changed.

We lived in our first house for a couple of years before we became parents, and reminiscing about that period before we had children feels like a hazy hedonistic fortnight now. With long lie-ins at weekends. Eating breakfast in bed watching *CD:UK*. Pure decadence. I joined a Blockbuster down the road, well I tried to, but they wouldn't let me without proof of ID. I even saw one of my live DVDs for hire on the shelf. I felt like holding it up and saying, 'Does this qualify as proof?' But I didn't. I just went back with my driving licence and a recent utility bill.

Leaving my mum was hard. I knew one day it would be inevitable. I pushed it to the back of my mind as it was something I'd been dreading for a long time. I tried to ease the situation by moving out slowly. Taking a few things every time (in fact I think she's still got some of my stuff). It wasn't so much the house I'd miss; it was the relationship we had living together. What can I say, I'm sentimental.

My mum loved our new house and was often up for Sunday dinner. She particularly enjoyed our garden, especially as we'd never had one growing up. When we had a heatwave, I immediately rushed to Toys 'R' Us for a paddling pool. The children were so excited when I brought it home. Then it took about four hours to pump up. The sun was setting when I finally rolled the family paddling pool into place and accidentally straight onto a thorn bush. I almost wept when I heard a very faint 'Sssssssssssss' as it slowly deflated. I've always been a big fan of paddling pools. I once wrote to Jimmy Savile to see if he could 'Fix It' for me to swim in a pool filled with ice-cold Vimto (a bit weird, I know). Unfortunately, Jim never replied (he was probably too busy being a prolific sexual predator).

Nevertheless, I decided to try it myself one summer. Vimto was far too expensive, so I had to make do with two-litre bottles of Rola Cola. I bought fifteen (they were only 30p each) and filled up a paddling pool. Surprisingly thirty litres of Rola Cola only filled about half an inch. What a let-down. Ah well, I got in regardless and lay in the sun all hot and sticky. Covered in warm Rola Cola. Took ages to wash off all the syrup.

We never had much room for parking at our first house. We just had a very narrow ginnel up the side of the house so if Susan and I both parked at the same time one of us had to exit their car via their boot. Not ideal. One evening I'd arrived home first, but before I had the chance to get out of my car Susan arrived and parked directly behind me. She obviously didn't see me clambering over the seat, so went into the house, leaving me trapped and unable to open my car boot as her car was parked right behind me. There wasn't much point in my shouting, she'd never hear me. Now at the time I had two phones (no, I wasn't dealing drugs). I had one phone with work numbers and one for family. Frustratingly my family phone was inside the house and the only person I felt I could contact on my work phone to explain my current predicament was the local priest, Father Philip.

'Hi Philip, is there any chance you could bob round to our house? I'm trapped in the boot of my car. It's a long story.'

'I'd love to, Peter, but I'm in Lourdes with a special needs group. Say hello to Peter, everybody.' Then I heard a load of cheering and jeering. Fortunately, Father Philip called Susan, who came out and freed me.

A similar thing happened another night. I was getting out via the boot as usual when I spotted one of the children's toys stuck down the side of a car seat. I reached to get it, fell forward, and found myself wedged head first between two seats. Upside down and flummoxed. I was there for ages. I couldn't even reach my phone to call Susan and tell her I was stuck outside. I ended up shouting for help. Luckily a neighbouring dog walker spotted my legs sticking out of the boot. They rang the bell and Susan helped me out again.

The first year we lived in the house I was away a lot as I was on tour. That's the only problem I've found with touring, being away from home. That's why I decided to do a residency at Manchester Arena. The Tour That Didn't Tour tour meant I could get home every night. I was also able to put my children to bed before I left for the show which was a joy. Then I'd drive myself to the arena. Literally arriving with minutes to spare with the audience already inside.

I'll never forget the first night. I came off stage, dripping with sweat, ran to my car, headed out of the back gates of the arena before the audience had a chance to leave their seats. I was back home so quickly that Susan thought I was a burglar. She was ready to batter me with a rolling pin.

A quick shower and then I was sat on the couch watching telly. What a gear change. Hard to process that an hour earlier I was on stage. Now I was halfway through *Silent Witness* and a packet of bourbons. I treasured that period of my life, playing those shows, while still being able to be a dad.

\* \* \*

May bank holidays mess you up. We had one yesterday and I'm still convinced it's Monday again today (it's Tuesday). They mess up your week. They also seem to increase the pressure to do something on bank holidays. We usually waste half the day trying to decide what to do. Then end up in a garden centre buying potted plants or a tin opener. Even worse is a DIY store. Those places were made for bank holidays. As I said earlier, I'm pretty crap at DIY. But I certainly never lacked enthusiasm growing up. My dad just never let me help him. Branding me a liability ever since I 'helped' him saw through a door frame.

He shouted, 'Could you sit on this door frame as a weight while I saw it?' I did as he asked. He started sawing and I started daydreaming. Then halfway through I just got up and wandered off. With no weight, the door flipped up and hit my dad in the head. He slipped off course with his saw which went straight through his leg.

Well, he grazed it but by the way he was screaming you'd have thought he'd amputated his leg. I wouldn't mind but Dad wasn't much good at DIY himself. He spent hours hanging the door frame.

'What do you think?' he said proudly.

'Why's the handle so low to the floor?'

He was livid. He'd hung the door the wrong way up.

When it comes to my occasional dabble at DIY, I'm far more encouraging with my children. Making them feel important, getting them involved. 'Oh, I can't do it without you.' The sad truth is I'm that bad at DIY I really can't do it without them. I bought a load of units from IKEA last year and put half of them up the wrong way round. Luckily, they're for storage in the loft so nobody will see what a shit job I've done.

I'm currently upcycling a garden bench and I'm making a right bloody mess of it. Paint splashed everywhere. Somehow completely missing the dust sheets and splattering the walls. The bench was reclaimed. A habit I've definitely picked up from my dad and grandad. They were reclaiming and upcycling years before it was fashionable. My grandad would scour backstreets for skips. Then rush home to tell my dad. 'Hey, Michael, I've found a crackin' door frame down the road. Can you give me a lift with it after tea?'

As soon as night fell, they were both off. That time they let me come with them. What a thrill to be involved. Stealthily we retrieved the door frame out of the skip and scarpered as quick as we could. Then we heard a fella shouting up the road behind us. 'Hey, where the bloody hell do you think you're going with that?' My grandad shouted over his shoulder 'Home' as we hurried home.

May Sunday was another important event in our hectic church calendar, and it was deemed a great honour for a child to be involved in the religious festivity, the May Day procession and crowning. The tension was palpable in class three when Sister Scissors picked names out of her upturned veil. Debbie Loftus let out a high-pitched squeal when she was picked to be May Queen. The starring role. Brian Loftus (no relation) was picked to be Earl Marshal. His job was to guard the May Queen and her crown during the procession (ironically, he was sent down for knocking off a Securicor van in his twenties). I was chosen to be one of the guards who escorts the May Queen and her maids of honour, during the big procession which took place around the streets of our parish.

It was a huge spectacle, with a brass band and hundreds of parishioners. The St Ethelbert's RC School banner was proudly hoisted high, as police stopped traffic on busy main roads. My mum was so proud I'd been picked as a guard. She's still got the navy-blue ruffle I wore down the front of my shirt.

Spectators lined the streets watching us pass. It was common at the time for churches to parade around streets with a band. Often, we'd be having our Sunday breakfast then we'd hear the unmistakeable 'rum-pum-pum' of a brass band approaching. We'd rush to our front door. Alongside neighbours. Nodding at familiar faces parading up the street dolled up to the nines. Such a shame it's all a thing of the past. Probably not a bad thing these days as they'd probably all get mowed down by some dickhead on an e-scooter.

After a few miles, the May Sunday procession would make its way back to a church packed to the rafters. Proud families huddled in benches, clutching instamatic cameras with cube flashes. Hoping for a glimpse of their child. The service climaxed with Debbie Loftus climbing up a stepladder until she was eye level with a statue of Our Lady (that's Jesus's mum for any heathens reading). The congregation belted out the wonderful, heart-wrenching hymn 'Bring Flowers of the Rarest'. Debbie had to wait for the specific lyrics 'Oh Mary, we crown thee with blossoms today, queen of the angels and queen of the May', then she leaned forward and crowned Our Lady's statue with a garland of flowers. I'm getting emotional just thinking about that moment. My mum said they crowned Mary with a halo of glow sticks at church last Sunday. Tacky. It's May Sunday, not a bloody hen do.

After the May Sunday service, I couldn't wait to get out of my fancy guard's outfit and back into my regular clothes: t-shirt and shorts. Before you could say 'immaculate Mary', I was up the local park on my sister's bike trying some off-roading through the bushes. That's when I spun out of control down a sharp incline and with a sudden jolt I managed to wedge my foot between the bike pedal and a tree stump. Ouch! It really hurt. Searing pain. It felt as though I'd broken something. In shock, I sat where I landed for a few minutes letting it all sink in. A lump swelled on my foot the size of a Kinder egg. Slowly I hobbled home via the backstreets. Embarrassed and in agony. When my dad saw my foot, he only inflamed the situation further by ordering my mum to 'go and get my saw from the shed, Deirdre. His foot will have to come off.' This only caused me to go into hysterics. Maybe his revenge for the incident with the door frame. My mum took me to A&E on the bus (no ambulance for me). The nurse said it was badly sprained and bandaged it up. Thank God it hadn't happened the day before or the May Queen would've been down a guard.

Miraculously I got the week off school. Rumours spread like wildfire that I'd severed my foot. When my dad mentioned it to the owner of the video shop, he kindly let my dad pick some videos for me that I could borrow for the whole week. For free. Get in!

That gesture blew me away. The fact I'm still writing about it forty years later goes to show how impressed I was. My dad chose *Flash Gordon*, *The Wild Geese* and *Cannon & Ball Live*. Bizarre choices I know; he must have been in a rush for the pub. I watched each of those videos about ten times that week and I still know almost every word. Especially *Cannon & Ball Live*.

Years later I was fortunate to meet Bobby Ball, who was a big influence on me as well as many other comedians of my generation. He was one of those rare people who was blessed with funny bones and comedy was effortlessly ingrained into everything he did.

I told him this when we met. Also, about spraining my foot and borrowing *Cannon & Ball Live* from the video shop. Bobby was so chuffed he organised a copy of the video on DVD. So kind of him and so good to see it again after all those years. I still knew all the words and the comedy still worked. I watched it with my children, and they laughed a lot. So much so that we went to see Cannon & Ball every year after that in panto. We travelled all over; it gave us something to do at Christmas. Bobby and Tommy were always lovely to us. The last time we saw them was in *Peter Pan* at the Crewe Lyceum with Chico (remember him from

*The X Factor*?). Chico managed to crowbar his hit song 'It's Chico Time' into the panto three times. Then Covid arrived. There were no pantos for a couple of years. Then Bobby caught Covid himself and sadly passed away. I discussed his passing with Billy Connolly, and he was upset too. As I said, Bobby was a big influence on a lot of comedians and loved by so many.

The last time I was with Bobby was when I went to visit him and Yvonne, his wife, in Lytham St Annes. We went out for a meal and then ended up back at their house, Bobby proudly showing off his new Alexa smart speaker on the floor in the corner of the front room.

'Have you got one of these things, Peter? They're bloody marvellous. Alexa, play "Smoke Gets in Your Eyes" – The Platters.'

A few seconds later the song started, and Bobby's face lit up like a Christmas tree. He was chuffed to bits and stood in the middle of the front room serenading Yvonne and myself. Then it all went wrong. As many of you might know, Alexa smart speakers can be unpredictable. Ten minutes later Bobby was on his knees in the corner of the room shouting at the smart speaker which was now playing the wrong songs. 'ALEXA, WHAT ARE YOU DOIN'? NOT THAT ONE. BLOODY HELL! ALEXA, ARE YOU PIGGIN' DEAF ALEXA?'

Unfortunately for many children, May is exam time. The most stressful month of the year. The worry is tangible as millions of pupils revise and succumb to pressure and panic. It's a trial and there's not much we can do as it's a process most of us have to go through.

Revision was never one of my strongest attributes. (What am I saying? The whole school curriculum wasn't a strong attribute.) Every time I tried to revise, I'd end up alphabetising my books/LPs/cassettes or watering plants around the house. Anything to distract me from revision. (If you happen to be reading this book as a distraction from revising, why not go water some plants, it never did me any harm and the plants will be glad of it.)

Plus, I'd been picked to play the Lion in a school production of *The Wizard of Oz* which completely clashed with my exams. So, when it came to my GSCEs I knew I was doomed. I didn't half feel thick at the time. Sat in the assembly hall day after day. Struggling to understand every exam that was put in front of me. It was soul-destroying. Pupils around me scribbled away while I panicked 'I'm going to end up a failure'.

But that's what we were told: 'Mess up these exams and your life is over.' Such an outrageous statement that only increases anxiety. There were far more opportunities in life than what the school curriculum could offer. It was only when I enrolled on a media performance course at Salford University that I finally began to excel academically. Finally doing practical work I felt enthusiastic about.

As I predicted, my GCSE results were poor. Other than my one fraudulent GCSE in Art that I'd manipulated the teacher to award me, I failed everything else miserably. Even receiving an appalling grade 'U' in my Electronics exam.

I'm still convinced I only got that because I spelt my name right.

The final day of school for fifth years (year elevens now) always landed at the end of May. Leavers have a school prom now. We've gone all American. And it's gone a bit ridiculous. Hiring limousines and hummers. Wearing high heels and ball gowns (and that's just the lads). All we got when we left school was a WHSmith's book token and a firm handshake from Sister Sledge.

The nuns knew the school leavers had a tendency to be rambunctious with high jinks and horseplay. Like trashing their uniforms and throwing flour and eggs over each other. That's why the rest of the school was carted off for our annual trip to Alton Towers – for many, the highlight of the school year.

I'd be looking forward to it for months and couldn't sleep with excitement. Waking early on May mornings, sunshine blasting my curtains, lying in bed planning what rides I'd be going on and how many doughnuts I'd buy. OMG! The doughnuts they sold would melt in the mouth. Freshly made, live on the premises. You could actually watch the individual dough plop straight into the scalding fat and cook right before your eyes. Once golden brown they'd be scooped up, placed in a paper bag, and doused in sugar. Manna from heaven. Bugger the corkscrew, I was happy with my annual doughnut fix.

We'd all meet up, bright and early outside the convent. Cacophonous chaos as nuns in blue cagoules (God's play clothes) tried to get three hundred hyped-up kids onto fifteen full-size coaches. A big operation. Though the nuns did have some help from the real teachers. Humans, who'd also be sporting their play clothes. We'd be in hysterics eyeing up their fashions as they endeavoured to dress down with the kids. Some teachers wearing the bluest of blue jeans. Pale sky blue with the biggest turn-ups I've still ever seen. You could hide a small child in either leg.

We'd charge straight to the school to check the notice board and see what coach we were on. Everybody wanted to bagsy the back seat, it was the cool place to sit, plus you'd get a chance to flick the 'V's at other motorists. I remember some girls pretending to be drunk because they'd eaten half a shandy lolly on the way to school. 'Oh, I'm pissed, get me to my seat,' they'd slur, staggering up the aisle.

I always preferred sitting at the front because I suffered from travel sickness, and it was handy if I needed to get off in a rush. It happened once; we were literally about a mile from Alton Towers. I couldn't hold it any longer. The driver pulled the coach over so I could puke up by the side of the road. How embarrassing. Spewing my ring to the deafening sound of cheering and banging on the windows ... the nuns could be so childish.

It probably didn't help that I'd eaten my packed lunch before we'd even got out of Bolton. I couldn't help it. Caught up in the hedonism of day-trip decadence. I'd wolfed down four tuna sandwiches, a packet of Monster Munch and two Blue Ribands. All swilled down with a beaker of Vimto (with some cling film over the lid so it wouldn't spill in my bag). No wonder I was bilious.

We'd arrive at Alton Towers, and we'd be off like firecrackers. First stop was the doughnut stall (regardless of me puking ten minutes earlier). Then with hot paper bag in my hand, I'd leg to the other end of the park to get on as many white-knuckle rides as I could. To be honest I was never keen on rollercoasters but fell victim to peer pressure. Queuing for hours we'd probably only end up going on about five or six rides. Stood baking in the sun, passing time trying to scare each other. Telling horror stories about how someone fell off the ride we're about to go on and had their head cut off.

Alton Towers has remained a familiar part of our lives. We took our children when they were old enough. Obviously, they were too young to go on the rollercoasters, so we spent the day on the kids' rides, but one of them turned out to be worse than any white-knuckle ride. I can't remember its name. It was a mini version of that adult ride where people sit in a row, then the ride shoots high up in the air and then you suddenly drop on a bungee cord. It always plays hell with my testicles. They're usually called something like Drop Zone or The Tower of Terror. Though I think Ball Buster would be more appropriate.

Anyway, the kids' version was gentle enough. No uncomfortable sensations in the testicle region as it only went up a few feet, and then came down quite slowly. My children were strapped in either side of me. We had those heavy harnesses over our shoulders and across our chests, so we were secure. The ride ended and we waited for the harnesses to automatically rise and release us from our seats. Nothing happened. A few seconds passed, but still nothing. My children asked, 'What's happening, Dad?' and I said, 'I think we're just waiting for some people to exit from the other side,' but I really hadn't got a clue. Slightly concerned, I looked at Susan, who just shrugged. The sun was beating down and suddenly I started to freak out. Restricted by the harnesses I started to feel like I was going to pass out … Oh my God, it was awful. Everything began to fade as I started to see stars. Susan could see I was slowly turning white and asked if I was OK. Thankfully my children couldn't see me because I was clearly having a panic attack. My heart beating, trapped and feeling helpless less than two feet off the floor. What the hell was going on? Finally, after what seemed like ten minutes (it was probably only three) the harness lifted, and we were free. I fell to my knees like a rag doll. I wanted to kiss the ground but thought it would be too weird in front of the children. Dizzy and lightheaded, I sat on a small wall and drank some water. It must have been claustrophobia. I never found out what the problem was with the ride, but I never did anything else the rest of the day. Except the doughnut shop.

My body can't tolerate rides and rollercoasters as I've got older. I think it's a bit of an inner vertigo and motion sickness. But it's quite hard to say no when you've got children, so then you go on and immediately regret it. I was on a ride last summer and threw up in my mouth halfway round. I tried to act discreetly but we saw the ride photo as we left (through the obligatory shop) and you could tell I was clearly holding something in my cheeks, so I didn't buy the picture. I never do. I just slyly take a photo of the screen on my phone when the shop assistant isn't looking.

My friend had his stag do at Alton Towers and I'll never forget that day for two reasons. Firstly, I was queuing up for Rita: Queen of Speed when I got a call from Richard Curtis telling me that '(Is This the Way To) Amarillo' had gone to number one.

It remained there for seven weeks, only to be knocked off the top spot later by that Crazy 'little bastard' Frog song that everybody had as their ringtone.

The second reason was what happened when I rode a ride called Oblivion. Strapped in, we slowly ascended the vertical tracks towards a thrilling climax. We were just about to tip over the edge when the ride suddenly stopped. Stuck? Then over the speaker system, I heard the familiar words 'Garlic? Bread?' followed by the sound of giggles. The ride staff pissing themselves laughing. Then after a few seconds, the ride shot forward and sent us hurtling downwards into oblivion. Literally.

I was gobsmacked. When I got off the ride two of the ride assistants jogged over with huge grins on their faces. Then one of them in a thick Brummie accent said, 'Hey, did you hear us shouting "GARLIC? BREAD?" when were you hanging over the edge?' I thought, 'Yeah I did. I'm not deaf. The whole bloody ride heard you, nobhead.'

# MAY

Garlic Bread. I've become synonymous with the stuff for years and probably always will be. Those two words have become one of the weirdest catchphrases imaginable. Tommy Cooper had 'Just like that'. Bruce Forsyth had 'Nice to see you, nice' and I've got 'Garlic? Bread?' It all started when I talked about garlic bread in a stand-up routine on my first live video, *Live at the Top of the Tower* in Blackpool. The context was my dad's reaction when he was first offered garlic bread. He couldn't comprehend the juxtaposition of the two words in one food. 'Garlic? Bread?' Somehow that observation touched a nerve with the public. Perhaps it was the recognition of their own parents' incomprehension of foreign food.

Then I perpetuated the catchphrase by writing it into a scene in *Phoenix Nights*. Brian Potter's trying to resurrect the Phoenix club and tantalises the staff with the prospect of a bigger, better club that would serve food, like garlic bread. Max, the doorman, repeats Brian: 'Garlic? Bread?' To which Brian replies, 'Yes Max, garlic bread. It's the future. I've tasted it.'

Fast forward to 2017. I've been asked to film an advert for Warburtons bread. A Bolton business and national success. Their iconic adverts had previously featured The Muppets, Robert De Niro, Sylvester Stallone and George Clooney so I felt I was among marvellous company. The advert featured Jonathan Warburton in his office. I burst in unannounced, pulling a tartan shopping trolley with a new idea for an advert. I'm midway through my pitch when I'm interrupted by a call from my auntie Barbara 'R Babs'. My phone's ringtone is the theme from *Phoenix Nights*. R Babs wants me to ask Jonathan Warburton if they sell garlic bread. Jonathan Warburton replies 'Garlic? Bread?' And there it was again. I suppose it's my own fault for keeping it going. But I was filming a bread advert. It felt wrong not to include it.

My favourite story about the garlic bread catchphrase happened when I went to watch a performance of Michael Flatley's *Lord of the Dance* in Preston. It was a treat for the in-laws, and it wasn't a bad show, in fact, I enjoyed it more than *Riverdance*. Anyway, it got to the big number in the middle of the show where all the Celtic dancers are effortlessly strutting their incredible stuff to the recognisable main theme. Then the orchestra goes quiet so the audience can hear the speed of the dancers' dazzling syncopated footwork. Then in between the silence, the chorus of dancers all suddenly shouted 'Garlic?' This was immediately followed by more stomping footwork and then the word 'Bread?' I spat my drink out. Turning to Susan I said, 'Did you just hear that?' She nodded. Unbelievable.

We bumped into some of the dancers on our way out of the theatre and they couldn't wait to confirm exactly what we'd heard. 'Did you hear us? Did you hear us all shouting "Garlic? Bread?"' in their strong Irish accents. I told them I did and thought I was having a mental breakdown. I'm sure if Michael Flatley had been there, he'd have pasted the lot of them.

*   *   *

# MAY

In May 1993 I went to one of the best live concerts I've ever seen, Peter Gabriel.

It was a seminal moment that doesn't happen often at music gigs. When the musicians on stage and the audience are unified by some otherworldly joy. I know it sounds pretentious but there really was a positive vibe that night. I often feel it when I do stand-up. Sometimes the energy or synchronicity between myself and the audience is perfect. And the more they give, I give.

Maybe I subconsciously needed that Peter Gabriel concert at that time in my life.

I'd split up with my girlfriend. I'll not tell you her name. I'll allow her some privacy. It was Helen Owen. Well, bollocks to her, she broke my heart.

She dumped me for another lad not long after she went off to Uni. Then got back in touch a few months later to say she 'thought' she'd made a mistake. Suddenly I was presented with a unique situation that every broken-hearted person craves. Talk about a boost to my damaged ego. A chance for retribution? No, unfortunately, I was still smitten and the familiar pain she'd left in the pit of my stomach resurfaced. (Perversely I'd secretly been missing that as much as her.)

I was working as a cashier at the Esso garage (sounds like a line from the Human League). The other lads I worked with were fed up with me whining and when Helen got in touch they begged me not to take her back. But like a fool I agreed to meet her. Now (and here's the excruciatingly embarrassing bit), I really wanted her to think I'd changed as a person (I hadn't changed at all). So I asked Lee, a lad I worked with who was into skateboarding if I could borrow some of his skater clothes. They were quite fashionable at the time in a grungy kind of way.

Lee obliged, so off I went to meet Helen in a pair of very long, baggy checked shorts, a long paisley shirt and a back-to-front skater's cap. I looked like a kid from one of those movies where he's swapped places with his dad. Basically, a right tit.

Lee was also a bit of a stoner. So, I bought a joint off him. It cost me four quid. I thought for some reason it'd complete the façade. I met Helen at the local park. I wanted to glide up to her on Lee's skateboard, but because I couldn't skate to save my life, I just decided to casually walk with the skateboard tucked under my arm. I'd never been able to ride a skateboard, even as a child. I had one but used to lay on my belly as I rolled down Daisy Street and into a lamppost.

What must Helen have thought as I strolled towards her I'll never know, but I'm sure I saw her giggle. God, I'd missed her, but at the same time I wanted her to realise how much heartbreak she'd caused me. It was a real dichotomy. We went for a drive in her dad's car and I insisted on playing her a song on a cassette I'd brought with me (of course I did. Such a drama queen). It was a song by Phil Collins, 'You Know What I Mean'. I thought the lyrics summed up my feelings. Look it up on YouTube. It'll break your heart (mine was still broken so any song would have tipped me over the edge).

I've just listened to the Phil Collins song again. Christ I'm squirming. It isn't very grunge considering I was dressed as a skater. I fought back the tears as we sat parked in her dad's Sierra. Helen didn't seem arsed at all. Heartless. Time for plan B. I got out my joint. It took four Swan Vesta matches to finally get it lit. I think she might have guessed it was my first time. Actually, it was my second; the first time I'd tried to take my pants off over my head. I handed the lit joint to Helen; she took a drag and coughed her guts up. 'What an absolute waste of four quid,' I thought as I put out the joint and shoved it back in my pocket. 'I'll smoke that later when I get home.'

We sat in silence, not knowing what to say. It was awkward between us. I suppose playing that song didn't help. Not knowing what to do we somehow ended up back at her parents', watching *Heartbeat*. What a washout. As Nick Berry sang the end theme tune, I got up to leave. There was only so much I could take. Helen offered me a lift home but then as we were walking down the path her dad came tearing after us. 'Hey, what's this?' We turned to see her dad holding what looked like a joint. My joint. It must have rolled out the pocket of my bloody baggy skater shorts when I'd stood up to leave. We all just stared at each other. Desperately Helen said 'Er … is it not Grandma's?'

'No Grandma smokes Embassy tipped,' her dad replied.

Followed by more awkward silence while her dad lifted the joint to his nostrils and sniffed it. His eyes widening with surprise.

'I think I know what this is.' Then he stormed back up the path taking the joint with him. 'There goes my night strung out on the ganja,' I thought as her dad slammed the front door.

Helen started to cry and went into a complete panic.

'What am I going to do? Oh my God, what am I going to do now!?'

'It'll be alright.'

'How? My dad's got a joint. What if he smokes it?'

'Well, if he's sat on the shed roof singing "One Love" by Bob Marley when you get back home, you'll know he's had a puff.'

'It's not fucking funny. What if my mum smokes it?'

'Likewise, if you see her silhouette in the upstairs bedroom doing that dance from *Tales of the Unexpected*, you'll know she's off her tits.'

Helen was not amused. But I was, and I was still chuckling when she drove home.

I never did find out what happened, and I never saw Helen again.

# June

And so commences the trilogy of summer months. June, swiftly followed by July and August. The subsequent twelve weeks assume their rightful place as the crowning glory of the calendar. Halcyon days bathed in sunshine. Or so we believe.

How the people of Britain can remain so completely naive when it comes to the weather here is beyond me. Surely, we'd know by now how completely unpredictable summer weather can be and yet we remain genuinely shocked and appalled. Like now, I've just received a text from a friend – 'Surely it's not meant to rain in June.' It's lashing it down outside. Flood warnings on the news. Damp, cold, I've even had the heating on for an hour and it's June!! Yesterday it was roasting, cracking the bloody flags, and now I don't know what coat to wear.

We holidayed in Britain for many years until my dad couldn't cope with the weather any more. He'd get incandescent with rage, as if the state of the weather was some kind of personal vendetta (hey, that almost rhymed). He'd look to the heavens and complain, 'You work all bloody year, and you get this. They really should do something about it.' Who? And do what? It's not the government's fault. It's the British climate.

My dad took us on two holidays a year. One in June, and one in September. Though September was usually a long weekend in Blackpool if we could afford it. My earliest recollections of the June holidays were trips to Butlin's holiday camps in Pwllheli, Filey and Skegness (where we had an infestation of earwigs climbing up our beds. That wasn't in the brochure).

My recollections of Butlin's all merge. I was young, six to eight, but I never recall much sunshine. Mind you, I don't think you really notice the weather much when you're a child. You just get on with things. Like the long coach trip from Bolton, during the annual exodus, as thousands fled the town for the seaside and beyond.

We'd dive headfirst into pandemonium down at the bus station. It'd be mayhem as crowds gathered, suitcases in tow. All frantically trying to figure out which coach was leaving from which bus stand. Usually, it was stand Z at the far end. I remember passing this info on to Auntie Kathleen only for her to go in search of a pub called The Stan's Head and miss her coach.

Most of the coaches were the same, a decrepit sixty-seater that unsurprisingly stunk of vomit (and if it didn't, it certainly would by the time I'd arrive). They all boasted 'ventilation' which was via those individual circular air vents that sat in the ceiling above each seat and released the tiniest stream of air. It was a bit like somebody blowing in your face through a straw. They always came alongside a crappy reading light carrying a 2-watt bulb.

These coaches were hammered constantly. Not just by weekly runs to Butlin's but also daily coach trips here, there and everywhere. We'd book day trips via our local newsagent. The coach would even pick up there. The only downside was that it'd pick up from all the other newsagents too, so it could take hours to finally get to our final destination.

On our way home my dad would always try and blag the driver to let us off nearer home. It'd be so embarrassing when he'd sidle down the aisle and say, 'You couldn't drop us off anywhere here, could you pal?' 'I'm sorry but if I do it for you, they'll ALL want it.' Peeved, my dad would go back to his seat. We were only going to the newsagents at the top of the street, lazy pig.

Mystery tours were popular day trips. Hilarious when you think you'd literally buy a ticket and never know where you were going. I suppose that was the thrill. I knew a bloke who worked at Bolton Fish Market. He went to Blackpool for a week and booked on a mystery tour that went to Bolton Fish Market. He turned up back at work. What a let-down.

I'd pass hours on the coach to Butlin's with a colouring book and some felt tips. Once I had a plastic picture puzzle of a lion holding a sunflower. My mum would shuffle around tiles of the image. Then I'd have to re-arrange them back into the correct order. Who needs an iPhone?

Pulling into motorway services would always be a treat. Especially when my dad bought me a *Beano Holiday Special*. Which featured longer versions of the usual comic strips with all the characters on their holidays. I'd be made up. Once he bought me a summer special of *Look-In* magazine which featured a double-page pin-up of Roger Moore in the new 007 film, *Moonraker*. I was ecstatic. How exciting, there was James Bond wearing a space suit, holding a gun, surrounded by scantily clad women. A bold proclamation at the top of the pin-up 'Bond Goes into Outer Space'. When we got to Butlin's I sellotaped it to the wall of my bottom bunk.

We never bought much at services. It was far too expensive. We just ate our packed lunch by the side of the motorway, inhaling fumes from the passing HGVs. We did splash out on a tin of boiled sweets once with a picture of Her Majesty on the lid. All the sweets were covered in white powder for some reason, and we kept the tin forever. Never throw away a good tin.

My ambition for many years was to earn enough money so I could buy a meal from motorway services. Then one night after a stand-up gig in Birmingham I did it. I strolled into the granary and bought myself steak & kidney pie, chips, beans and gravy. It wasn't cheap but it was a dream come true. Proudly I sat down and tipped a sachet of sugar all over my meal. Bugger! I thought it was salt. Sheepishly I went back to the lady on the till and told her what I'd just done. 'Can't you read?' she said sarcastically. I was half hoping she'd offer a replacement meal. No chance. I sat back down and tried to pick individual grains of sugar out of my beans with a fork.

The chalets at Butlin's left a lot to be desired. Basic but functional, they all had the same layout, a living room/kitchen/bedroom with doors off to other bedrooms and a small bathroom with zero windows and a noisy ceiling fan that whirred for ten minutes after you'd flushed. I wonder how many of the chalets are basically the same today but with a fresh lick of paint, a broadband router and a couple of pictures from The Range. Regardless of Butlin's bragging about booking big acts like Diversity and Mr Tumble.

The chalet windows always seemed to be dripping in condensation, caused by either the relentless rainfall or my mum trying to deep fry chips. I remember my dad struggling to get a clear picture on the black and white TV, so he could watch the news and *Happy Days*.

Drawing the short straw, I'd often end up sleeping in the living room/kitchen on a corner sofa that converted into a double bed via a collapsible kitchen table. Snazzy but crap if you wanted a lie-in as your bed would be needed for breakfast. Every day my dad would be up at the crack of dawn. Off for a mooch down the beach and a morning paper. He'd come back and find us still in our pyjamas. 'Come on, get up, you're missing the holiday.'

But that's how we wanted to spend our time. Wasn't that the whole point of a holiday? That you did what you wanted? But my dad never understood it. He'd go mad because it'd take us ages to go out for the day. My sister was the worst.

When she got older, she'd always take a friend on holiday, and they'd both lie in bed until mid-afternoon which drove my dad insane. He just saw it as time-wasting.

Butlin's were strange places. One camp we visited had a swimming pool with a glazed section underneath the water which meant you could swim and wave to people in a café. Equally, that meant people in the café could see kids swim past and flash their arses at the glass. That wouldn't be allowed today. It'd be a paedophile's dream.

When we visited Butlin's they had a couple of camp mascots (by that I don't mean two blokes talking effeminately and mincing when they walked). They were a couple of space aliens called Toot & Ploot. They both resembled The Creature from the Black Lagoon, but with turquoise faces and googly eyes. They featured heavily in the Butlin's brochures and adverts that year. Cashing in on the success of *Star Wars* and the sci-fi boom.

Toot & Ploot would make public appearances on the Butlin's circuit, flanked by security (red coats). Campers would react like they were meeting The Beatles. Paying to have souvenir photos taken with them both. When they turned up at the camp in Filey where we were staying, I begged my dad to let me have an official photo with them. But he wouldn't pay, he just told me to stand near them while he took a sneaky photo on his Instamatic. (Like father, like son.) Then when the pictures were developed we could see Toot & Ploot clearly posing with some other child. All looking in the opposite direction while I stood alongside, my thumbs raised half-heartedly like some oddball.

# JUNE

Every time we went on holiday my dad would always tell me to 'go and find a friend'. Like it was that easy. I'd always try, but it was tough starting a conversation with somebody queuing for the big bumpy slide. I'd resort to showing them my party piece. I'd slap my fingers against the palm of my hand so fast it made a really loud slapping sound. I know it sounds rubbish but apart from my mum I've never met anybody else who can do it (or want to). I'd show 'my party piece' but never succeeded in making any friends (or going to many parties either). Kids would just look at me like I was deranged, as I followed them up the bumpy slide flapping my hands.

Shit! I've just tried it after all these years, and I can no longer do it. I'm gutted.

Sadly, we've only got a handful of photos from those Butlin's holidays. People didn't take as many photos as it was expensive. It's not like these days where we have thousands of images on a single phone. Back then you had to buy a film for your camera that allowed you to take twenty-four or thirty-six pictures. Then you'd have to pay to get the film developed. I was trying to explain all this to my children. Having to delicately remove the camera film and keep it away from daylight so its negatives wouldn't get overexposed and ruin the pictures.

I was telling them that chemists used to develop photos, as well as dispensing prescriptions and selling whistle lollies. Bizarre really, when you think, it's a bit like shoe menders cutting keys. Later, dedicated shops like Supasnaps and

Prontaprint popped up on the high street specifically for developing photos in all shapes and sizes. Though it'd still take a few days to get them back. You'd see eager customers keen to view their photos outside the shop, almost getting knocked down by passing cars as they jay-walked in front of traffic. Laughing and screaming while they tried concealing photos from each other – 'Oh my God you're not seeing that one!'

Photos rarely came out as well as you'd imagine. Sometimes, they'd have a 'Quality Control' sticker stuck on by the chemist. A kind of patronising critique of your photography skills. I particularly enjoyed those mundane photos that were taken just to use up the camera film. Like pics of your parents raising a glass sat in the backyard or the dog asleep in front of the gas fire.

I've just been looking through my old photos from Butlin's. They're really poor quality. One with my nan posing in The Safari Bar with a macaque monkey on her shoulder. Do you remember that phase when it was acceptable to get your photo taken with one of those God-awful squealing monkeys? You'd be walking along a prom, and somebody would throw a monkey on your back and shout 'Do you want your photo taken with the monkey?' When it was already tearing your hair out. My nan looks terrified in that photo.

There's another picture of me riding on a cable car in Skegness with my grandad. I loved the rides at Butlin's especially because they were all-inclusive. I could go on as many times as I liked, and I certainly made the most of it. Dragging my mum and dad around the fair all day. Unfortunately, the

130

arcades weren't free, and because of the rain (which it often did), I'd be in there a lot. Playing bingo with my mum or racing camels on The Arabian Derby. That was a racing game run by guys dressed as Arabs, who did commentary on a microphone. You'd have to keep rolling a small wooden ball up a ramp into a hole so that your numbered plastic camel could race to the finish line and hopefully win you some tokens. The weather must have been really crap that year because my mum won enough tokens to get a set of bathroom scales.

One arcade had a fantastic shooting game. It was a full-size replica of a wild west saloon. You'd fire at various targets, including one on a wooden toilet door. If you hit it the door would fly open to reveal the mannequin of an old cowboy taking a shit. Being seven years old I thought that was the funniest thing I'd ever seen and fired at that bog door as often as I possibly could.

Another game we all loved to play was air hockey. You know the one where you bat a puck across a flat table to score. We'd spend ages playing each other. Stacking our 10ps on the side so we could bagsy the next game. I also devoted a load of time to electronic arcade games like Space Invaders and Pac-Man. They were addictive. Then I'd be back badgering my mum and dad for some 'more money please'.

Butlin's camps had cinemas too. They were all one-screen flea pits, but I loved films, so found them exciting. We watched many films, *The Muppet Movie*, *Digby – The Biggest Dog in the World*, *Live and Let Die* and *Emanuelle in Bangkok*, to name but a few. One time when we were leaving a busy cinema after the film, I took hold of what I thought was my dad's hand but when I glanced up to say something I saw that it was some strange bloke. He had the denim jeans like my dad, but I was only waist-high and didn't look up. I let go of his hand and panicked: where was my family? Nowhere. I started welling up. It's an awful feeling being lost when you're a child (it's not much better when you're an adult either). Then I saw my dad standing near a kiosk with the rest of my family all laughing, watching me in tears panicking, the sick sods, but I was very relieved to see them.

Thinking of that I've just remembered Butlin's used to offer a babysitting facility.

Parents could go out for the evening within the campsite and book somebody to patrol outside of your chalet. They obviously thought nothing of it in those days but how weird is that? A stranger patrolling the campsite listening for kids crying. If they heard a disturbance they'd report to the main ballroom, and it'd get written on a giant blackboard sat on stage, 'Child crying in chalet 46', while some magician would be sawing his female assistant in half.

I still can't even believe that was acceptable. My mum and dad did it for us once. They went off to the ballroom to watch some act from *Opportunity Knocks* while R Julie and me lay in our dark chalet, petrified by the creepy silhouette of a strange person walking past our window every few minutes. Who was this person? Had they been CRB checked? Not likely.

# JUNE

We were both so traumatised that my mum refused to leave us again. I've just been reminded by a couple of the photos I've just found. R Julie and me tucked up in bed with my mum, both with a book each. R Julie's got an Enid Blyton, while I'm reading *Noddy: Gets Left Alone at Butlin's While Some Weirdo Patrols His Chalet*. A classic.

Inevitably it would always be my birthday when we were on holiday. Now I don't mean to jump the gun (or the month), my birthday is 2 July but our holiday would always fall on the last week in June and straddle my birthday. It was a fortnight known as Wakes Week (or more commonly now, half-term). This meant I'd get presents that were always a bit useless for the rest of the year. Like a lilo, a snorkel set or when we were in Torquay an inflatable dinghy. I'd badgered my parents for it since we'd arrived. Then on my birthday they caved in. Hooray! I had my own dinghy which was fantastic at the seaside but useless back in Bolton, forty miles inland. It was a bit like winning the speedboat on *Bullseye* and living in Tamworth.

My dad spent ages inflating it with a foot pump. We all had a go, even my grandad with his angina. Finally, I sailed out to sea and fell fast asleep. How I nodded off I still can't remember. I was only ten, it's not like I took daily naps. I just remember lying back, relaxing in a 'this is the life' sort of thing. The next thing I felt was cold water being splashed on me. I opened my eyes to see two blokes swimming towards me. I was miles from shore. Shit!! How had that happened? I'd only closed my eyes for a few seconds. 'Hey, wake up, you've gone out too far, you need to get back to shore,' one of the fellas panted in a Devon accent. Grabbing for my oars I frantically started to paddle back to the beach. One bloke grabbed the string at the front of my dinghy and yanked me back to shore. I could make out my family, waving in the distance. My mum hysterical. My dad's face crimson. I was grateful for those two blokes swimming out to save me. Otherwise, I might have been spending my eleventh birthday in France.

When we were at Butlin's, my dad put in a sneaky birthday request with the red coats. This meant the whole dining hall would sing 'Happy Birthday' to me. They did it every morning at breakfast for anybody celebrating their birthday. That person was then required to smile and stand on their chair. Unbeknown to me it was my turn. I was mortified when they read my name out over the microphone. My family beamed as three hundred people started to sing. I wanted to hide. A red coat bellowed down the mic, 'Stand on your chair, Peter.' Not a bloody chance. I slid under the table in tears. My dad kept trying to yank me back up. I sobbed, humiliated. And he was fuming because I wouldn't join in and I was fuming with him because I didn't want the attention. It was one of the few times we ever fell out.

Saying that, there was another time when I thought it'd be a brilliant idea to run through some smouldering hot ashes in the backstreet. All the local kids were doing it. Mr Callaghan's shed had burnt down the night before. The embers were still burning red as we took turns running through them. I felt fearless, even stopping to do a little jig at one point, midway through the cinders, anything to get a laugh. But the fun ended when I noticed the soles of my new school shoes had melted.

My mum was furious, but my dad went berserk. He slapped the back of my legs and sent me off to an early bed. Then I heard the front door bang; he'd gone out, it was Friday night. Ten minutes later my mum said I could come downstairs and watch *The Gentle Touch* on ITV. I'd have preferred to have stayed in bed.

It's the same these days. Sending your children to bed is no punishment. They're not bothered, they spend most of their time up in their bedrooms anyway. It'd be more of a punishment forcing them to sit and watch *The One Show* with you.

It sounds abhorrent that my dad slapped the back of my legs, but I understand it was the time we lived in (that's not an excuse, it's a fact). Don't get me wrong, it wasn't pleasant but hitting children was the norm back then. Nuns would often batter us at school. Sister O' Mercy slapped me across the face once because I was talking in assembly. I was so upset I marched straight out of school, went home, and told my mum. She went straight up to school to have it out with the headmistress, Sister Sledge.

My mum said when she was in Sister Sledge's office listening to her trying to explain why I got a backhander, a volley of toilet rolls came flying out of the classroom window on the top floor. Suddenly Sister Sledge snapped and dropped her façade, flung open her office window and wailed 'Whoever's doing that is going to get a wallop' in her thick Dublin accent. Then she composed herself and continued her reasoning.

Another nun, Sister Meen-ol-bitch (picture Miss Trunchbowl from *Matilda* in a black veil and cassock), grabbed me by my hair and dragged me around the chemistry lab just because I didn't shut the door properly. And she once hung Paul McGregor on a coat peg for the whole lesson. He was still limping from that wedgy till the new year. I've already told you about them throwing board dusters. One of them gashed Keith Walsh's eye open. So, trust me when I tell you that having the back of my legs slapped by Dad was tame in comparison to the punishments dished out by The Sisters of The Cross & Passion.

My dad wasn't perfect. I'm a father and neither am I. But what I appreciate now are the complexities of parenting. Every generation tries to compensate for what they believe are their parents' mistakes but in doing so they create more mistakes themselves. My view is that my generation has swung too far the other way. We now over-love our children. I keep expecting to flick on the TV and see some Jeremy Kyle-style show with the episode title 'My Parents Loved Me Too Much', featuring kids complaining about their parents. 'I was smothered in love. They told me they loved me fifty times a day.'

But I'm just as guilty. One minute I'll be spouting clichéd lines at my children: 'When I was your age, I'd walk everywhere,' etc. Then five minutes later I'll be offering them a lift somewhere because it's started raining.

I mentioned that we never had a car growing up. My mum passed her driving test but unfortunately we could never afford a car and my dad never learnt to drive. My dad's parents didn't really encourage much aspiration. I don't believe it was deliberate, it was the reality of that generation. Their aspirations were probably to stay alive and put food on the table both during World War II and its aftermath. Fundamentally their lives were all mapped out. Leave school, work in a factory, create a family, retire, die, oh and try and visit Butlin's once a year if you were lucky.

The only interest or hobby they ever nurtured in my dad was going to the pub. That was the only real release working classes had back then. Graft all week and let loose at the weekend. So sadly, the main memories I have of my dad are of him working, sleeping or going to the pub. It was all learnt behaviour from his parents. I'll give my dad his due though, he did like to go for a walk, to the pub. He'd go on walks with me in summer, that were basically disguised as a pub crawl. It would often start with a familiar proposition at the tea table: 'Fancy a walk later, son?'

We'd amble down the hill to Haslam Park. Thirsty, my dad would pick up pace and swiftly target The King's Head. Thankfully it had a beer garden and some swings which meant I could entertain myself before we headed across the road to The Stag's Head for a drink. Immediately followed up by a quick one in The Queen Anne next door. Then we'd mosey over the road to MY favourite part of the walk, Sou's Chippy, for a portion of chips in a tray with pea wet (pea juice poured over the chips with a ladle) and scraps (bits of crispy batter left over from cooking fish).

My dad would say, 'You always have to have that little bit extra.' Which was ironic: we'd just visited three pubs in two miles. 'Your eyes are bigger than your belly,' he'd say, while nicking a fistful of chips.

We'd cut up the backstreets towards home. Frustratingly he'd always call for one last pint at The Willows. My least favourite pub, as it didn't have a play area, we were less than two hundred yards from home, and I'd eaten all my chips. I'd pass the time standing in the vestibule studying the drink prices and opening the big door for incoming patrons. Some men 'thanked me', but most didn't. The ones that did got a salute. Which I think they appreciated.

My dad came out to check on me once, pint in hand. I was fed up with waiting, so when he went to take a swig I pushed the pint glass into his face. Not viciously, only jokingly to hurry him up. But he didn't see the funny side. Beer spilt all down his cardigan. 'YOU COULD HAVE CUT THE BLOODY MOUTH OF ME.' This was the second time I got my legs slapped. We walked home in silence.

My dad was a right drama queen when it came to pain. Like the time we went to the Bolton Marathon. This was a huge event that took place every year. The marathon was one of the first outside London. Twenty-six miles, televised within the Granada region. One year we were on camera for a nanosecond when my family stood in the pissing rain for hours, waiting for Jimmy Savile to run past flanked by nonces. What fools were we?

Apparently, the final few miles of the marathon were the toughest, as runners struggled to climb Smethurst Lane (or as it was nicknamed 'Heartbreak Hill'). Once over the peak, it was all downhill, literally, straight to the finish line on a packed Hulton Lane playing fields – the hub of the day's events. Thousands gathered to celebrate. There was a funfair, a 'fun' bus, featuring top celebrity DJs from our local radio station Piccadilly 261, as well as a big beer tent. My dad's favourite.

I'd take a small transistor radio with me so I could listen to Piccadilly Radio during the marathon and simultaneously watch the DJs broadcasting live from their open-top 'fun' bus. Desperately trying to catch the occasional bit of merch as they threw t-shirts and window stickers into the frenzied crowd below.

Me and R Julie would always head to the funfair. My dad chaperoning us, clutching a pint from the beer tent. 'Make sure they give you the right change,' he'd shout as we clambered onto the speedway. Bagsying a bike each. 'These gypo's will fleece you.' (Now I fully appreciate that word isn't appropriate but I'm quoting my dad in 1983. Is that allowed? Surely a person's memories can't fall foul of political correctness. Anyway, I'll soon find out when the publishers make me remove that last line from the book and then you won't even be reading this. Mind you, if they do let me leave it in, I'll probably wake to find the lead stripped from the roof of my house as retribution.)

The lads collecting money on the funfair rides were always cool. Walking backwards as the ride hurtled around at 100mph. Casually eyeing up girls and counting change. What a skill.

My dad was jogging alongside the speedway as it gathered momentum. 'Oi! Are you listening to me? I said make sure you get your chaaaaaange,' and that was the last thing he shouted before he tripped over a cable and disappeared under the ride. You're laughing. He lost both his legs ... well he didn't but you'd have thought he had the way he cried all the way home.

Ten minutes later we were hobbling home. My dad's arms wrapped around both our necks. Shouting 'WALK SLOWER' and 'GO DOWN THE BACKSTREETS. I DON'T WANT ANY BUGGER SEEING ME LIKE THIS.' He was quite a sensitive man.

Like the time he was in Bolton town centre, standing at the top of a very steep hill eating a pastie, watching a lady struggle up the vertical slope towards him. She reached the top, put down her shopping bags as she paused to breathe.

My dad said, 'Are you OK, love? It's a steep hill, isn't it?'

She took a beat, contemplating what he'd said. Then replied: 'Fuck off, you ugly pig.'

My dad was crushed.

Another time he was walking out of Bolton Market Hall when he saw a woman keel over right in front of him. A crowd quickly gathered. My dad bent down by the side of her. 'Quick, somebody call an ambulance. Is everything OK?' The lady lifted herself and whispered to my dad, 'We're filming,' and nodded towards a camera crew on the opposite side of the street. We were in hysterics when he told us.

June half-term always reminds me of the time I was on tour in London and Paddy was with me. I was playing shows at the Hammersmith Apollo at night but during the day I had plenty of time to kill, so decided to head into central London to see some sights. I'd been going to the capital for years but had never taken the time to enjoy any cultural high points. Paddy and I caught a bus to the Science Museum. It was enormous with a smorgasbord of exhibits. I felt like I was back in primary school on a trip, which was ironic as it was half-term and the place was packed with kids on trips. Paddy and I couldn't go on any of the exhibits because we felt like a right couple of predators. Awkwardly queuing. When it eventually came to our turn, we bottled it and left. An utter waste.

Speaking of June half-term, one of my all-time musical heroes is Eric Clapton the legendary guitarist. My dad used to play his LPs, so I'd grown up listening to his music. I'd also seen him play live quite a few times. (In fact, one of my most favourite songs of all time is 'Badge' by Cream if you're interested.) Anyway, thanks to my fortunate work in comedy I once found myself backstage at Manchester Arena meeting Eric Clapton. What an honour. A friend of mine worked on the production side of the touring show and managed to organise a meet and greet. I didn't believe him at first and thought it was a wind-up. Sceptically sitting in my seat after the concert, but true to his word he came to get me and before you could say 'Layla' I was backstage shaking hands with Eric 'flipping' Clapton. Not too hard though as his fingers were probably insured.

I tried to convey just how big a fan I was, only for him to acknowledge he was a big fan of mine. I responded with 'Bollocks'. But then he began quoting lines from my stand-up routines and *Phoenix Nights*. It turned out he regularly watched my DVDs on the tour bus with the rest of his band. This was overwhelming as you can imagine, especially as most of his band were American. I didn't think they'd understand my humour, let alone jokes about social clubs. Steve Gadd, his drummer, said, 'what's not to understand about *Phoenix Nights*? There's a horse trying to shag a bucking bronco.' I suppose he had a point.

Our whole conversation backstage was surreal, then as we parted Eric Clapton asked if we could exchange emails. I thought nothing would ever come of it. Then a few days later a message from Eric Clapton popped into my inbox. 'Hi Peter, how are you? I've just come off stage at Madison Square Garden.'

How mental was that? I replied, 'That's amazing. I've just been to my nan's flat for my tea.' It was the truth. Anyway, how could I compare with coming off stage at Madison Square Garden? We were in two different worlds.

Remarkably we kept in touch. Often chatting via email. Occasionally on the phone. It felt genuine. It *was* genuine but deep down I couldn't help but keep thinking 'It's Eric fecking Clapton'. Like I said, I'd always been a huge fan, but we never talked about work, just life and family. Normal things, so it wasn't difficult to separate the art from the artist.

What I did discover was how generous he was. We were talking about holidays, and he said I was more than welcome to go and stop at one of his houses. I was blown away. He said he had a house in the south of France if I ever fancied staying there with my family. I was straight on Jet2.com. How could I refuse an offer like that? Not because it was Eric Clapton's house but because it sounded stunning. And it was.

A sixteen-bedroomed chateau in Provence, surrounded by acres of greenery. A magnificent outdoor pool with a diving board and a TV with Sky. We felt like competition winners.

Giddy to get in the pool, we flung open the cases and started to unpack as quickly as we could. I grabbed an armful of toiletries. Susan unpacked clothes. I opened a drawer and was shocked to find Eric Clapton had the same underpants as me. Gobsmacked, I told Susan as I held up a pair of budgie smugglers with a hole in its arse. Susan shook her head. 'They're yours. I've just put them in the drawer.' Hilarious. I thought what are the odds of Eric Clapton getting his underpants from George at Asda.

We headed out into the sunshine and to the pool which, despite the June heat, was surprisingly cold. Really cold. We were only in the water for a few minutes, and we noticed the sides of the children's lips were turning blue. They were freezing, shivering, so we had to get out. How disappointing. Undeterred, I drove to the local supermarché and bought a massive paddling pool. Foot pump and a packet of Les Cadbury's Fingres, for old times' sake.

The children were beyond excited but that all faded when it took hours to inflate. My foot was still pumping in my sleep.

I sat the huge paddling pool on a patio outside four enormous French doors (I wonder what the French call them?). It was laid on some sandstone flags which I thought might be a bit hard for the children if they banged their heads so to cushion things I padded the floor out underneath the paddling pool with some black and gold Versace bathmats I found in a cupboard downstairs. Like you do.

It took a further five hours to fill the paddling pool up with water. By that time the children were fed up. I also couldn't find a hose anywhere, so had to fill up the paddling pool with buckets of hot water. Trekking each one of them from the kitchen to the patio. By the time I was finished I had arms like Mr Tickle. But it was all worthwhile as I lay in the hot water with my family, sipping a glass of Baileys, watching *Only Fools and Horses* on a giant TV through the French doors. Heaven on Earth.

I'll never forget the look of confusion on the housekeeper's face when she arrived to tend to her garden and found us all sat in a paddling pool on the patio just by the side of an enormous swimming pool. I bet she thought who are these people?

What are they doing in there? They've got to be blackmailing Eric Clapton.

We all had great fun in the paddling pool, but finally it came time to leave and empty the water. I released the little plug at the bottom of the pool, but nothing happened. Three thousand litres of water and not even a trickle. We were going to miss the plane home. So, I did what any sane thinking person would do: I got us all to lay our full body weights over the sides of the paddling pool, allowing a tsunami of water to come flooding out. 'Woo-hoo!' I shouted as we aquaplaned on the patio. But our decadent joy quickly turned to terror when I remembered the housekeeper's flower bed was directly underneath the patio. 'Shit, stop!' Was it too late? Nervously we peered over the ledge only to discover her cherished flowers had washed away. Her prized hydrangeas, clematis and geraniums had all floated down the lawn.

Worse was to come. I lifted the paddling pool to find that the humongous water pressure from the paddling pool had caused the dye from the black and gold Versace bathmats to soak into the sandstone flags on the patio. Double shit!

Quickly I grabbed a few scourers from the kitchen, some fairy liquid and we all started scrubbing, but nothing was lifting. Panicking, I pegged it back to the supermarché and bought some steel wire brushes, industrial floor cleaner, a rake and some more Les Cadbury's Fingres. (Chocolate aids shock. Well, it does for me.)

Half an hour later my family were on all fours scrubbing the patio, while I was raking dead flowers back up the garden.

Foolishly trying to get them to stand up in what was once a flower bed. I resorted to sellotaping the flowers to lolly sticks and sticking them in the soil. What a disaster!

When we got home, I immediately rang Eric Clapton and offered to pay for his patio to be power washed and some new flowers replanted. He was just puzzled as to why I'd bought a paddling pool in the first place. I told him the swimming pool had been freezing and about the kids' lips turning blue. He said, 'But why didn't you just turn on the pool heating?' The bloody pool had heating. No bugger told me.

# July

It's my birthday today, so I thought I'd spend it with you. That may seem a bit sad, but I've loved writing this book and aren't you supposed to do what you love on your birthday? OK, I might slip off occasionally for the odd 'slither' of birthday cake but otherwise you have my full attention.

My family always ask, 'What would you like for your birthday?' 'World Peace' I always reply, either that or '*The Chase* not to be on ITV seven nights a week.' I don't actually mind it. It's just on too much.

One thing I've always wanted is to go sailing on a lake in the sunshine. I came close the other week when we went to the Lake District and hired a boat. Nothing fancy, just a little motorboat. I strolled up to the pier and asked a lady smoking a roll-up (I swear I smelt weed) how much they would be to hire. She briskly informed me 'We don't handle cash since Covid, so you'll have to book on their website.' I thought,

'Christ, play the game; I can see the boats. They're about eight feet away and they're empty,' but she was having none of it.

So then I had to stand in the baking midday sun while I tried to book a boat that was literally in front of me, online with a piss-poor intermittent 3G phone signal. When I finally got on the website, I was then forced to set up an account. Oh, Jesus, I was losing my mind and the children were about to keel over in the heat. I had to pick a password, confirm my password, register my email, confirm my email and then wait to receive a confirmation email. By now my children were foaming at the mouth. Then another woman waltzes up to the pier and says, 'Hi, I rang up earlier about hiring a boat. I don't have access to Wi-Fi so they said I could just pay when I got here with cash.' I was aghast.

'Oh yeah,' says the lady, 'just pay that man over there in the hut.'

What!? And I'm stood on one leg developing skin cancer, waving my phone in the air so I can get a confirmation email and she's paying cash?

I wasn't in a great mood. We finally got on board, then sailed straight across Windermere and onto a sandbank. We were stuck. So now I had to google the phone number of the boat company (that I could see across the lake) to ask them if they could send somebody to tow us off the sandbank. It went straight to voicemail. Fortunately, some chancer in a sailor's cap cruised over to us, tooting his horn, threw us a rope and yanked us free. The whole idyllic experience I'd envisioned was ruined.

If the pothead lady on the pier had told us to watch out for sandbanks we would have. When we got back to the pier, she said, 'Oh did you get stuck?' with a big smile on her face. She was probably high as a kite.

In an effort to restore the mood, I called at a shop across the road for some calming ice creams. The girl behind the counter said, 'Peter Kay? Did you get your boat stuck on the lake?' I thought, Christ, it'll be on the local news in an hour.

Fortunately, my story wasn't half as embarrassing as what happened to my plumber friend Keiron. He told me that he took one of those very same boats out on Windermere with his wife, one sun-drenched afternoon. They were in the middle of the lake for quite a while, drinking bottles of cider and lager. Then he was bursting for a wee. 'I didn't know where to go, so having no choice, I grabbed one of the empty lager bottles and let loose. There was nobody around, I stood up facing away from land, obviously. Then from out of nowhere one of those bloody big tourist boats came sailing past. Everybody waving at me and taking pictures. My wife shouted "STOP". I said, "I can't love, once I've started there's no going back."'

I know exactly what he means. I was watching Genesis at Knebworth and was bursting for a wee when Lisa Stansfield was on stage (she was the first support act at three o'clock). They had toilets there, but we had a great spot near the stage. I thought if I chanced it and got lost I might not find my way back to my mate and he was driving us home.

I had no choice but to hold it in. By the time Genesis came on stage my back teeth were floating. When they'd finally finished two hours later, I couldn't see colours. My kidneys were packing up. I needed a MASSIVE slash. We rushed back to the car where I fell to my knees and 'let go with the yellow flow'. But then I couldn't stop. It was like nothing I'd ever experienced. I was pissing like a racehorse. People were walking past and all I could do was smile and apologise. I couldn't even nip it as litres cascaded out. I think I created my own little Lake District, right there in that field.

Looking back, I've had some unforgettable birthdays. Though not always for the right reasons. I spent my eighteenth birthday blowing eggs in a caravan in Wales. One of my friends had heard that if you made a tiny incision with a pin at both ends of an egg you could blow out all the contents and then decorate it. Christ, I knew how to live. I've also got completely soaked while fully clothed stomping in the sea in Barmouth while listening to The Doors ('Love Her Madly') on my Walkman. That was a privilege of youth.

Later, we visited the otherworldly village of Portmeirion, where *The Prisoner* was filmed. With its colourful façades, lush gardens and iconic Bell Tower overlooking the bay. We called at a café, where I accidentally fell backwards through a fire door and cracked my head open on some gothic architecture. I ended up spending the night in A&E. Happy eighteenth.

When it was my twenty-first, I was working at Top Rank Bingo (the worst job I ever had). I went out with my family for something to eat at a pub restaurant that'd been highly recommended. We couldn't book in advance (I don't know why, they wouldn't accept reservations). So, we waited for hours. My nephew was teething at the time. Hungry and crying. Sadly, we had no choice but to throw the towel in and went to our local chippy instead.

Now I don't know if I ate something dodgy, but I felt dreadful and was up all night puking, with the Brad Pitts. Nevertheless, I still went to work the next day. 8am I was back down the Top Rank making sandwiches. When Jean the supervisor saw my ashen face, she sent me straight home. Said I couldn't be around food in my condition. The next day I got a written warning from the manager. He'd heard I'd turned twenty-one, presumed I'd been out on the lash and that was the real reason I was feeling rough because I'd been out celebrating. I told him, indignantly, in a very high-pitched angry voice that I didn't even drink, but he was having none of it. Arsehole.

My thirtieth wasn't too bad. Some friends came around and we played pin the tail on the donkey. You can't whack a parlour game. (Though I do draw the line at Murder in the Dark.) The night before had been the last show of my stand-up tour, so I was completely knackered. I really didn't want to get out of bed. I was knackered on my fortieth birthday too, which fell right in the middle of filming *Car Share*. Susan had booked a meal, but I was tired from filming and reluctant to go. I felt bad because we hadn't seen much of each other so decided to go. I was too weary to even put a belt on my pants. I thought, sod it, we'll just go to the restaurant, eat, and come straight home. Who needs a belt?

What I didn't know was that Susan had organised a forti-eth birthday party. I walked into the restaurant, and everybody I knew shouted 'surprise' and I thought 'shit' and yanked up my pants. Then I spent the rest of the night constantly pulling on my strides for fear of them falling. It was a great night but I did find you can't have as much fun when you're the centre of attention. I spent most of the night obligingly thanking people for 'taking the time to come' while watching family and friends having a right good dance. Wish I could have joined them. But my pants would have been around my ankles.

That fortieth was the first birthday party I'd had since I was four. Don't pity me. Birthday parties weren't really 'a thing' in the seventies and eighties. Well, not where I lived. And I'm probably going to sound like a whining pensioner now, but kids have it all these days. When I turned sixteen, I got the soundtrack from *Good Morning Vietnam* on LP, and I was made up. For my eighteenth, I got a CD player from my family … and I still chipped in thirty quid of my own money. We were skint. But kids today just mainly get money for their birthday. A ton of it too. I was over the moon just to find a few pound coins sellotaped inside my birthday card.

Can you remember when people actually did that? You could feel there was something inside just from the weight of the envelope. Heavy and misshapen before you'd even opened it. If I sellotaped some pound coins inside a birthday card today and gave it to a child, they'd look at me like I'd got two heads. I wouldn't be surprised if companies didn't start printing a section in birthday cards where you can put your sort code and account details. Cut out the middleman.

When I was growing up, I went through a phase of buying weird presents for my friends. Random things for a laugh, like crap LPs from charity shops, a tea cosy, some lady's plastic mac. A giant bag of cooking flour. I think you get the gist. I'd spend ages wrapping them up, then I'd be in hysterics watching their puzzled look when they opened it. I once glued three paperback books to a plank of wood.

I'd get decent presents too. I wasn't completely nuts. I'd spend a lot of my wages buying gifts for friends and making them personalised compilation tapes. As we spent time together over the year, I'd make notes of songs they liked or scenes they'd enjoyed when we'd watched TV or films. I'd then spend hours (and I mean hours) recording those same scenes from various videos and segue them in between their favourite songs. There was no YouTube or Spotify, so it was a case of searching and buying. I'd even make a cover for their compilation. An image of something they'd find funny, cut out, and pasted onto the inlay card of the cassette box. Please note I was single during this period of my life.

People bug me when they say, 'I didn't know what to get you!?' Just give a personal gift. It's much better to give somebody something unique. They'll love the fact you've made the effort. Frame them a picture? Make them a playlist? Bake a birthday cake?

As a society, I think we've gone birthday cake mad. Children get a cake from their parents, their grandparents; if their birthday isn't celebrated that day, they get another on their birthday or another down the soft play in the party room. It's a cake-fest. At any one time, we can have three cakes in the kitchen, half-covered in foil. You want to try walking past and not picking at the icing? It's tough.

The secrecy of birthday cakes always makes me chuckle. The annual charade of pretending a birthday cake is a big surprise. Everybody gets ushered into the kitchen or the front room with a whisper. A dead giveaway. Then you can see the glow of the candles as the cake approaches. Suddenly the lights go out and you've got to act shocked, like this has never happened before. Everybody starts singing 'Happy Birthday' at varying tempos and keys. My in-laws always sing an extra verse which will no doubt get passed on to future generations. You'll probably know it. 'I went to the zoo; I saw a fat monkey and I thought it was you' (then everybody points at the birthday boy or girl). No doubt political correctness will get that cancelled. The 'fat' monkey will soon be replaced with 'big boned' just so fat fuckers aren't offended.

My wife's birthday is two days after mine which means my cards get pride of place for about forty-eight hours before they're relegated to a side table or down in front of the fire. It tickles me that certain cards always get priority. Cards from the heads of the family always get prime position on top of the mantel (they used to go on top of the telly until they invented flat screens).

It's nice to keep cards for sentimental reasons but I've got three bags full (like Ba-Ba-Black Sheep – I bet you can't say that now either). Will I ever find time to read through these cards again? No, never. So, now my children are going to be left with these bags of cards when I've shuffled off. I'd just like to take this opportunity to apologise in advance: please feel free to shred them, because I never could.

I'm a bugger for accidentally leaving the price on the back of cards. Fecking price stickers. 'A pound from Tesco' stuck on the back. It's the same with flowers.

I can't tell you the number of times I've stood on the path in people's front gardens trying to rip the price tag off a bunch of flowers. I always end up tearing the label in half, so it looks shoddy. OK, I'll stop whingeing now, I sound like Victor Meldrew. Cheer up, Peter, it's your birthday FFS!

Let's talk briefly about July (I mean, it's what this chapter is supposed to be about). Let's talk about those last few weeks of the school year when nobody seems to do anything. Except wordsearches, while teachers 'tidy their storerooms' (shop on Amazon). Everyone's stalling, just for the end of term.

There's a sports day that's usually rescheduled twice because of the rain.

We used to trudge across to the park for our school sports day. I was crap at every event. Egg and spoon, obstacle course, three-legged race. Then we'd have to have a tug-of-war with the nuns. They were very competitive. So we always had to let them win or they'd sulk all the way back to the convent.

Right at the end of the school year comes the most boring day of them all. Prize giving, which feels like it lasts forever.

The entire school crammed inside a stifling assembly hall. Choking with hay fever, while a boring head dishes out copious awards that celebrate mediocrity. 'Here, have a cheap gold medal that we couldn't even bother to inscribe for coming SIXTH in a skipping race.'

Children are fainting left, right and centre while the self-obsessed head waffles through a lengthy, heartfelt speech written on ChatGPT. If you're lucky you might get to finish school an hour earlier than usual and then you're off for the summer. Dashing through the old school gates chanting the classic ditty, 'We broke up, we broke up, we're not fussed if the school blows up' to the tune of Knick, Knack, Paddywhack.

Then off for Wimbledon fortnight. All the kids near me would go tennis mad. Playing anywhere and everywhere they could, down the park, in the fields, up against the gable ends of houses. Neighbours coming out shouting because there's 'No Ball Games'.

I love the sound of tennis balls hitting rackets. I find it quite therapeutic. Perhaps because it instantly reminds me of summer. That and chimes of an ice cream van. I also enjoy the intoxicating smell of freshly cut grass (atchoo)! Horrible and debilitating if you suffer from allergies.

Wimbledon used to be plagued with rain. Matches extended for days due to British downpours. Diehard eccentrics would remain undeterred. Sat in torrential rain, clutching umbrellas, necking tea from a flask, while Cliff Richard performed an impromptu sing-along. Thank God they fitted a retractable roof.

# JULY

I still don't understand tennis. People have tried to explain it to me, but I just can't fathom it. I still enjoy watching though. Especially at the end when they show the funny highlights to music. I've even been lucky enough to go to Wimbledon, twice. The first time was when I was guest-hosting *The Big Breakfast* on Channel 4 and was offered an invite to watch the tennis.

Presenting *The Big Breakfast* was a great gig. Johnny Vaughan was on holiday, and I'd been invited to guest-host for two weeks, which just happened to coincide with Wimbledon fortnight. What I wasn't so chuffed about was getting up at half three each morning, but I'd be finished by nine and had the rest of the day to myself. So, I went to Wimbledon and fell asleep. I was shattered from my early start.

What I couldn't get over was how tiny Wimbledon was. It looked huge on the telly.

There was a great atmosphere, and what a gorgeous set-up. Impeccable grounds, with manicured lawns and lush green courts spreading off into the distance. I particularly loved the ivy-clad façades on the main building. The flower beds, dotted here and there, adding bursts of colour. Diligent smiling staff in their purple uniforms. Several stands selling succulent strawberries. (That was a proper tongue twister.) And all this before I'd watched any tennis.

What also surprised me was how residential the area was surrounding Wimbledon Tennis Club. Nestled in leafy suburbia, it feels like the whole place has been dropped from the sky. Lord knows how the locals cope with traffic each year, it was gridlocked when I arrived. I've heard that some residents pack up and leave during the tournament, renting out their properties for lucrative prices.

I don't blame them. I just hope they pack away ALL their private belongings. We rented a house near Brighton a few years back and couldn't get over how many personal items they left around the house. Pictures of family. Food in the fridge. Opened packets in the cupboard. I opened one drawer to find pairs of knickers and tights. Then I went to put my toiletries in a cupboard under the sink and found a packet of anti-depressants prescribed to the owner. I wasn't best pleased with the children running around so I texted 'Tell your wife she's forgotten her Sertraline.' The reply said, 'So sorry, they should have been locked away.' Pisstake.

So should all the other personal belongings, but I think they'd got greedy and lazy renting out their house over the years. When I looked back at the images on the emails I'd been sent nothing was out of place and there certainly weren't any photographs on display.

It wasn't cheap either. I mean, it was clean, but we felt like we were intruding the whole time. Like we'd broken in. The final straw came when the only channel I could get on the telly was ITV4. We had a choice between the Tour de France or *The Sweeney*. At that point, I started taking his wife's Sertraline myself.

\* \* \*

Before I return to Wimbledon let me tell you about the hotel they put me up in when I was hosting *The Big Breakfast*. It was a swish Holiday Inn at Canary Wharf.

A Holiday Inn. I'd never stopped anywhere like it before and wasted half a roll of camera film taking pictures of the 'hair-dryer in drawer' and 'mints on pillow'. While I was there Paddy came to stay for a night. I'll never forget it because it was the night England played Argentina in the World Cup. David Beckham got sent off and quickly became a national pariah. I don't know anything about football, but I remember it clearly because Paddy went bananas and when it came to half-time I said, 'Shall we nip to a shop and get some treats?' I did have a minibar in the room, but the prices were extortionate. 'Surely there must be an off-licence up the road or something.' So off we went, and we walked and walked. Nothing anywhere. The streets were deserted. It was like that film *28 Days Later*. Mind you, we were in Canary Wharf, surrounded by offices and skyscrapers, during the half-time of England vs Argentina.

Eventually, we spied one shop in the distance but when we reached it the shutters were down. They were probably watching the World Cup. Then suddenly we heard cheering coming from the open windows of swanky apartments above us. The second half had started already. Paddy lost his mind and made us run all the way back to the hotel. 'I got a stitch, Pat,' but he wasn't for stopping. When we got back England lost on penalties and Paddy was inconsolable.

One thing the Holiday Inn at Canary Wharf had was incredible bath towels. Very high standard. Really good thirsty ones. Absorbent and cosy. Massive too. So, I may have 'accidentally on purpose' dropped one into my holdall and took it home. God forgive me but I loved that bloody towel. I was bereft every time it was in the wash. My other towels just couldn't compete.

Anyway, fast forward a couple of years and I had a stand-up gig in Leeds. It was a Saturday night, Susan said she'd come with me, so we decided to make a weekend of it. I booked us into a Holiday Inn Express (no expense spared). Hey, don't judge. The reason I chose a Holiday Inn Express was because they'd started opening all over the UK, so everything was brand new. Nothing worn and decrepit. No shower mould. Just shiny new TVs and fluffy white duvets with a decent tog.

*Who Wants To Be A Millionaire* was really popular back then and I was a bit obsessed with it. So much so that I took my video recorder with me and wired it up to the TV in the hotel room, so I could tape the show while I was out doing the gig. Susan thought I was unhinged when I opened my bag to reveal a VHS recorder wrapped in a bath towel. And not just any bath towel. My most favourite massive bath towel, inadvertently removed from the Holiday Inn. I said, 'You won't be mocking me when we come back after the gig and we've both got something to watch.' And sure enough, she wasn't. The only problem was while we were out the maid did a turn-down service and took my towel.

I'd left it on the floor when I unfurled my video recorder. How could she? Probably quite easily with the words Holiday

Inn inscribed on it. My beloved bath towel. What to do? I could hardly complain to reception, could I? Susan thought it was hilarious. I was gutted. I just kept thinking about the maid pulling my towel out of the washing machine. Puzzled as to how it'd somehow grown two sizes bigger than all the other towels.

Anyway, where was I? Yes! I remember. It was the second time I went to Wimbledon which was Susan's birthday, she loves tennis, so I thought I'd pull the stops out. I was balls' deep (forgive the pun) filming *Car Share* for the BBC, so decided to try and blag a couple of tickets for Wimbledon via the head of BBC Sport. Boy, did I fall lucky; not only did they get us into the five-star hospitality suite, we were also going to be watching the women's final from the Royal Box. What an incredible treat.

We were spoilt like royalty the whole day: A three-course meal in the clubhouse; sat with dignitaries such as the head of the Australian Tennis Federation (not a clue); Billie Jean-King (I'm sure she dyes her hair) and her wife. Boy, can that woman shovel down trifle. Then we were all marched out to Centre Court where we sat behind Sir David Attenborough, Sir John Hurt and the American TV presenter Ellen DeGeneres. And that's when I made a complete cock of myself.

Ellen turned to me, waved, and said 'Hi'. I immediately responded in the only way I knew how. I leaned over, threw my arms around her neck, and gave her a kiss (a tad inappropriate, I know). I thought, how does Ellen DeGeneres know me? YouTube is international, I suppose. Maybe she'd caught a clip of '... Amarillo' when she was surfing t'internet.

Ellen appeared a little startled. I smiled politely and settled back into my seat. Then Ellen said something to her partner and for the second time turned towards me and mouthed 'Hi'. It was then I realised that Ellen wasn't saying 'hi' to me. It was the person sitting beside Susan. Fucking hell! I could have died of embarrassment.

'She was saying hello to her.'

'No shit,' whispered Susan.

The girl beside Susan immediately got up, went over to Ellen and they both embraced like old friends.

Susan said, 'I tried to tell you, but you'd already dived on her.'

The girl turned out to be an actress called Maisie Williams from *Game of Thrones*. I didn't know her. I'd never seen Game of Bloody Thrones. The reason I misread the signs was because Ellen was wearing sunglasses. I couldn't see her eyes; I didn't know she *wasn't* looking at me. Well, that's my excuse and I'm sticking to it.

Everybody was wearing sunglasses at Wimbledon. You needed them. The light was extremely bright on Centre Court. I tried to wear my sun hat but was told it wasn't in keeping with protocol. 'And I suppose sunstroke is' was my rebuttal. Then I dropped my sunglasses and like a clumsy arse I stood on them. Breaking the arm, rendering them unwearable.

I tried to watch the match, but my retinas were burning, so I told Susan I was nipping to the toilet and went off in search of a new pair of shades. 'Surely there must be some sunglasses in Wimbledon,' I mumbled to myself as I wandered down a staircase. Eventually, I ended up in a basement room full of soldiers. They were sat huddled around a portable TV shining their boots. I asked if anybody had a spare pair of sunglasses and a scouse soldier chirped up, 'You can have mine if you'll have a selfie with me.' The floodgates were open. I was down there for ages doing selfies. I certainly earned those sunglasses. Then when I put them on, they were too small for my head. I looked like Yoko Ono. Ah well, they'd have to do. I legged it back upstairs to Centre Court and retook my seat.

'Where have you been?' whispered Susan '... and where did you get those?' 'I'll tell you later. Who's winning?' Then ten minutes later I fell asleep, again! I know because the BBC cut to a close-up of me when Serena Williams was necking her Barley Water. 'And there's comedian Peter Kay having a snooze,' said the commentator. There was a picture of me asleep in all the papers the next day. And those sunglasses still looked shit.

For me July will forever be synonymous with Live Aid – the historic 'global jukebox' organised by Bob Geldof and Midge Ure that raised funds for famine relief in Ethiopia. It took place on Saturday 13 July 1985 at Wembley Stadium in London and John F Kennedy Stadium in Philadelphia. It was watched by 1.5 billion viewers in over 150 nations (but I still refused to miss *The A-Team* on ITV).

It featured an astonishing line-up including Paul McCartney, Led Zeppelin, The Who, Elton John, The Beach Boys, Bob Dylan, Madonna and Nik Kershaw (who I remember tripped as he walked towards his microphone. Then nonchalantly looked around to see if anyone had noticed. Only half the planet, Nik).

Queen stole the show, and their performance is frequently hailed as one of the greatest in rock history. I wholeheartedly agree.

People always remember where they were during Live Aid. We were travelling to Great Yarmouth for a fortnight's family holiday. The weather was stunning. Clear blue skies, warm winds. One of those rare days when the sun is beating down from dawn till dusk.

We caught the train from Bolton, and despite Jimmy Savile reassuring the British public that it was in fact 'the age of the train' (the dirty monster), every train we caught that day was in varying degrees of decline. Cleanliness left a lot to be desired. One was slower than Captain Tom Moore walking around his garden.

When we got to Sheffield station, I thought it'd be funny if I suddenly got off the train. Call it an impulsive spontaneous joke. I'll never forget the faces of my family through the carriage window as I casually strolled past them up the plat-form. To say they were shocked would be putting it mildly. My dad did a double take and spat his lager out. My beaming smile quickly transitioned to horror when the train began pulling out of the station. I ran to the doors as fast as I could.

Fortunately, they didn't lock automatically in those days. I could see my dad running parallel with me inside the carriage. He thrust open the train door, grabbed my outstretched arm and yanked me back onto the train. Then slapped the back of my legs for the third time in my life. I deserved it. What was I thinking? My family was furious and refused to speak to me until we changed trains in Peterborough.

I'm convinced our connecting train (the Captain Tom Moore one) was manufactured just after they'd phased out steam. As it was well past its sell-by date. Dirty, faded upholstery, seats marred with dark stains and sticky residue. The brown hue of the interior emphasising the dirt and grime. Scattered wrappers and fag packets strewn across the floor. It was also chock-full of holidaymakers like ourselves, en route to Great Yarmouth (and it certainly was ... Great that is).

We could hardly see anything through the carriage windows. They were coated in layers of gunk distorting the view and a section of glass right beside my head was streaked with dried vomit. I'm not kidding. There it was, baked in the summer heat. It was really hard to ignore, being parallel to my face. So continually I retched as we rode through the flat lands of Norfolk. Passing the occasional barge leisurely navigating on The Broads.

The reason this moment remains so vivid is because it was framed by the sound of Live Aid. A fellow passenger had a HUGE boom box. These types of big stereos were all the rage – 'The Bigger, The Better' was a popular mantra in the eighties. It might have been cool to walk around with a gigantic sound system on your shoulder. Pumping out enough bass to make your ears bleed. But those same people are now stone-deaf, trundling around on mobility scooters. Their spines crooked from carrying all that weight.

Funny how forty years on technology has completely reversed in the opposite direction. I've just bought a Bluetooth speaker the size of a tangerine and the sound is better than that boom box.

Every passenger in the carriage was unified, as we listened to Radio 1's broadcast of Live Aid pouring out of the ghetto blaster. Phil Collins was on stage singing 'Against All Odds' before he had to dash as Noel Edmonds was waiting in a helicopter backstage ready to whisk him to Heathrow. He was then flying on Concorde to perform at Live Aid in Philadelphia later that day. They should have a benefit concert now just to pay for Phil's carbon footprint. No wonder the planet's fucked.

The BBC tried to do an exclusive interview with Phil via a live link from Concorde and you couldn't make out a bloody thing. Just the sound of static with Richard Skinner looking embarrassed back at Wembley. But it wasn't as bad as Paul McCartney ending the concert singing 'Let It Be' and his mic not working for the first few minutes. What a balls-up.

It seemed the whole world was transfixed by Live Aid. When we arrived at the train station in Great Yarmouth, some local tech whizz had wired the platform monitors up to a TV and they were screening the concert. The tinny sound streaming through the station's speaker system. People had gathered to watch Howard Jones, as staff collected money for Band Aid with buckets.

We continued listening as we boarded our coach to Caister Holiday Park. The driver tapping his steering wheel as Bryan Ferry crooned a cover of 'Jealous Guy' on the radio and still there wasn't a cloud in the sky. We had to jog to our chalet because R Julie and her friend Sharon were massive fans of U2 and were desperate not to miss them. Flicking on the TV just as Bono and co took to the stage.

'Oh, don't help us with the cases whatever you do,' my dad moaned sarcastically. R Julie and Sharon were oblivious.

That performance changed U2's career forever. There was one particular moment when Bono jumped from the stage, picked an unsuspecting member from the audience and slow danced with her as U2 played Bad. Not as in they played badly, the song was called 'Bad'.

We had chippy tea as Dire Straits sang 'Money for Nothing' with Sting. (By the way, holiday camp chip shops are always substandard and being down south there was nowt moist.) Then came the Live Aid moment that everybody still talks about, Queen. They took the show to another level. Their energy was palpable, as they pounded out their classic anthems, one after the other. I stood at the door of the chalet and all I could hear was Queen's performance echoing across the campsite, as other people watched with their chalet doors open in the heat.

We sat around the TV mesmerised watching Freddie Mercury's interaction with the crowd. The shots of handclaps in unison on the chorus of 'Radio-Ga-Ga' brought the hairs up on my neck. He was masterful with his call and response. I'd never seen anything like it and knew we all were witnessing something very special. The whole world did.

The other iconic moment people have never forgotten from Live Aid was when Bob Geldof swore. He was sat in the makeshift studio at Wembley Stadium overlooking the stage. 'You're not giving enough; you've got to get on the phone, take the money out of your pockets. Don't go to the pub tonight please, stay in and give us the money. There are people dying now (bangs his fist on the table) so give me the money ...'

David Hepworth said, 'OK. Let's give them the address,' and then Bob Geldof interrupts, 'Fuck the address.' My mum choked on a chip. 'Did he just say that? On the telly?' I could hear cheers across the campsite. Billy Connolly and Pamela Stephenson who were sat beside Bob Geldof pissed themselves laughing. Poor David Hepworth didn't know what to do and cut to some naff graphics showing us how we could all donate via Williams & Glyn's Bank.

People think Bob Geldof said, 'Give us your fucking money,' but that's an urban myth. I met him once, coincidentally at Live 8, twenty years later. I would never have thought that'd ever happen when I was sat in that chalet aged twelve. It was at Hyde Park. I was stood by the side of the stage, and there he was wearing a creased white linen suit. Mike McCartney was taking official photos and asked me to pose with Bob Geldof.

# JULY

Now I don't know why (and still don't), but I made another one of those impulsive spontaneous decisions. I thought it'd look funny in the photo if I was kneeling down beside Bob Geldof. So, I did it. Not realising that my face would be level with Bob's crotch, which stank to high heaven. I thought, 'For Christ's sake, Mike, hurry up and take the picture.' My eyes watering from the stench. What kind of man doesn't wash his genitals? He's a knight of the realm FFS.

That holiday was tough for my dad. Not just because of the usual unpredictable British weather but because we all wanted to stop in and watch the *Brookside* siege on Channel 4. We couldn't miss it. That really tested my parents' marriage. My dad was furious – 'COME ON, YOU CAN WATCH THIS AT HOME. LET'S GO OUT. DUNCAN NORVELLE'S ON IN THE BALLROOM TONIGHT' – but we were having none of it. Kate the nurse had just been taken hostage.

My mum let me stay up late on Friday night and watch a horror film, *Theatre of Blood* on BBC1. There's a scene where Robert Morley is force-fed his own pet poodles in a pie and the power ran out on the meter in the chalet. By the time my mum had found a fifty-pence piece, the film had finished, and the snooker was on.

*Pick of the Pops* was on Radio 2 this afternoon, it was July 1985, and the music took me straight back to that holiday in Caister. They played 'Axel F' – Harold Faltermeyer, 'Head Over Heels' – Tears for Fears, 'The Word Girl' – Scritti Politti, and I went right back to mooching around the arcade on the campsite. Trying to find myself a friend, flapping my hands. Still no luck.

Number one on *Pick of the Pops*, this day in 1985, was 'Frankie' – Sister Sledge. Watch the video on YouTube, they're basically stalking an elderly postman who appears to have some kind of learning difficulty. Sister Sledge are taunting him everywhere he goes. Poor sod.

As I was saying, R Julie brought her friend Sharon on holiday, but I was a bit lonesome. The only thing keeping me going was my Walkman and a carrier bag of cassettes I'd brought from home. I adored music and was enthralled by a DJ who was on in the ballroom each night called Paul Mack.

He was a huge inspiration. Playing the hits of the day, but he was also quite innovative and had projection screens on either side of him showing things he'd recorded off TV. He'd taken time to put the footage to music. Playing 'It's Raining Men' by The Weather Girls over a scene from *Dallas* where Bobby Ewing turned up in the shower. It'd only been on BBC1 the previous night and there he was referencing it already. The audience loved it. I'd never seen anything like it before. It really had a great influence on me. Years later I was basically doing the same thing when I presented 'My World of Entertainment' on *The Sunday Show*. Referencing clips from TV shows and playing music. I'm still doing the same act now. Hey, if it ain't broke.

So, we're reaching the end of this chapter and also my birthday. I've never written a chapter in a day before. It's such a joy writing these monthly memories and being transported back to moments in my life. I keep mentioning how furious my dad would get with the British weather. Well, when we were at Caister-on-Sea, it rained almost all of the time and yet weirdly all I remember is sunshine. Dappled, flickering through the window of a bus we caught to the Odeon one evening, to watch the new Bond film (I was still obsessed). *A View to a Kill*. One too many for Roger Moore in my opinion. He was fifty-seven at the time and was that knackered I'm sure he had a stuntman playing him when he drank his vodka martinis (shaken not stirred). The best thing about *A View to a Kill* was the Duran Duran theme song. Which was the first seven-inch single I ever bought, on limited edition white vinyl from Woolworths. I bet that's worth a bob or two now. I better hang on to it for when the comedy dries up.

My dad never joined us that night at the cinema; he went for one of his explorative holiday wanders, which inevitably involved him having several swift pints in a pub somewhere. He loved discovering pubs. 'I've found a nice little pub, follow me,' and then he'd lead us for miles up some obscure country lane. We'd all be shattered. Aching feet. 'Dad? We're in the middle of nowhere.'

'Just round this bend, it'll be worth it,' he'd shout.

But it was never worth it. It was always just another boozer like all the others he'd taken us to.

'They do a great pint in here.' That meant nothing. We were teetotal.

We'd had enough and my dad was fed up with the weather. But all that was about to change because the following year we decided to holiday abroad. Arriving on the sun-drenched shores of Malta. It was 1986, and it was August … (see what I've done? This book's not just thrown together).

# August

'Malta, we love Malta, there's nothing that we'd alter' – the lyrics from the 'Maltese Calypso', a song played constantly during our holiday in August 1986. We all went for a fortnight. The same crew that went to Great Yarmouth the previous year. Finally caving to my dad's long-time desire for guaranteed sunshine.

Our accommodation was self-catering. Soulless grey concrete apartments. Sterile and impersonal. The interiors always felt uninviting due to minimal natural light. And I didn't have a telly. I think my dad was fully aware we didn't have a telly when he booked; perhaps it was his revenge for us being glued to the *Brookside* siege the year before. It was probably for the best as there would have been zero channels in English. A fear confirmed when I managed to view some TV in a pub one night, a three-hour Maltese version of *The Generation Game*.

So, we had to go cold turkey without a telly. The only entertainment we had in the apartment, other than Uno, was R Julie's ghetto blaster. Which was almost as big as one of our suitcases. It took a whopping eight double-D batteries and weighed a ton.

When R Julie wasn't struggling to carry her boom box down to the pool (it took both her and Sharon to carry it), I'd borrow it to play some of my own cassettes which mainly consisted of episodes of *Only Fools and Horses* that I'd taped off the telly and *Now That's What I Call Music 7*. (How ancient do I feel? I saw an advert for *Now 208* the other day.)

*Now 7* became the soundtrack to that holiday in Malta and whenever I hear any songs from that double compilation I'm transported back to St Paul's Bay in Bugibba 1986. Back to our utilitarian apartment. 'The Edge of Heaven' – Wham, 'Let's Go All the Way' – Sly Fox, 'Invisible Touch' – Genesis, reverberating off the concrete walls. Competing with other music being played by guests in adjacent apartments. I'd just whack up the volume on the 'Brixton Briefcase'. None of them could compete with the level of sound that thing pumped out.

Another song that's synonymous with our holiday to Malta is 'Baker Street' – Gerry Rafferty. We went for a meal, and it came on a jukebox. I recognised the iconic saxophone melody. I love this song. 'Who sings this, Dad?'

'Baker Street' reminds me of spaghetti bolognese as it was playing the first, and only time, I ever tried it. When the song finished, I went over to the jukebox and for a laugh picked 'White Christmas' – Bing Crosby. Much to my dad's disgust.

'Only you could do this in August.' Then to my amazement, all the people in the bar started to sing along. Quite a surreal moment in the forty-degree heat. My spag bol resurfaced later when I threw up back at the apartment. I've never had it since.

It was on that holiday that my dad first discovered the existence of garlic bread. He came from a generation where foreign food was clandestine. So, when a waiter offered him some garlic bread, his brain seized up. 'What?' He couldn't process what he was saying. 'Garlic? Bread?' he said to the waiter inquisitively.

'Yes, garlic bread.'

'Garlic? And bread? Together?' My dad was dumbfounded. 'Am I hearing you right? Am I hearing him right, Deirdre?'

'Would you like some?' the waiter said, equally confused.

'ME?! Oh God NO thank you buddy,' my dad openly retching.

My dad sporadically mumbled 'Garlic? Bread?' to himself the rest of the night. The penny never did drop. He simply couldn't comprehend it.

You know they don't have garlic bread in Italy? A friend of mine runs an Italian restaurant in Bolton and he told me about his elderly grandfather. They flew him over from Italy to meet his family in the UK. Now this man had never been out of Italy, he was eighty-eight years old and didn't speak a word of English. They threw a big party for him; all the relatives were there. Generations of grandchildren and great-grandchildren he'd never met. As you can imagine he was pretty overwhelmed. They put on a big buffet, and he sat at the table, everybody watching when he picked up a piece of garlic bread. He started to eat it and with every mouthful he swallowed he looked confused. 'What's this?' he said in Italian. They replied 'garlic bread' but of course he didn't understand. Another member of the family had to translate. 'What's Italian for garlic bread?' One of them said 'Pane Al' Aglio' to the grandfather. He took another bite and, shocked, he said 'Pane? Al' Aglio?' Together?' Just like my dad with 'Garlic? Bread?' Apparently, the grandfather couldn't eat enough of it. And took some back to Italy. The irony.

Meanwhile, back in our Eastern bloc apartment, I stared at my spag bol as it lay at the bottom of a washing-up bowl. I felt dreadful, with cold sweats and the Brad Pitts. I'm convinced it'd given me food poisoning and spent the next few days in bed, listening to *Now 7* on heavy rotation. I hung netting around my bed to keep out the mosquitoes. It was like a scene from *Tenko*. This wasn't something I'd invented; the nets were there when we arrived. We spent the fortnight spraying ourselves with insect repellent. Or in my dad's case insect repellent, with a splash of Hai Karate. A formidable smell that I can still taste to this day.

My dad blamed the tap water for my bout of sickness. 'I said don't drink it.' But I hadn't, not unless you count brushing my teeth. Every day my dad would traipse over the road to a little off-licence and buy bottled water in bulk but then discovered it was cheaper to buy a case of Coca-Cola instead, so he got that. At the time I'd developed this nifty trick where I was able to talk while simultaneously holding liquid in both of my cheeks. It was right up there with my hand-flapping trick.

How reckless was I holding coke in my cheeks? All that sugar in the back of my mouth. By the following summer I'd had that many fillings my teeth looked like the keys on a piano. Such an idiot.

There are a few things I distinctly remember about Malta. The skyline being chock-full of cranes was one of them. Funny, my friend went a few weeks ago and said exactly the same thing. It's almost forty years later. There were building works on the horizon as far as I could see. It was like the set of *Carry on Abroad* looking out of our apartment window. Workmen and diggers grafting round the clock. It's a pity the council didn't pay as much attention to the potholes in the roads. Jesus wept. Talk about vibrations. I got an erection every time I went on the bus. And that was every day. I was almost passing out from the lack of blood to my head.

The Maltese bus service was legendary for being completely treacherous. Combined with the potholes it was an action scene from a Bond film. Swerving all over the road. You seriously felt like you were taking your life in your hands. I'm really not exaggerating. Ask anybody who rode one of those green buses in Malta.

The drivers used to be sat surrounded by religious paraphernalia inside their cabins. It wasn't uncommon to see a pair of rosary beads swinging from the rear-view mirror or a statue of the Virgin Mary glued to the dashboard. And trust me, the drivers needed some divine intervention. All I could hear were passengers shrieking and screaming at the near misses, as the bus dodged cars, cyclists or pedestrians crossing the road. I'd be mumbling a novena to myself as I sat at the back with a hard-on.

Malta is predominantly Catholic. Which suited my mum right down to the ground. We even brought an extra bag for all the religious tat my mum bought. It was like being back at Knock Shrine. I'll never forget the faces of the customs officers when they opened my dad's Tetley Bitter holdall to find fourteen Jesus candles, a crucifix, six sets of rosary beads and a statue of St Martin de Porres (our family's patron saint).

We visited several religious landmarks, including the Rotunda in Mosta, a church devoted entirely to the Assumption of Mary. The Luftwaffe blitzed the church during World War II (the sequel) and a bomb struck the dome. It hit the deck, skidded across the altar where three hundred people were waiting for evening mass but miraculously the bomb never exploded. It was later defused by Bomb Disposal experts and put on display as part of the tour. You could even buy souvenir silver chains from the gift shop with a replica figurine of our lady straddling a bomb. My mum bought two (I'm kidding … she only bought one).

We also booked on a trip to a religious festival. The streets were heaving, as locals paraded a giant statue of Jesus over their heads through narrow streets. It was like a scene from *The Godfather*. My mum was moved to tears, but all I wanted was some nougat, which is apparently the sweet of religious feasts. All the shops were selling it. More fodder for my back teeth. The celebration ended with a huge firework display then we were herded back on 'the green bus of death' for more prayers on the journey home, and another boner.

Gozo is a little island off the coast of Malta. We took a day boat trip there. We could have booked a glass-bottomed boat trip which we all really fancied but my dad wouldn't shell out an extra twenty lira.

Sailing past dramatic cliffs, a sweaty tour guide with an eye patch took great pride in telling the passengers that the cliffs were used as a location in *The Guns of Navarone*; many took photos as we bobbed up and down on rough waters. It was my first day out since the spag bol incident and I still felt a bit queasy. The smell of diesel burning my eyes.

Next, we drifted into Anchor Bay, also famous as a film location, this time for 1980 musical *Popeye*. I was thrilled when I heard there was going to be a film version of my favourite cartoon character. And one of my favourite comedians, Robin Williams, would be playing the lead role. Talk about a double whammy. I was first in the queue the day it was released at the cinema. In anticipation, my mum bought me an official *Popeye* magazine that folded out into a big poster of Robin Williams and Shelley Duvall as Popeye and Olive Oyl. Proudly I hung it on my bedroom wall next to a pin-up of *Mork & Mindy* I'd got from *Look-In*. Sadly, the film wasn't good. I wanted to like it but it didn't make much sense and was a big flop at the box office. It failed to capture the magic of the Popeye cartoons. Which I loved, especially *The All-New Popeye Show* when I got home from school. I even had a Popeye hand puppet that rarely left my fingers (that just sounds wrong on many levels). I'd drive my family crazy. Imitating Popeye's gravelly voice and reciting his familiar theme song 'I'm strong to the finish 'cause I eats me spinach, I'm Popeye the sailor man, toot, toot.' My dad would roll his eyes and shout, 'You'd want to go out and get a job, you're nineteen.'

And then six years later I was staring at Popeye's dilapidated film set. What a dump. Fortunately, the boat trip was slightly more successful than the film.

As you know, I'm quite partial to a boat trip. I went on another one last week during a visit to Windsor. We sailed down the river near Henley-on-Thames, a stunning part of the world. The guide pointing out the houses of the rich and famous. 'That house belongs to the late Sir Michael Parkinson and his wife Mary, and a few doors down was where Rolf Harris used to live.' I noticed he'd dropped the 'Sir' from Rolf Harris's name. Quite rightly too. He was another knight of the realm who was up to no good, just like 'Sir' Jimmy Savile. What were we thinking?

Now I know I might appear to be a bit fixated with Jimmy Savile. I notice I've mentioned him in almost every chapter so far and I've thought about this. I'm not obsessed; if I'm honest I'm still in shock. That somebody so prominent in public throughout the whole of my life could turn out to be a prolific sexual predator is hard to take in. We trusted him and it turned out he had hundreds of allegations spanning decades. I think the whole nation was stunned. I know people say 'there were always rumours' but it's the betrayal of trust by someone who was seen as a national treasure that still staggers me. And he never replied to any of my *Jim'll Fix It* letters.

That last paragraph has led me to think about the tone of this book. Obviously it's more on the lighter side, as I imagine you'd expect from a comedian. (Just look at the cover.) But I've always preferred to write about joy than pain. I acknowledge life is filled with its fair share of sorrow and believe me when I tell you I've had plenty of sadness and tears. But by highlighting the positive and the lighter side I can hopefully offer some kind of escape and distraction from the challenges we all face. Nothing more, nothing less. Some joy and maybe some laughs. That's always been my vocation and I'm sticking to it.

One of the most memorable boat trips we ever took was in the picturesque town of Dingle. A small seaport in County Kerry on the southwest coast of Ireland. It was home to Fungie, a solitary dolphin who'd swam into the bay in 1983 and over the years became a national treasure (like Jimmy Savile, sorry), as well as a massive tourist attraction for Dingle.

A large portion of the town was dedicated to Fungie. They named pubs after him, shops after him, and a café with a Fungie wall mural painted on the side. They even had a Fungie statue outside a Fungie souvenir shop that sold Fungie merchandise. Fungie plates, Fungie keyrings, bracelets, t-shirts, cups, towels … But the main source of Fungie income was the daily boat trips that sailed into the bay hoping to catch a glimpse of Fungie himself.

Like the Kardashians to cameras, we couldn't resist and booked on a boat trip. Hoping to catch a glimpse of the legendary Fungie. Fat chance. For two hours we swayed around on choppy waters. I had motion sickness and the only time we saw Fungie was on the lid of a tin of Fungie fudge Susan bought from the onboard shop.

The Fungie phenomenon got me thinking. What would happen if Fungie suddenly disappeared? What would Dingle do? Because Fungie had clearly become big business for the town. I imagined the heads of the town holding an emergency meeting. Panicking. Desperate to come up with a solution, so they could keep the Fungie money rolling in.

*(County Kerry accents)*

'Jesus lads, we're knackered without that fecking dolphin.'

'Oh I hear ya. I've just ordered a thousand Fungie vapes and now the little fecker's done a bunk.'

'What are we going to do?'

'What about animatronics, Shamus? Surely we could make a fake dolphin and keep it floating in the bay?'

'Anima-what Pat?'

'Tronics.'

'You're talking shite, Pat.'

Well, a few years later Fungie did disappear. Nobody could find him, and nobody ever found out what happened. He either swam away or sadly died. The Fungie dream was over.

So, what did the people of Dingle do? They started selling Fungie memorabilia. Hilarious.

My dad was always a big fan of the Irish (well, he did marry my mum, and she's as Irish as they come). When we were in Malta my dad went out for one of his famous holiday wanders and stumbled upon 'Paddy's Bar', up a side street. He instantly found kinship within those blarney stone walls, and rarely a day went by over the remaining fortnight that my dad failed to call into 'Paddy's Bar' for a few scoops of the old black stuff (and I don't mean Pepsi). Reluctantly he'd insist on dragging my mum and me with him.

The owners, Paddy and Marie, were amiable enough. A laugh, a joke and a ton of junk from the emerald isle spattered all over the walls. Oh, and a mammoth jukebox in the corner, laden with tunes from the old country. We spent hours in that pub. My mum sipping a single glass of water that she'd make last all night, while I drank cheap coke, ate crisps, and was mauled by middle-aged, inebriated women as I wowed them with my party pieces. Flapping my hands and singing with coke in my cheeks. Yes, the craic was definitely mighty in Paddy's Bar.

The songs on that jukebox became a big part of my life. I still play many of them to this day. Paddy, the landlord, even sold compilation tapes. My dad bought one. What's funny is that Paddy simply recorded the songs straight from the jukebox onto the cassette tape. You can hear the hubbub of the bar in the background. Glasses clinking, bog doors opening, the fruit machine in the corner. You can even hear the regulars occasionally ordering pints and chatting while the songs played. Over the years I've managed to learn all the songs and incorporate all of that bar noise. In fact, I still can't sing 'The Fields of Athenry' without shouting 'two cold ones when you're fecking ready Paddy' after the second chorus.

I got a surprise after the last song on side two of the cassette. It was a message from Paddy himself in his distinctive Dublin accent. 'Er ... hello this is Paddy and Marie from Paddy's bar in Malta, we hope you all enjoyed your holidays, and we hope please God to see you all again soon. Good luck and God bless you all.' Marvellous. I'd like to think that Paddy recorded that message especially for my family but I'm pretty sure it was on all the tapes that he sold behind the bar for six lira each.

It was during our holiday to Malta that I started to notice cracks appearing in my parents' marriage. Maybe they'd always been there, maybe I'd just been too young to notice. My dad pestering my mum to go on a pedalo didn't help matters. I still don't know why she agreed because she's terrified of water.

We went to a beach in Mellieha. A beautiful stretch of golden sand. Popular with families because the water remains remarkably shallow quite a distance from the shore. There were the three of us on this yellow pedalo. My dad, myself and my mum shitting bangers at every move we made. The water was only three feet deep, and my mum was losing her mind. 'Pedal slower. Go slower, I don't like it. Michael, we're going too far out!' as she hyperventilated.

Then my dad, like a proper bell-end, winked at me and whispered 'Watch this' and threw himself over the side of the pedalo into the sea. My mum completely lost it. 'Oh Mary mother of God. Michael! Michael!' But my dad had disappeared beneath the waves, just so he could get a reaction from my mum. Which he certainly achieved: she stopped pedalling and started a novena.

But my dad's prank backfired massively. Without realising, we'd pedalled off course and drifted beyond the shallow waters. He was still expecting the water to be three feet deep and had no idea we'd drifted into the deep sea. Not being a competent swimmer, he sank like a stone, only to resurface a few seconds later blue in the face, sputtering for breath. Blinded by salt water he grabbed the side of the pedalo. 'Help me back on board, Peter,' he shouted. Tipping the pedalo with his weight. My mum batting him with her handbag. 'Get off, Michael, you're going to sink us. You're going to sink us!' My dad panting 'I can't breathe Deirdre, I can't breathe!' as I tried to push his skinny arse back on the pedalo and navigate us back to shallow waters. Lord knows what the families on the beach thought was going on. My mum hardly said two words to my dad for the rest of the holiday.

Unbeknown to us at the time that was to be our last family holiday. Everybody was growing apart in different directions. R Julie and her friend Sharon were now typical teenagers. They wanted to sleep late, laze by the pool in the afternoon and go out on their own at night – visiting discotheques (or whatever 'the young 'uns call them' my dad would say).

Concerned for R Julie and Sharon's safety, my dad made it his duty each night to surreptitiously chaperone them both back to our Soviet communist bloc apartment. I kept expecting him to get his collar felt by the Maltese police for stalking young girls and wake up in the cells.

He also used this nightly assignment as an excuse to stay out on the lash till all hours. He seemed to prefer drinking on his own and was becoming more isolated. It felt as if my mum and me were cramping his style. Looking back, I wonder if he was experiencing a mid-life crisis. He seemed blissfully happy holding court, stood at the bar in Paddy's Bar. Laughing, which is something he rarely seemed to do with us any more, unless he was watching *Only Fools and Horses* or *Rising Damp*.

I was at a loss and naturally sided with my mum. We both preferred staying in the apartment anyway (despite it having no telly and being twinned with Chernobyl). We'd listen to *Now 7* again or play Uno. But deep down I really missed us all spending time together. And yearned to rekindle memories reminiscent of our first holiday abroad to Spain in 1982. Lloret De Mar to be precise.

We were outrageously excited the morning we travelled to the airport. The night before was reminiscent of Christmas Eve, as I couldn't sleep a wink. I just kept thinking this time tomorrow we'll be abroad. I wouldn't have got much sleep anyway; the alarm was set for ridiculous o'clock. Frantically we all rushed around bleary-eyed. Packing last-minute essentials.

# AUGUST

And we all wore our Sunday best for the plane journey. What was all that about?

'The taxi's here,' shouted R Julie, which only caused more panic. My family were incapable of keeping a taxi waiting. The meter would be running. It'd cost more money. The frenzy revved up a notch. My parents completed their last-minute ticklist. Note out for the milkman. Turn off appliances but not the fridge. We would have adjusted the thermostat, but we didn't have any central heating. Just an immersion heater that had to be strategically flicked on three hours before a bath.

My dad would turn off the stopcock, while my mum would put all our house plants in the sink. I still don't know why. The suitcases were already in the boot of the taxi as my dad wailed, 'ARE YOU COMING DEIRDRE OR WHAT? WE'RE GONNA MISS THE BLOODY PLANE.' Informing the whole neighbourhood that we were going on our holiday. Net curtains would be twitching over the road. So much for sneaking away quietly.

My mum locked up after activating our security system. No, not a house alarm, a small transistor radio which was left playing in the kitchen. The ideology being that if any unsuspecting burglars heard the radio playing, they'd naturally assume the house was occupied and think twice before breaking in. But the radio idea was flawed. If I were a burglar, I'd be listening in outside the back door and as soon as I heard music playing, bang, I'd be straight in. Having a dance while I robbed the house.

Another device we bought specifically for the purpose of protecting our family riches (of which we had none) was a plug-in timer from Argos that flicked on a single lamp in the front room. Once again perpetuating the myth that we were still home. All we needed were some cardboard cutouts of ourselves and we'd be Kevin McCallister, eight years before *Home Alone*. The only problem with the plug-in timer was that nobody could fathom its twenty-four-hour clock. So when we went on holiday the lamp was on during the day and off all night.

I've just recalled a further tactic we had in our arsenal: my nana and grandad who lived around the corner. They had the unenviable task of opening and closing our curtains each and every day. Once again to perpetuate the illusion we were all home as usual. I think there was less fuss protecting the Tower of London.

All the way to the airport my mum would be twisting my dad's melon. 'What have we forgotten, Michael?' 'Nothing, Deirdre.' Running through the checklist. 'Have you got the passports? The Spanish money? Did you turn off the stopcock?' 'YES, YES AND THRICE YES, NOW LET'S JUST ENJOY OURSELVES.'

Going on holiday was exhausting.

Security at UK airports was practically non-existent in the early eighties. A quick shufty through your luggage if you were chosen at 'random'. Unless you were of foreign descent or spoke with a Northern Irish accent. After security you were free to enjoy the wonders of airport hospitality. For some, it was the best part of the holiday. Perhaps a browse around Dixons. Top up on some sun oil from Boots (sunscreen wasn't a popular purchase back then. People wanted to be brown, not safe). You treat yourself to a book from WHSmith's. One of the most intoxicating smells in the world is a new book. Just smell the pages on this book for a second. Hmmm, a slightly sweet aroma with hints of wood and vanilla from the paper and freshly painted ink (unless you've picked a dog-eared copy up from Help the Aged). I could inhale the evocative perfume of books all day long. Maybe that's why I'm often escorted out of Waterstones by their store security.

We'd roam around Duty Free. Eyeing up the giant Toblerones (the only confectionery that physically hurts when you eat it). Perhaps a bottle of Yardley Gold perfume for Mum? Maybe four hundred B&H for Uncle Tony and his chain-smoking wife Cath? She now smokes through a hole in her neck. Surely, at that point, you'd contemplate nicotine patches.

Giddily we boarded our plane to España. Flying with the now defunct Dan Air. Sadly they didn't have any TVs on board (something I was particularly looking forward to) but we did have ashtrays in the seat arms. The plane felt dated in 1982 but as my dad used to say, 'It'll get us from A to B, and from B to A.' I threw up mid-flight in one of those paper bags they supply. I'm not usually travel sick on planes. I think it was either the early start and the hullaballoo OR the full English breakfast, Cornetto and can of Lilt I downed before boarding the plane.

... and two Caramacs and an orange Aero. I was on my holiday. I got up to vomit in the toilet, but it was engaged. Sod's law. I felt like a right spanner handing my bag of puke to the stewardess. She didn't pull any punches. Snatching it from my hand with a face like a bull mastiff licking piss off a nettle. I thought, sorry love but isn't this your job?

I'll never forget experiencing the change in climate. That first blast of heat I felt as I walked down the steps of the plane. It wrapped around me like a blanket. So, this was what everybody had been raving about? Scorchio. A deep blue cloudless sky, warm winds, the sun blazing down. My dad burst into tears on the runway. And he was still struggling to compose himself at the baggage carousel. Involuntarily sobbing as he hunted for our cases.

Locating our cases was made much easier as my mum had tied a red ribbon around each of the handles so we could locate them quicker. It would have worked too if other passengers hadn't had the same idea. Instead, it took twice as long as my dad argued over whose case had whose red ribbon.

Eventually, we arrived in Lloret De Mar. Our accommodation was the 'formidable' Don Juan Hotel. I've just had a nosey on TripAdvisor and it's still going. It's been retitled The Don Juan Resort, but it still looks the same to me forty-odd years later. I notice it's still only got three stars.

I think it's amazing that we can study accommodation nowadays. You can do a 360-degree search around a hotel room, read countless reviews, and look at hundreds of travellers' photos before even parting with any money. In 1982 the only guidance people got before they booked holidays was watching Judith Chalmers on *Wish You Were Here …?* or seeing two or three pictures in a holiday brochure from the travel agents.

It's no wonder so many holidaymakers got ripped off. Arriving at some crap accommodation or the ruins of a building site. Another huge gamble, that didn't even offer any images, was booking a holiday via your TV remote on Teletext.

You were basically booking a holiday blind. How ridiculous? Everybody knew people who'd brag about booking on Teletext.

'You can get some fantastic deals. It only took me and Sheena five minutes to find something. Then we booked it, packed it and fucked off, for a week to Gran Canaria. All-inclusive, two hundred quid. We were on the beach the next day.' Horseshit!

We never once got lucky. Sat on the sofa for hours. Mesmerised by all the offers on Teletext. Poised with pen and paper in hand. If you did finally glimpse something you liked and missed it, you'd have to wait half an hour before the page came around again. Then we'd always bottle it. Scared we'd end up in a right dump or starring in an episode of *Holidays from Hell*. Susan pointing at some cockroaches in a shower, while I jumped from the top deck of a ship with my legs on fire.

Fortunately, the Don Juan in Lloret wasn't that bad. Apart from two dodgy lifts that guests kept getting stuck in. It must have been a regular occurrence as the staff on reception didn't bat an eyelid. Guests could often be seen climbing up out of the lift shaft while it was wedged between floors. Terrifying. I don't think the Spanish gave a shite about health and safety.

I've a few scattershot memories from our time staying at the Don Juan. Like the obligatory excursion we booked on with our holiday rep. A day trip to a champagne factory in the morning, followed by a perilous journey up Monserrat Mountain in the afternoon. It was a breathtaking view, but the coach driver had to navigate some precariously narrow roads as we ascended the mountain. Suffering from vertigo I was genuinely frightened. And couldn't believe how high we were.

I'd had a fear of hills since I was a toddler. I can't recall how it started but whenever I was on the slope of a hill I was scared that somehow I'd roll down. I'd cling on to my mum's hand for dear life. Like when we came out of the chemist on the slope of Derby Street. I was terrified I'd roll down the hill and under a car. Weird. I've just googled that, and the condition has a name. 'Bathmophobia – an extreme fear of slopes and steep hills.' Crikey! I feel vindicated.

My dad went on a day trip to Barcelona. Years later I did the same when I visited Spain again in 1989 with my friend Paul. We booked on a similar coach trip to Barcelona, but I was so worried about getting lost that I insisted we follow the coach driver. My logic being that if we could always see the driver there'd be no chance we could get lost or miss the coach because he was driving it.

The only flaw with that plan was we kept bumping into the coach driver everywhere he went. It was painful. When he sat for a coffee, he saw us. When he decided to look at some postcards and spun the carousel around, we were there again. When he visited a brothel, we were in the next bed. I'm joking, but he definitely thought we were stalking him.

I'd honestly never seen my dad as happy. Not only did the glorious weather warm his bones but for the first time ever he truly seemed to relax in Spain. He'd always make me laugh when we'd get back to Bolton and friends would ask him about a holiday – 'How big was your hotel room, Michael?' My dad would draw comparisons with the weirdest measurements. Starting from wherever he was. 'Er … let me think, well the length from where I'm stood right now to that kitchen door (pointing) and width wise the room was from where the telly is to those ladders in the backyard' (points out through the kitchen window). WTF?

'How far were you from the sea, Mick?' My dad would mumble the question back to himself, 'How far from the sea?', and he'd suss out some weird geographical reference from where we lived in Bolton. 'Er … well you know the video shop on the main road? Next to the dry cleaners? I'd say we were from about there to here from the beach.' He couldn't have made it sound more unglamorous if he tried.

He'd also proudly rate the destination by how clean it was. 'It was absolutely spotless, no litter anywhere and not a bit of dogshit. Not like round here.' Well, it wouldn't be like where we lived. We were in Spain.

When we were in Lloret my dad went off on *yet another* of his legendary holiday wanders and found a bar called The Red Lion run by a couple of ex-pats from Leeds. He couldn't wait to take us. 'Come with me. You're going to love this place, it's like an old English pub. Look, they've even got a British phone box outside. They serve Tetley's bitter. It's just like being back at home.'

'Do you fancy some food? Because they've got your favourite on the menu, Peter, steak and kidney pie, chips and beans. And you can watch British telly while you're eating it. I had a cottage pie yesterday watching *Hi-de-Hi!* Like I said, it's just like being at home BUT we've got the weather. Look, they've got framed pictures on the wall of dogs playing snooker – it's comical. Pull up a chair and grab that Connect 4, I'll have a game with you.' His mind was completely blown. This genuinely was heaven on Earth. I swear if he didn't have to be back at work he'd have never come home. He talked about emigrating.

We were down The Red Lion every day. Not only did they show British TV, but they also showed films too. A lot of the bars in Spain did. They put blackboards outside listing the films they were showing. Now I thought that was incredible (maybe a chip off the old block). Though some of the films they showed weren't really for children. I watched *Mad Max*, *Alien*, *Stir Crazy* (with about a million eff words), *Friday the 13th*, *The Wild Geese* (which I still love) and *The Life of Brian*. Which was completely inappropriate. Thank God my mum didn't know. When my dad mentioned it later, she was furious. 'You're only nine. You shouldn't be watching blasphemous filth like that. Sending up Jesus and the bible.' She was right, though it was funny. Especially the bit where Brian opens his bedroom window and stands naked in front of hundreds of followers. And it was exactly at that point the landlord froze the film for an interval, and I ate my fish fingers while Graham Chapman's cock and balls paused on the TV.

When we weren't down The Red Lion, we were back at the Don Juan and I'd always be in the pool floating around on my birthday lilo. Trying to avoid honeymoon couples necking in the deep end. Would you ever? Didn't they know petting wasn't allowed?

Every day my dad would bring us yesterday's UK newspapers. He found a shop down the road that sold them. Copies of the *Daily Mirror* and *The Star* that he'd pay double the price for. We thought it was giddy being able to see what was happening back home, the day after it'd happened. That's completely alien today having t'internet but back then it was exciting. I'd be lying on the sun lounger with a beach towel over my head studying the previous day's TV guide – gutted about what I'd missed.

Speaking of sun loungers, we were lucky if we got one. The ratio per guest was shocking. Every morning my dad would get up at the crack of dawn just so he could go down to the pool and commandeer a few sun loungers for us. Securing them with beach towels before the Germans got in there first. Such a cliché but true. Over the course of the holiday, my dad and the Germans tried to outsmart each other. Setting their alarm clocks earlier each day. By the end of the holiday my dad resorted to laying out his beach towels the night before he went to bed.

Mind you, my dad fell foul to the twisted hands of fate when he commandeered a defective sun lounger that almost cost him his family jewels. It was one of those cheap and nasty sun loungers with a nasty hairline crack running up the inside of a white plastic slat. Fresh from a dip in the pool, my dad leapt from the water like a gazelle. Then he sat astride the lounger towelling himself off, completely unaware his full body weight was causing the plastic slat to gape open. Its jaws ready to devour my father's testicles as they hung through the hole. Completely unaware he was straddling a mantrap. He asked my mum if she'd pass him yesterday's *Daily Mirror*. Innocently he reached forward as she handed him the paper, causing the crack in the lounger to fully widen. Then as he lay back the plastic snapped shut on his genitals. A hammer blow. His cry was so loud a waiter on the opposite side of the pool dropped a tray of drinks.

The Germans were pissing themselves laughing when five of us lifted my dad into the back of an ambulance. Delirious from the pain and still straddling the sun lounger. He pleaded for my mum to 'Quick, go and pick my dick up, Deirdre, before it rolls into the pool.' He spent the rest of the fortnight kicking his balls down the beach … well at least *they* got a tan.

# September

I was married in September 2001. A week before the attack on the World Trade Center. Obviously, nobody knew that at the time, well nobody except Osama bin Laden and his cronies. The world was thrown into chaos. Everybody remembers where they were on 9/11 (and when the tram crashed in *Corrie*). I was in Mexico, waking up on my honeymoon drowsily flicking on the TV to find a plane had hit the World Trade Center in New York. I could see plumes of black smoke pouring out of the iconic skyscraper. Total shock and pandemonium. The sound of approaching sirens, people screaming. I presumed I'd flicked on one of the hotel's movie channels. They'd been showing a film called *The Siege* about terrorist attacks in New York City. I thought this must be it, but when I couldn't see hide nor hair of Bruce Willis or Denzel Washington I began to realise that what I was watching was real. It was happening right now. Holy Shit!

# SEPTEMBER

I woke Susan and like the rest of the planet we watched in astonishment. Maybe it had just been some horrible accident. Nobody knew the size and scale of the plane but then suddenly a second plane hit the other tower and terror swept through everybody. This was deliberate.

How could this be happening? I could hear people's shocked reactions in the other rooms in the hotel. The phone rang and a couple we'd met told us what was happening. It was indescribable, we couldn't take our eyes off it. As far as we were concerned the honeymoon was over.

The whole resort was flung into grief, as you'd expect. We really wanted to go back home but thousands of planes were grounded. It was an unprecedented move to thwart any further attacks from hijacked planes. That backlog lasted for weeks. We tried calling home but queues for any public phones were huge. Mainly Americans calling family and friends.

The feeling was eerie. All joy evaporated. All music stopped. It was a surreal juxtaposition; we were in such idyllic surroundings while all this tragedy was happening. We'd tried to continue with normal holiday activities, but we felt guilty. I had a kayak lesson booked for the 12th; that went out the window.

We'd lie in the sun, we'd swim without smiling, we'd eat (well, it was all-inclusive) and then we'd go back to our room and watch the news, all the time. Every channel in every language was covering the attacks. The most heartbreaking scenes were of people searching for loved ones. Putting pictures on lampposts, walls, anywhere, desperate to find whoever was missing.

Christ, this is a cheery chapter.

After 9/11 the world changed forever in so many ways. For the first few years, it was hard to avoid footage of 9/11, especially when the anniversary came around and somehow even more unseen footage was unearthed. The famous footage of the falling man. Heartbreaking documentaries about phone calls made by people trapped in the towers. Footage people had filmed on camcorders. You've got to remember this was before we could film properly on phones. God forbid anything like that happened now. Tik-Tok would go into meltdown.

When our children arrived in our life we tried to shield them from inevitable annual coverage of 9/11 in the media. It was too traumatic and upsetting. We'd just casually flick channels when it occasionally popped up. We didn't want them to endure something we still couldn't comprehend. I think the whole world was in shock for years. When it finally got discussed in our house, it was really hard to answer the children's questions 'Why and how had it happened?' There was no real explanation for such an inhuman act. Sometimes the world can be a horrible place, and it ruined our honeymoon.

We got back home six days later than scheduled. We were so grateful to get a flight back. We'd been waiting in a packed airport in Cancun for seven hours. We flew with another airline. The crew looked completely knackered as they walked through the terminal. Concerned passengers nudging each other, mouthing the words 'Are they flying us?' Everybody was on pins.

I did consider telling somebody in charge that we'd paid extra for a honeymoon upgrade but thought it inappropriate. On our flight over to Mexico, we'd had napkins and access to bowls of Quality Street. Now we were back to ashtrays in the seat arms. It was like being back on that Dan Air flight to Spain. There was no in-flight entertainment. Well, not unless you count a fat woman from Stockport getting trapped in the bog for over an hour. Faulty door. But at least we were finally heading home. Fucking Al-Qaeda.

I'll never forget the passengers clapped and cheered when we landed in Manchester. Such a relief to be back on terra firma. Though nowhere would feel safe for a long time to come. Fucking Al-Qaeda.

So September … well the big summer holidays are over and everybody's back on life's treadmill. Nose to the grindstone, the daily routine, back to school. My children despise seeing 'back to school' adverts, it's a reminder of the one place they don't want to be. 'Why are they showing back-to-school ads now? We've not even finished our summer holidays yet.' They have got a point.

It's the tried and tested way of flogging product. It's the same with Easter eggs in January, or Halloween gear in September, which they were in The Range last week. Have you ever been to The Range? It's the only place I know where you wander in for a relaxing browse and walk out with a load of crap you never needed to buy.

We used to go there for the posters for the children. You know those poster racks that you used to see in Woolworths and HMV. You'd flick big vertical frames in a rack (not Iraq), from left to right. If you found one you liked, you'd buy the corresponding poster rolled up in a tube underneath. You could get pop stars, football teams, a map of the world (though I don't know who that appealed to). I wanted *Gremlins* but picked up the wrong tube and ended up with Sam Fox with her busters out.

They've stopped selling those posters in The Range since Covid. Probably something to do with touching things. McDonald's stopped doing porridge during the pandemic, and fish fingers (though I never even knew fish had fingers). I've never fathomed how fish fingers fell under Covid restrictions. I think the staff just couldn't be arsed cooking them. For a time during Covid, Domino's wouldn't let you create your own pizza. Eh?

I think a lot of people used the pandemic to put their feet up. It was a golden pass.

'Er ... I'm sorry, no, we can't add pineapple to your ten-inch Hawaiian.'

Fucking Al-Qaeda.

Strangely, I quite like when normal service resumes in September. Don't get me wrong, I love the summer, but by the end of the holidays I can't wait for the children to go back. After two months of decadence, the children's sleeping patterns are out of sorts. They become a bit shapeless and aimless. They need the daily structure. Saying that, going back to early mornings can be a real shock to the system.

I love sleep. I think I'll get that printed on a t-shirt. I've never enjoyed waking up, and most mornings I'd gladly sell my house and contents for an extra hour in bed. I find the night version of me is constantly at war with the morning version of me. I'll wake knackered and swear to myself 'I'm definitely having an early night tonight; I need more sleep.' Then slowly I transition into the night version and he's like 'You don't have to go to bed. Stay awake, you'll get up in the morning no problem.' It's proper Jekyll and Hyde shit and it never changes.

When the alarm goes off, I always have to round the time up. I'd never get up at 7.03 or 7.04, God forbid. It's got to be rounded up to 7.05 … or even better just after a song that's playing ends. One thing I never enjoy is randomly waking up before your alarm is due to go off. There's not enough time to get back to sleep. I just lay in bed trying to convince myself I don't need a wee (when I really know I want one). The first thing I do is check my phone for messages. Usually, it's junk mail asking if I'd like a longer thicker penis (how do they know?).

And why do mums lie about time? 'ARE YOU GETTING UP? IT'S HALF SEVEN!' And yet the clock clearly states it's 7.15. It's scare tactics. Just like fucking Al-Qaeda (alright I won't do it again, promise).

As my school was only a few minutes away, I'd push my luck and always be there last-minute. My mates would call for me each morning. They'd come in and catch a bit of *TV-am*, as I wolfed down my Sugar Puffs and threw my shoes on. My mum would be blowing a gasket. 'YOU'RE GOING TO BE LATE, IT'S NINE O'CLOCK.' It was 8.40.

Quite controversially I really looked forward to getting back to school in September. I enjoyed the big summer holidays, but they were overrated. Too much of a good thing. I'd be bored after a few weeks. There were only so many episodes of *Why Don't You?* I could watch or play raindrop races on the windows. School didn't seem too bad by comparison, apart from the lessons, they spoilt it ... and the nuns.

I'd always be fascinated by how much everybody's appearance had altered in September after just a few weeks off. It's as if everybody had been through a puberty-powered transformation chamber. Some lads were completely unrecognisable. Towering over their former selves after having a huge growth spurt. Pants half-mast. Hormones raging through their bodies. They suddenly had muscles. Yodelled when they spoke, their voices teetering on the edge of breaking. A thin line of bum fluff on their top lips. And the pungent smell of body odour and Right Guard. The girls had transformed too, in both size and shape. Some now with breasts as big as my own (I'd had far too many Sugar Puffs).

Rushing to get to school, we'd cross with Ethel, the lollipop lady (or crossing guard as they're called now ... Jesus). She was a lovely lady in her seventies, and I'd been pals with her since I'd crossed at primary school. The first time we met I decided to play a really elaborate prank on her. I had a reversible coat. Do you remember them? I could turn it inside out and wear the opposing side. It even sported a nifty reversible zip.

So, I crossed over with Ethel wearing one side of the jacket, then ran around the back of the Methodist church. Turned my jacket inside out, so I was wearing the opposite side. Ruffled my hair. Then ran back up the road and crossed over with Ethel again a second time. She looked confused. I managed to convince her that I was/had an identical twin brother who'd gone ahead without me. 'R Trevor never waits for me. What's he like?'

Can you believe I kept this convoluted charade up every day for weeks? In all kinds of weather. It was exhausting. I don't know how Ethel never twigged. Because R Trevor and me never crossed together. Then R Julie grassed me up, she told Ethel I didn't even have a brother and I was a space cadet with a screw loose. I felt like a right idiot. Ethel thought it was hilarious and we kept in touch for many years until she retired and emigrated to Australia.

Eventually, my mates and I would arrive at school just in time for assembly. Sister Sledge would be on stage reminding us all to 'simmer down. You're not on your holidays any more.' I always wanted there to be one boy wearing trunks, lying on a lilo applying sun cream. Jumping to his feet shouting, 'Nobody told me.'

After I left school, I missed assemblies. It's one of those things you don't realise you quite like at the time. Sister Actoo playing the guitar and singing 'Dan, Dan the Leper

Man' or the time Keith Walsh dressed the giant crucifix of Jesus in a body warmer and Bolton Wanderers hat. That must have taken some planning. I still don't know how he got that body warmer over each end of the crucifix. The nuns weren't happy. The older sisters had to be wheeled out with oxygen.

I'd struggle for a few days to adjust after the big summer holidays. I'd somehow forgotten how to use a pen. My hand was all wobbly. Six weeks of watching *Why Don't You?* And now I couldn't write.

A new school year meant new stationery. And who doesn't love stationery? A brand-new pencil case (that would be doodled on and covered in graffiti in no time). Inside the pencil case would be chock-full of useless junk I'd never need. Like a protractor? A set-square? And a compass. Which was only ever used twice. Once for carving my initials into the lid of a desk (for which I got two detentions) and secondly when I shoved it up Tom Vernon's arse in self-defence (another detention). Tom Vernon was constantly hyper and drove me insane, singing 'Jack Your Body' in my ear during Physics. That was the only altercation I had in school, though I did twat Clive Marsh on the nose with my torch during a camping trip to Aberystwyth.

He was another wild child. Forever twitching and beeping. But he was cracking at drawing. He always added his own sound effects. If he was drawing a car or a bike, he'd be making engine noises the whole time. Looking back, it's clear now that he must have had ADHD but sadly kids went undiagnosed in those days. The nuns just labelled him a fruit cake and stuck him on the thick table.

Now when I say thick table, I don't mean the table was made from a thick piece of wood. I mean it was for thick kids or academically challenged. I know first-hand because I was on the thick table. However, I was only put on the thick table as punishment. Can you believe that? Sister Mary-Juana said, 'If you're going to act stupid, then you can sit with the stupid.' Talk about double discrimination.

There had to be a permanent stigma from being labelled thick. Jason Patel was forever bullied as a result; I'd often see him stuffed into a school bin arse-first. He'd be there for hours with the caretaker trying to pull him free. Such a shame. Now Jason collects trolleys at Morrisons. I heard he tried to commit suicide by jumping out of a window at home but failed, as it was the lounge window. He landed in a bush in the front garden and sprained his ankle. The thick sod.

Sadly, bullying was common. If some older boys didn't like the look of you, you'd be pushed to the floor or punched in the face. It was brutal.

Once I was head-butted by a random boy. No reason whatsoever. It was agony. I fell to the floor with my nose bleeding. He walked off. It really shook me up. When my dad asked me why my nose was swollen with a cut on it I just said I'd banged into a door at school. Two days later that head-butting caused two black eyes. I looked like a panda. I know I probably should have told a member of staff, but it wasn't worth the hassle. They probably wouldn't deal with it properly. The nuns were never subtle, so I'd probably get another beating for grassing somebody up. It was just the way things were.

Anyway, I found out who the boy was who head-butted me and even though it's over forty years later if I ever see him I'll mount the kerb in my car and knock the fucker down. Not that I hold a grudge, you understand.

First year (or year seven as it's called now) was by far the worst for bullying. A very scary time. It was all about hierarchy. Six weeks before I'd been in the top class at primary school, full of confidence, and then I was tossed into the viper's pit of secondary school. Where my tie was forever flicked, or I'd be flipped upside down and my dinner money nicked. I was once fastened to a wire fence with my own school tie.

It was a tough time. I felt lonely and lost. Not only did I have a whole new school to contend with, but I didn't know where anything was. The place was a labyrinth. It's funny that years later I can literally remember almost every nook and cranny of my secondary school and the grounds within. Even the smells of the classrooms. In particular the art room where I spent a lot of time. Occasionally when I can't sleep, I visualise floating around the corridors of my old school so I can eventually drift off. A bit like the last scene in *Titanic* when the camera roams through the ship, up the staircase to find Jack waiting for Rose and then everybody claps. I'm filling up just thinking about it.

First-year pupils were always easy to spot. Wandering around looking terrified, clutching a tear-stained timetable, crumpled on a piece of A4. I just simply kept my head down for fear of getting it kicked in.

First years were an easy target as they were always dressed the smartest. In their brand-new uniforms (unless you had an older sibling, then your uniform would be handed down). I always liked uniforms, they're like overalls. They also put a stop to the inevitable hierarchy of fashion. Everybody was the same. Except on the last day of term when you were allowed to wear your own clothes. Then you could easily spot all the stylish kids. On 'wear your own clothes day' I'd always wear my uniform. It was MY uniform. It wasn't rented.

What never failed to impress me was the way pupils would manipulate the rules of a uniform. Our school uniform was primarily a brown jumper and a gold shirt, but we'd always push the boundaries. Just little tweaks to try and be rebellious. Like wearing a white shirt, with no jumper. Black pants instead of brown. Ditch the school blazer immediately. I know it'd cost my mum a fortune but it had to go unless I wanted a beating every day of the week.

Boys would adapt their ties. Placing the widest point of their tie on the inside of their shirts, so they could sport a thin tie. Girls would try and wear skirts as short as they possibly could, until the nuns performed random inspections with a ruler. Pupils would and always will create a new style within any restrictions imposed. It's adolescent nature. Or to quote a line from *School of Rock*, 'stick it to the man', or the nun in our case.

One place where I could always hide from the tyranny of

bullying was the school 'Recreation Centre'. A newly constructed building set beside the convent. Apparently, past pupils had to vote between a swimming pool or a recreation centre. Lord knows why but they chose the latter.

I had a recreation card which allowed me unlimited access to ALL the unbridled pleasures of 'the rec', as it was ingeniously nicknamed. Including ping-pong, Twister, Tiddly Winks and a half-empty box of Spirograph. There was a small tuck shop on a trestle table manned by two sixth-form girls, who sold cartons of Vimto and Chipsticks.

The best thing to happen at 'the rec' was the annual school talent contest. Which everybody loved as it meant an afternoon off lessons. How could we not enjoy watching three first-year girls wrapped in white bandages dancing to 'Ghostbusters', or a rock band of five fifth-year girls singing 'New England' – Kirsty MacColl. Which contains the lyrics 'I put you on a pedestal, you put me on the pill.'

When the Sisters of the Cross & Passion heard that, the curtains were quickly closed and guitars unplugged. The nuns had the staunch views of the Catholic Church to uphold. Like the time they forced us to sit through a slide show on anti-abortion. I still wince when I recall the graphic images that were projected on to a twelve-foot screen. The nuns even passed around a plastic replica of an aborted foetus for us each to hold. The exact size and scale. Can you believe this traumatic shit? When Natalie Sergeant stood up and suggested there were two sides to the argument of abortion, the nuns hastily bundled her out of 'the rec'.

# SEPTEMBER

The only other thing 'the rec' was good for was school discos. An unmissable event, the last Thursday of every month. I've many a happy memory of dancing badly to 'Bad Boys' – Wham, 'Uptown Girl' – Billy Joel and 'Superman' – Black Lace. All the while Sister Sledge would sit at the back of 'the rec', overseeing proceedings and knitting.

Those school discos were a turning point in my life. Music had started to consume me. I'd always been exposed to it growing up. A few steadfast albums played in heavy rotation on the family record player. The best of The Beach Boys, The Carpenters and Simon & Garfunkel. Those LPs were enough to keep me going until my teenage years. That's when music really took hold of me, and I couldn't consume quick enough. I began exploring my dad's collection of singles. An important education. Jaunty pop melodies at short lengths. Then I discovered The Beatles. A massive game changer. I couldn't comprehend the number of songs they produced over an eight-year period. Just their ability to evolve and experiment with so many different styles. Covering so many different musical genres. Truly phenomenal.

I'd listen to everything and anything. The radio, *Top of the Pops*, R Julie's record collection. I joined the local library and hired music constantly. It was a glorious time; music was colour, contrasting the greyness of school. I'd get home each night, go straight upstairs, and play my music.

Embarrassingly I even took an old piece of cardboard and made a sign that read 'DJ PK', colouring individual letters. Then I'd play music and record my own intros in between the tracks. Just for myself. I can feel my arse tightening as I type this, but hey, I was only eleven. All this was an epiphany. I knew I really wanted to have a go at being a DJ at the school discos.

Monthly discos at 'the rec' became the focus of my world. I'd hang around the stage, watching the fifth-year boys DJ-ing. I'd help them pack up, struggling to carry the enormous double turntable, infinity lights and speakers back to the convent where they were stored. I'd have visons of the nuns cracking out the disco equipment at the weekend and cavorting around the corridors to the *Sound of Music* soundtrack.

On Thursday 25 September 1986 our monthly school disco was hijacked by the one and only Timmy Mallett and was broadcast live on our local radio station, Piccadilly 261. Timmy had an evening show each night from eight till ten which was a massive hit. Each week a school in the region could nominate themselves to have Timmy Mallett's radio show (or 'Timmy on the Tranny' as it was called) broadcast live on air. And our school was chosen.

It was incredibly exciting as production vans started arriving at 'the rec' with Piccadilly Radio logos on the side. Then an enormous aerial was erected. Cables were laid. Signs were posted. 'The rec' was packed. Everybody wanted to be there.

We all just stood in front of the stage mesmerised as Timmy played the hits of the day, took requests, and threw bundles of Piccadilly Radio stickers into the audience. It was a thrill to hear the names of pupils you knew read out on air. He even played a cheeky request for the nuns – 'Sisters Are Doin' It For Themselves' by Annie Lennox and Aretha Franklin.

Timmy Mallett was a natural broadcaster with natural charisma. He'd later swap the radio for hosting *The Wide Awake Club*, Saturday mornings on ITV. Then later *Wacaday* with his big pink mallet. Followed by national fame having a number one with 'Itsy Bitsy Teeny Weeny Yellow Polka Dot Bikini'.

During the live broadcast from our school Timmy was joined on stage by a young assistant, Chris Evans, who played a regular character on the show called Nobby Nolevel. And as you'll no doubt be aware Chris Evans would also go on to huge fame himself as a DJ, broadcaster, and star as Captain America in the Marvel films. When I met Chris Evans at Radio 2, I mentioned his appearance at my school disco, but of course he'd no recollection of it. Ah well, at least I've still got a battered old cassette as proof it wasn't all a dream.

Inspired by Timmy Mallett's show at school I started to integrate myself more with the fifth-year DJs on Thursday nights. Even lending them a few of my own records. It wasn't too long before they invited me to help on stage and choose a few records. The food chain ran its course and when they eventually left school it became my turn to run the monthly school discos. Also, because nobody else wanted to do it.

Completely distracted, I'd spend time in lessons writing lists of songs. Meticulously planning my playlists. Spending all my pocket and paper round money buying records from a stall on Bolton market that sold ex-jukebox singles for 50p. Then on the last Thursday of every month I'd load up my mum's shopping trolley with records and pull it up to school. The wheels buckling under the weight.

Like most people I'd tape the charts on Sunday afternoon and desperately try to stop the recording before the DJ spoke. Then I hooked up my tape player to the speaker system at school. This allowed me to play the current hits without blowing all my money.

DJ-ing at those discos was the only thing I was interested in at school. I suppose it was my first real step on the road to performing. Well, that and being an altar boy but I don't think Father Michael would be up for me to 'spin the discs' at Sunday mass.

I'm still just as obsessed with music, and I still occasionally play the role of 'DJ PK' when I curate an event called Dance for Life. They're enormous discos in arenas across Britain, with all the profits going to cancer research. I've hosted over twenty-five Dance for Life shows since 2015 for over fifty thousand people. You should come. They're joyous. I just love seeing people happy, dancing, it's just like being back at 'the rec'.

As I was saying, September is the first month of the school year and one thing we always had to do was back our books. I'd spend my weekends on my hands and knees in the front room with an assortment of left-over wallpaper, backing my books. A bit of woodchip, anaglypta, my dad's copy of *Razzle*. Apparently, the point of backing your books was to keep them well protected. But it was a complete waste of time because I spent the rest of the year graffitiing on the backing. Practising my signature and doodling, bored while the teacher droned on.

It was very hard to concentrate on what teachers were saying at school. I retained virtually nothing. I just couldn't seem to process what they were saying but I could certainly bluff, acting the part of somebody who understood. Writing things down and nodding on the surface but internally there was a panic and sinking feeling that marred my entire time at school. The only subjects where I felt I had an ounce of ability were Art (which as you know was my only GCSE, albeit fraudulently) and English language where I held a whiff of proficiency in writing stories, but then I only got a grade D. Yet here I am, still having a go at it.

My worst subjects were everything else on my timetable except lunch. Lord knows why I took Electronics as an option. It was possibly the opportunity of making a disco rope light which I thought would come in handy at the school discos. But I literally couldn't understand anything Mr Booth said. It's like he was speaking a foreign language and the more I tried to concentrate the less I could comprehend. I resorted to copying everything from Pamela Dawson who sat next to me and had a glass eye. I sat on the right side of her eye, so she was completely unaware of my skulduggery. Then Mr Booth shifted her down to the front of the class and I failed miserably.

In Science, Mr Harper, who was a bit cool, once said, 'If you ever need any help my door is always open, except for Thursday nights when I play jazz guitar in a band.' He also told us to back our books but said we could draw anything we liked on the cover as long as the theme was 'science-based'. I thought that was ace. And decided to draw a scene from *Young Frankenstein* which was one of my favourite films. It was the moment Dr Frankenstein (Gene Wilder) tried to bring the monster to life. I admit it was a bit tenuous on the science-based theme but at least there was plenty of lab equipment.

My parents also loved *Young Frankenstein*. My mum said when they watched it down the Odeon my dad laughed so hard that he slid off his chair and onto the floor.

I loved it too. Instantly adoring anything that made my parents laugh. I think basically children enjoy seeing their parents happy. My parents laughed at the 'Pink Panther' films, with Peter Sellers as Inspector Clouseau. The slapstick of Laurel & Hardy. The incredible wit in *Porridge*. The inventiveness and mania of Robin Williams. One of their big favourites was Mel Brooks. My mum let me stay up late and watch *The Producers* on BBC1 when I was ten and it was a pivotal moment seeing it for the first time, and another huge influence.

Fast forward over thirty years later and I got a chance to take my mum and nan to watch Mel Brooks' new musical version of *Young Frankenstein* on Broadway. The show was still in previews, with changes still being made before opening night. Mel Brooks himself was doing the changes.

I'd contacted his film company, Brooksfilms, and they put me in touch with his PA who replied saying Mel would love to meet all of us after the show. What an absolute thrill. Now just to be clear, I'm not a stalker. I did have a vague connection to Mel Brooks, having spoken to him once on the phone when I played a part in *The Producers* musical in 2007.

He phoned my hotel when I was in rehearsals in London and left a message in his unmistakable raspy voice. I couldn't believe it. I'd watched and studied everything he'd ever done. Collected his film posters, bought his records. Read his autobiographies. I even drew a pencil portrait of Gene Wilder and Zero Mostel in *The Producers* for my GCSE art exam. (On reflection I suppose I was a bit of a stalker.) And now Mel Brooks had called my hotel room. Wow!

After playing back the message several times in disbelief I called him back at Brooksfilms in LA (Lord knows how much that cost). His secretary, Shelby, put me through and suddenly there he was, chatting away with all his trademark vim and vigour. It felt like we'd known each other for years. To be honest I was so overwhelmed I can't really recall what we said to each other. Except for one moment when we discussed my rehearsing for the show and he said, 'You're a comedian, trust your instinct. You've got my permission to try and make the show as funny as it can possibly be.' Oh my God. Mel Brooks is telling me this!

The only problem with that sage advice was how do you convey it to the rest of the cast and crew. It's not as if I can just start adding lines here and say, 'It's OK, I've got Mel Brooks' permission.' So I said nothing to nobody. I didn't even mention we'd spoken, but very slowly over the next few months I started to try things. The odd line here, a bit of improvisation there. Even breaking the fourth wall on occasion and talking to the audience. Commenting on the price of the theatre ice creams in the interval. It must have worked because after I'd finished *The Producers* I was invited to return for the last week of the tour in Cardiff. Of course, I said yes.

Working in *The Producers* was one of the happiest experiences of my career and occasionally I dream I'm still performing in the show and when I wake I'm gutted it's a dream. So, you can imagine my surprise later that year when I received another call from Mel Brooks. I was in Ireland on holiday and didn't have much of a phone signal. Frustratingly we kept missing each other's calls and then when I finally spoke to Mel Brooks he said, 'Do you not take calls from Jews?' Hilarious. He asked if I'd consider appearing in *The Producers* again on a national tour all around the UK. I was SO flattered but honestly, I knew it wasn't what I wanted. I told him that we had a young family, and I really didn't want to be away from them. He said he understood that family should always come first, and I was making the right decision. I was relieved he understood, it made me love him even more.

So now we were sat in the Hilton theatre on Broadway eager to see *Young Frankenstein* the musical and finally get to meet Mel Brooks. By the way, the tickets cost a small fortune but hey! We only go around once, and it was my mum's sixtieth birthday.

The show started, it was strange seeing the characters in colour as the original film is in black and white. The cast were great but sadly I couldn't help but compare them to the cast in the movie. I missed Gene Wilder, Marty Feldman, Cloris Leachman and the extraordinary Madeline Kahn. Unfortunately the story didn't lend itself to the theatre as well as *The Producers*, as that show satirised the world of theatre and made you feel part of the joke. *Young Frankenstein* was an isolated story, set in Transylvania. It wasn't crap but sadly it wasn't brill. I think that was reflected when they closed on Broadway after only five hundred shows. Either that or it was because the tickets cost an arm and a leg. *The Producers* had won a record-breaking twelve Tony Awards, so I think somebody wanted to seriously cash in on its success.

Anyway, all I was really interested in now was meeting one of my all-time comedy heroes. I was distracted and found myself scanning the audience to see where Mel Brooks was sat. After the show his PA came to meet us and took us backstage. What an honour. There he was, little old Mel Brooks. We hugged long and hard. I was so chuffed to meet him. Then with the energy of a toddler he grabbed hold of my hand and pulled me towards the dressing rooms of the main cast. My mum and nan struggling to keep up the pace. Mel knocked on the first door which was opened by Roger Bart, who was playing Dr Frankenstein. He looked completely worn out, hot and perspiring. Mel dived into a list of performance notes that he read from a dog-eared jotter scribbled in writing. Roger Bart nodded while simultaneously wiping sweat from his neck with a towel. Then just as he was about to close his door Mel Brooks said, 'Oh and by the way, Roger, I'd like you to meet Peter Kay,' and he turned to me. 'He's one of the UK's top comedians and he's here with his mum and his nan.' Coyly I waved at Roger, he smiled back. Before I had a chance to say 'hello' Mel was already knocking on the next dressing room door which belonged to the actress Megan Mullally (she was in *Will & Grace*).

She opened the door, looking equally exhausted. Mel fervently read her some notes from his jotter on her performance and then again, just as she was about to close the door Mel said, 'Megan, I'd like you to meet Peter Kay, he's one of the top comedians in the UK.' We exchanged polite smiles but, honestly, she didn't look the least bit interested. 'He's here with his mum and his nan,' and then he was off again. So much energy for a man his age. We had to chase after him.

I pleaded with him, 'You don't have to keep introducing me, they haven't a clue who I am.' 'Nonsense, you're Peter Kay, you're a funny guy and they need to know it.' I was blown away. Not only by his compliments but also his kindness. Taking the time to introduce me to everybody. And that sequence of events was repeated at every dressing room door along the corridor. The cast got their performance notes and Mel introduced me as the king of British comedy, right until we reached the back doors of the theatre. It was there that we stood and chatted. Mel and my nana reminiscing showtunes and singing to each other. That was a moment to cherish. I always judge people on how they treat my family and friends. Mel was exemplary.

Sadly, after quite a while chatting, we reluctantly had to say our goodbyes. I could have stayed and talked forever. The four of us left the theatre and walked into the Manhattan night air. The city buzzing with noise and traffic. We each hugged Mel and I asked him if he was getting a taxi (or a cab as the Yanks say). He said, 'No, it looks like a nice night. I think I'll walk,' and off he went. I watched him as he walked off up the sidewalk and into the distance. It made me sad.

Mel's wife, the actress Anne Bancroft, died a few years before and I'd heard that Mel was completely lost without her. Working on the musical to distract himself. Maybe I just felt sad because he was on his own. But I might have been completely wrong. He could have been off to a vibrant showbiz party or heading home via a brothel. Either way it was the greatest pleasure to meet the great Mel Brooks.

# October

A radio station in Preston re-branded October as Rock-tober, playing soft and hard rock classics for the whole month each year. I went on the station once to promote a stand-up tour. It was inside an old church. I brought their milk in with me.

One of their station jingles boldly stated, 'broadcasting to a nation'. I said, 'Well, I couldn't pick up the station on my radio until I pulled into the car park.' The presenter wasn't so chuffed as I was live on air at the time.

Rock-tober is a month of transition. Dark nights creep in slowly as the sun sets earlier. And skies are coloured with hues of orange and pink. Leaves begin their descent, fluttering to the ground on cool and crisp air. October's full moon, or blood moon, is mystical, mysterious and more than fitting for Halloween, which looms over the month like Pennywise, the terrifying clown from Stephen King's *IT*. One of horror's most unforgettable and chilling characters. I was never a fan of *IT* or anything horror related. So, Halloween never lit my pumpkin. In fact, we couldn't even afford pumpkins. We used to carve out turnips or swedes and stick a candle in them.

There was never that much of a fuss about Halloween when I was growing up. We were always more interested in Bonfire Night five days later. We did play Halloween parlour games. Like bobbing for apples hung from a piece of string or we'd take turns bobbing for apples in a washing-up bowl. Then bobbing for chips in the deep fat fryer, but we soon had to stop after R Julie got third-degree burns.

Now we've all gone nuts over Halloween. We celebrate it like America, where it's been a huge holiday for decades. They're selling costumes and decorations in UK shops from August. People love decorating their houses inside and out with all kinds of grotesque paraphernalia. Ghosts, skeletons, bats hanging up, witches, photos of Jimmy Savile. Some Halloween masks are horrible, and people wear them while they're trick-or-treating. A lot of pensioners shit themselves but that's nothing to do with Halloween. That's just a fact.

Trick-or-treating is just begging, pure and simple. Most people refuse to answer the door. I don't blame them, it's not worth it, just to give some scallies a few Celebrations or Heroes in fear. And if you don't answer the door, you get a lighted rag chucked through your letterbox. Or maybe that's just in Bolton.

The most frightening thing about Halloween is how much sugar kids consume after trick-or-treating. It's at epidemic proportions. Big corporations don't even want the word sugar in the name of their products. They've rebranded Sugar Puffs to Wheat Puffs. Poor Honey Monster must be signing on. I'm sure I saw him outside the Job Centre. It was either him or it was someone trick-or-treating.

So, the house is decorated all spookily for Halloween, the children are cosied up inside in their creepy costumes. Eating their stash from trick-or-treating, watching scary films. Well, kids' scary films like *Hotel Transylvania*, *Goosebumps*, *The Texas Chainsaw Massacre*. OK, the last one isn't for kids, but I wish somebody would have told my granny; she let me watch it when I was just seven. I was petrified. Sat behind a cushion watching it with my cousins in Ireland. Then when it was finished my granny put on John Carpenter's *Halloween*. What was she thinking? Maybe that it was all just a bit of fun, but I didn't sleep for weeks and kept wetting the bed. Which was traumatic, as I had an electric blanket at the time and kept getting shocked in my sleep.

As I said before I've never been a fan of horror and have always given scary films a swerve. I've seen some classics like *Psycho*, *The Omen*, *Poltergeist*, *The Exorcist* (which was really disturbing, although I did enjoy the bloopers at the end). We'd rarely hire a horror film from the video shop. But if my dad ever rented one, he'd discreetly lean over and flick off the lamp in the front room. Plunging us into darkness, then he'd make a ghostly 'Whoooaaa' sound, so we'd jump out of our seats. It never worked. And the only time we ever saw my dad jump out of his seat was when he balanced his plate of Sunday dinner on the arm of the comfy chair. Then, just before he sat, the plate slid off the arm and onto the seat cushion, burning his arse when he sat down. So funny. He was distraught. Quickly trying to salvage mixed veg and roast beef smeared down the back of his pants.

My dad loved trying to frighten us. Like the time we stayed at his favourite B&B in Blackpool, The Royle Palace (please don't be fooled by the name, though my dad clearly was). It had definitely seen better days and certainly wasn't a palace by any stretch of the imagination.

The B&B was owned by Jean and Graham 'Royle' and boasted a sea view (yeah, if you stood on a ladder with a pair of binoculars). Hot and cold running water (big deal) and a fervent promise that whoever stayed would 'Arrive as guests but leave as friends'. This pledge was permanently displayed on a piece of A4, sellotaped in the front lounge window, hand-written in green felt tip. Which also happened to be the colour of the toast they served at breakfast. But my dad loved The Royle Palace for one reason. Graham would let my dad go behind their tiny lounge bar and pull his own pints. This was heaven on Earth and I witnessed a look of ecstasy on my dad's face I'd never seen before or since.

The Royle Palace did have one redeeming feature: a Pac-Man arcade game, a flat tabletop console which was the saving grace from boredom for R Julie and me. We played for hours in the centre of the lounge bar. Sat facing each other surrounded by mock Tudor décor. Artificial beams attached to the low ceiling. The front façade of the lounge bar was padded in a brown faux studded leather. Classy. Once-white walls were now a muted shade of nicotine yellow and covered in ornamental brasses. And the whole B&B stunk of cigarette smoke. Our clothes reeked of it, even our room smelled of smoke, four floors up. Back then 'non-smoking' rooms weren't even an option. We shared a 'family' room (a family of dwarves), with a communal toilet just down the corridor. I wasn't keen. The last thing I needed was another guest rattling the bog door handle while I was mid thrutch. So, I refused to empty my bowels until we got back to Bolton. However, I did develop a hump and I began to hallucinate before the end of the holiday.

Jean, the landlady, always kept a pile of disposable paper bags on the cistern in the communal toilet. They were for female guests who were experiencing their lady time. Each bag featured the figure of a Victorian lady strolling with an umbrella. I hadn't a clue what they were for and used to use them for drawing on. Jean looked perplexed when she kept finding these disposable bags dotted around The Royle Palace, with inane crayon doodles of Popeye the Sailor and James Bond on the back of them.

We stopped at The Royle Palace quite a few times over several years. Much to my mum's disgust. She loathed the place, but somehow my dad managed to soft-soap her into staying again. Once with the enticement that all the bedrooms now boasted en suite facilities. Graham had finally got compensation for breathing in asbestos during his time in national service. Every cloud.

# OCTOBER

The en suite was hardly state of the art. Somehow, Graham and Jean had managed to convert a wardrobe-sized space into a cubicle where a guest could have a shower, a shave and a sit-down shit all at the same time. I swear if I'd had a cat, I couldn't have swung it.

Every Friday night was party night at The Royle Palace. Whoopee! This consisted of all guests assembling in the lounge bar for a mixture of high jinks and horseplay. Jean (who had an uncanny resemblance to an adult version of Little Orphan Annie, complete with ginger afro) masterfully fingered the keyboard on an upright Bontempi organ, while her husband Graham inflated balloons in the corner of the lounge bar. Occasionally sucking in helium, so he could accompany Jean on the chorus of 'Tragedy' – The Bee Gees. Even as a child I recognised tripe when I saw it and was fully aware that they'd been rolling out this *tired* and tested routine every Friday for years.

To make matters worse the Pac-Man game was covered up with a plastic tablecloth in lieu of the night's frivolities. R Julie and me were bereft and all we could do was smile politely as we tried to watch *Blankety Blank* through everybody's legs.

Blackpool was full-on. Like grabbing an electric cable. A sensory overload of sights, sounds and bingo. Occasionally when we needed some respite, we'd retreat to the conservatory at The Royle Palace, a glazed sitting room at the front of the B&B facing the main road. A few soft furnishings, cosy table lamps, and some dog-eared board games positioned on a bookcase. Not dissimilar to a day room in a hospice. And all lit up by a red neon 'no vacancies' sign which pulsated in the window.

Jean would often brag 'We never have any vacancies, we're chock-a-block all year round.' But I was suspicious, the place always appeared half empty to me. I think a permanent declaration of 'no vacancies' was more of a cutthroat statement for the neighbouring B&Bs. As ironically, they all said 'no vacancies' but all appeared to be deserted.

Halloween was fast approaching so the BBC were showing a new mini-series called *Salem's Lot*. Based on the book by horror maestro Stephen King. It starred the late David Soul from *Starsky & Hutch* fame. Who legend has it broke his arse jumping on a car roof in the opening titles.

*Salem's Lot* was scary. And we all sat watching it in The Royle Palace conservatory. In one particularly creepy scene a character called Ralphie Glick, who'd transformed into a vampire, returned from the dead to suck the blood of his brother Danny. We watched anxiously through cushions as Ralphie floated towards Danny's bedroom and tapped on his windowpane. Just as my dad thumped loudly on the window.

We jumped out of our skins; my mum even screamed. My dad relished our reactions. Pointing through the glass and laughing before swiftly exiting back behind the lounge bar to pull some pints.

\* \* \*

Watching horror films was all the rage in the eighties. Video nasties they were labelled by the media, and R Julie couldn't get enough of them. She'd gather in the front room with her friends. I was far too young to watch, so would quickly get booted out of the front room while they revelled in an abundance of gore. Films like *The Burning*, *Driller Killer*, *Zombie Flesh Eaters*, *I Spit on Your Grave* to name but a few. As well as ALL the *Friday the 13th* films. I'd sneakily watch them later when they'd gone out – fast forwarding through the gruesome bits with my eyes squinted.

There has only ever been one thing that truly frightened me: a series on ITV called *Armchair Thriller*. Search up the opening credits on YouTube. Even they sent me scurrying behind the couch. The shadow of a man creeping towards an armchair. He slowly sits and splays his fingers as the camera zooms in on the last note of the eerie theme tune (composed by Andy Mackay from Roxy Music – a little factoid for you).

*Armchair Thriller* was always preceded by a familiar TV ident for Thames Television. This normally showed an image of well-known London landmarks by day. But for *Armchair Thriller* the ident was specially revised to a spooky night-time setting of London. That put the willies right up me.

*Armchair Thriller*'s opening titles were chilling enough but there was one series storyline that really disturbed me, it was called *Quiet as a Nun*. Set in a convent, it was about the death of a nun that's being investigated by a lady sleuth (well, that's what I've just read on IMDb). There was one particular scene that petrified me. The lady sleuth is doing a bit of snooping at night. She climbs some ladders up to an attic within the convent. She hears a rhythmical creaking noise, so shines her torch which reveals a nun sat in a rocking chair, swaying back and forth BUT the nun hasn't got a face. Just a black veil. Christ on a bike. I've got goosebumps just writing that last sentence. That's how it still affects me after all this time.

I literally sobbed in fear as a child. Undeniably due to the fact I was taught by nuns and was heavily ensconced in Catholicism. I've shown that scene to people who aren't Catholic, and it doesn't bother them in the slightest.

My mum found a paperback book of *Quiet as a Nun* in a sale at our local library. When she brought it home and showed it to me, I snatched it out of her hand and threw it across the room. It freaked me out. Occasionally when I get up for a wee in the middle of the night, I anticipate the nun with no face appearing from behind the bathroom door. Now that's a deep-seated fear.

Can you believe *Armchair Thriller – Quiet as a Nun* went out on ITV on a Tuesday night at 8pm? After it'd finished, I'd plead with my parents to let me stay up and watch *Robin's Nest*. I hoped the change of programme would calm me down before bed.

On Wednesdays in infant school, Sister Mary-Christmas used to wheel a TV on gigantic legs into the classroom so we could watch children's programmes. One afternoon she flicked the TV on too early and would you believe *Armchair Thriller* was on ITV. The episode was *Quiet as a Nun*. Not only that but it was just at the attic scene where the faceless nun is on the rocking chair. What were the odds?

I let out a yelp and legged it to the boys' toilets crying. Ironically it was a nun that came into the toilets to comfort me. At least she had a face. What sick sod at ITV chose to repeat that *Armchair Thriller* in the afternoon?

For pupils, October can be a gruelling month. It runs straight through the longest term of the academic year, when there's still a lot of adjustment taking place. I found leaving school to be hard. The pressure of what to do next. Should I go to sixth form? It was very tempting; all my mates would be going. But I wasn't academic, so it wouldn't necessarily be the best choice. I'd really enjoyed performing as the Lion in our school production of *The Wizard of Oz* earlier in the year. It left me with a desire to perform, to follow that path.

Lo and behold I discovered that there was a brand-new Performing Arts course starting at Bolton College, so I applied. Miraculously I was offered a place. Christ knows how. My informal chat with one of the lecturers seemed to go down well. I managed to make him laugh; that must have counted for something because my single GCSE in Art probably didn't.

So, I was off to Bolton College, which was only down the road in town but felt a million miles away and very grown up. No uniforms, no assemblies, now I'd be calling teachers by their Christian names. That felt ridiculous.

Those first few weeks were tough. I was really unhappy. Everything had changed so fast; it was hard to process. I'd also got a job working in a factory packing toilet rolls in the evenings, 5 till 9 (like Dolly Parton in reverse). All these sudden changes manifested themselves through negativity and cynicism. Internally I was scolding and judgemental of everything and everybody.

Performing Arts. What was I thinking? A load of pretentious theatrical types. I was expecting the Kids from Fame, dancing on car roofs and singing 'Starmaker' but this was Bolton in 1989. Kids were into the Stone Roses, Happy Mondays, and the only time I ever saw any dancing on a car roof they were off their tits on ecstasy.

Why was I so depressed? What I didn't realise at the time was I was grieving school. Upset that such a big part of my life had gone forever. Quite literally, as the council demolished the building three weeks after we left. I couldn't even go back and reminisce with the nuns. Who I was starting to miss. Who'd have thought?

This wasn't me. I'd never felt like this before. The students on my course weren't unfriendly, it was me who wouldn't really socialise. But there was one girl I managed to get close to. She stood out from everybody else. Tall, light-coloured long hair, attractive but well out of my league, which is probably why I had the confidence to speak to her.

She was living in a bedsit in Bolton but didn't know anything or anybody. Sophie Bruce was from London, but for some reason had ended up on the performing arts course in Bolton. Talk about a fish out of water, which is exactly how I felt. Perhaps that's why we clicked.

I wanted to make her feel welcome in my hometown. We spent time together. Most days we'd go for lunch, walking from college to Ye Olde Pastie Shoppe on Churchgate where we'd buy a couple of pasties and then head off to eat them sitting in the grounds of the parish church overlooking the bypass (I knew how to treat a girl). The grass was now littered with gold, crimson and amber leaves. We chatted endlessly about anything and everything. Mainly music. I made her a few mix tapes. We bonded over Billy Joel, my favourite, and Supertramp. I even invited her round to our house for Sunday dinner as she'd just be alone in her bedsit.

We went to see *Dead Poets Society* at the local cinema (where I'd later end up working as an usher). The actress Susannah York (who played Superman's mum) was sat in front of us. She was appearing in a play at the Bolton Octagon Theatre (where I'd also end up working). It was a brilliant film. Robin Williams gave an incredible performance. Those few hours, that film, that day had an enduring effect on me. I don't think I'd ever been moved by a film so much. The final scene where the pupils rebel, standing on their desks, each of them exclaiming 'Oh captain my captain' was extremely affecting. And we sobbed over the end credits (Susannah York too). The cinematography in the film was also stunning. Rich autumnal colours that coincided with the seasonal weather we were also experiencing at that time.

My friendship with Sophie had a big effect on me. I'd never met anybody like her but sadly before the October half-term she left. It was all a bit sudden, but the course just wasn't for her. I understood the isolation she was feeling, living in a new town on her own. I was bereft, because I was losing a good friend, and our relationship was helping me cope with the changes in my life. Suddenly I felt back to square one.

We said we'd keep in touch, and we did. Letters and postcards (remember those). We also chatted on the phone. The connection and affection we had never waned. I didn't see Sophie again for four years; when I did it was in an emergency.

Fast forward to October 1993. I'd been working as a cashier at a local Esso garage for a few years. The pay was crap, but the job was fun and cushy. For most of my shifts I worked with Iqbal. He was older than me, a really deep enigmatic character who was fanatical about Prince, The Doors and writing poetry. He also smoked a lot of weed and was prone to melancholic mood swings. We spent a lot of time together outside of work, usually on the weekends. I'll forever treasure Iqbal taking me to a late-night showing of *Total Recall* at the new multiplex in Bury. I'd never seen or heard anything like it before. But the highlight was Iqbal driving us in his dad's Mitsubishi Eclipse. I'm not into cars, but what a vehicle. So comfortable, smooth and exhilarating. We seemed to glide to the cinema. Travelling in that car was a sporadic luxury, as most of the time Iqbal was relegated to his Mini Metro but hey, at least he had a car. I was still learning to drive.

Iqbal also left the garage and Bolton. He relocated to London with his wife, child and extended family. We occasionally spoke on the phone, and he kept begging me to come and stay. So, after saving up I nervously booked a train ticket to the big smoke. Arriving at Euston I expected to be greeted by Iqbal but was greeted by another familiar face, his cousin Jamal. I'd met him a few times when he'd visited Bolton. I'd always found him a bit of a tool, but I was glad, and surprised to see him at the end of the platform. He said Iqbal had been caught up with some 'business'. Obviously, I'd have preferred Iqbal to pick me up but at least somebody had met me. You've got to remember this was before mobiles and I'd come all the way to London based on a phone call I'd had with Iqbal the previous week.

It's unthinkable now that we'd live our lives like that. I'd say to a mate on a Friday, 'I'll meet you outside WHSmith's next Tuesday at 10am,' and they'd be there. Nowadays I receive a constant flurry of updates via text: 'Just setting off', 'I'll be there in 5 mins' and 'I'm just parking up'. Too much communication? Just turn up.

The heat was stifling as we headed north from Euston. London intimidated me. The hustle and bustle of the capital. Continual gridlock. It didn't help that Jamal only had one cassette tape, 'Rhythm Is a Dancer' – Snap!, that he played in a loop for the whole journey. I wanted to snap his cassette, as he kept reminding me it was a banging tune.

We arrived at a small, terraced house nestled beside a stone railway bridge adorned with maroon-coloured ivy. Gusts of wind swirled autumn leaves as Jamal rang the doorbell. Iqbal's younger sister opened the door. She seemed surprised to see me. So did Iqbal's mum, who appeared over her shoulder.

# OCTOBER

I was welcomed inside and sat in the lounge, while the three of them had a heated conversation in a side room in a language I couldn't understand. Though I did recognise 'baka-vaas kya hai', which is Hindi for 'what the fuck'. But what I did understand quite clearly was nobody knew that I was coming to stay. Awkward.

We sat in silence waiting for Iqbal to return, which seemed like forever. I was offered several cups of tea. Politely I declined, recalling the last time Iqbal's mum had made me a cup of tea. She heated the water in a saucepan with about six teabags. It was the colour of tar and tasted like it.

An hour or so agonisingly passed. Any conversation had long run dry, as we watched *Countdown* with the sound virtually off. Finally, we heard the scrape of keys and the front door opened. It was Iqbal; what a relief. His beaming smile lit the lounge. We hugged, then he immediately disappeared behind some glazed sliding doors for a massive barney with his family. It didn't sound good. I heard tempers rise and 'bakavaas kya hai' uttered several more times. I was tempted to grab my rucksack and leg it, but go where? My return train ticket wasn't until Monday, and it was Thursday.

God forbid I'd buy another train ticket and head home, but I was young and poor and to be honest the thought didn't enter my head. The glazed doors slid open, Iqbal beamed as nothing had happened and said, 'Would you like something to eat?' Twenty minutes later I was eating a plate of fish fingers and sweetcorn. A bizarre choice of food. Iqbal said, 'Let's get out of here.' I still had a fish finger left.

Sitting in the front seat of his familiar Mini Metro, we headed to Christ knows where. It all looked the same to me. We played music and we chatted. Just like old times. It was good to see him again, but he seemed preoccupied. As I said, Iqbal had always been a dark horse when we'd worked together. Blowing hot and cold, and I'd forgotten about his gloomy side.

We pulled up outside a block of flats that looked straight out of an episode of *The Bill*. 'I won't be long,' Iqbal said. 'You wait here and keep the doors locked. Don't open them for anybody,' then off he went. I sat and waited. He returned about half an hour later, strolling across some spare land with a grin on his face. When he got back in the car, I noticed his pupils were dilated. He was high.

We drove to another similar block of flats on another housing estate and off again he went. It was dark when he eventually came back, and I was beyond perturbed. Anxiously watching some kids setting fire to a pram.

And this entire pattern was repeated the whole weekend. (Iqbal bunking off, not the prams on fire.) Apart from one perfect moment sat beside a lake, eating a Burger King, and listening to P.M. Dawn while the sun set. I felt like an uninvited guest. Kipping uncomfortably on a lounge sofa at night. Sitting in a Mini Metro by day with the doors locked while Iqbal clearly dealt drugs around the east end of London. I thought we'd be seeing the sights, Tower Bridge, Buckingham Palace. Anything would have been better. This was worse than my trip to London at primary school.

# OCTOBER

That must have taken some organising. The full school went, two hundred kids commandeering the whole train. They printed our picture in the local paper. We only went for the day. It was an eight-hour round trip and hardly worth it at all.

We were put into groups with a member of staff. I ended up with Sister Hood, she was a heavy nun. She weighed about thirty stone and carried a bag with 'big shopper' written on the side. I never knew if she was aware of the double meaning or not. Sister Hood didn't have the energy to walk very far so the furthest we ventured was the Spudulike on Euston station. The other groups came bounding back with stories of visiting Big Ben, Trafalgar Square and St Paul's Cathedral. All we saw was Sister Hood wolfing a jacket potato with tuna mayo and a shifty-looking Arab selling knock-off cosmetics from a holdall, till the transport police yanked him away. I wouldn't mind but Sister Hood had just bought some lip gloss from him, and she was a woman of the cloth too.

Well, my weekend with Iqbal went from bad to worse when his cousin Jamal gatecrashed the Mini Metro with his 'Rhythm Is a Dancer' cassette single. Which I did snap. When he got out of the car with Iqbal for another drug deal, I ejected the tape and pulled it apart.

I couldn't take it any more and was desperate to get out of this situation. But how? I didn't know anybody in London. Then I remembered Sophie. Thank the Lord I'd packed my address book. Bravely, I unlocked the Mini Metro doors and nipped over to a piss-stained payphone without a door. I called Sophie's number. It turned out to be her mum who answered and gave me Sophie's work number. It was noisy when Sophie answered but I managed to convey I was in a pickle. Miraculously she said I could come and stay with her. RESULT.

I can't remember what excuse I told Iqbal, but I managed to get away as fast as possible. He dropped me at an underground station, and we said our goodbyes. Somehow, I knew that would be the last time I'd ever see Iqbal.

To say I was happy would be putting it mildly; my heart was thumping with delight as I rode the tube into central London towards Sophie. I could've kicked myself. Why hadn't I thought of visiting Sophie in the first place? Maybe the weekend could be salvaged after all.

Sophie worked downstairs in a pizza restaurant called 'Slice, Slice, Baby' (what a great name). We hugged for so long Sophie got a verbal warning. I waited around until she finished her shift, got some free pizza, then we talked and talked like no time had passed. She lived with a friend called Louise, a feisty Welsh midwife, and they kindly let me sleep on a futon in the front room of their tiny flat. I was just chuffed to get away from the Muslim cast of *Trainspotting*.

We ate, we drank, I felt welcomed. We even walked round to the local video shop and hired a film, *Cinema Paradiso*. What a tearjerker that turned out to be. A beautiful film, stunning music. Almost as sad as *Dead Poets Society*. What a fantastic end to a really strange weekend.

From then on myself and Sophie kept in touch as often as we could. I returned to London the following year to see Billy

Joel when he played Earls Court. That was a real treat for both of us, finally watching him together after all those years. Life's definitely about moments like that. Then again, in 1995, staying for the weekend. Sophie was now living above a KFC in Bayswater; can you believe she didn't even get any discount off the menu? We went to the half-price ticket booth in Leicester Square and got tickets to see a Neil Simon play called *Chapter Two*. Sadly, not one of his better plays. Sharon Gless was in it, one of Cagney & Lacey. When we were walking to the theatre, I bobbed into a newsagent to buy some pop, crisps and chocolate. I was off to see a show after all. Though I don't think a trip up the West End was in the same league as Cannon & Ball in *Mother Goose*.

We had great seats very close to the stage. I'll never forget Sharon Gless's piercing glance when she heard the audible fizz of me opening a bottle of Fanta. It was right in the middle of an emotional scene.

Anyway, there's a reason I'm telling you about Sophie, and it's because she's working on this very book. More importantly we're still good friends and she's very much a part of my life. Sophie is a successful literary agent and has worked extremely hard on the last few books I've written. She'll no doubt be blushing at this surprise recognition, but I think it's a remarkable testament to our friendship after all these years. I mean, would we have ever believed it back in 1989? When we were sat overlooking the bypass eating pasties. Not a chance.

\*   \*   \*

Back to cosy autumn nights, it's dark at seven o'clock now. The older I've got the more I resent the darker evenings. I'm convinced I suffer from seasonal affective disorder. As the light slowly slips each day, I start to feel deprived. I wish I could hibernate until the clocks go forward again.

It's Harvest Festival time again which means any forgotten tins lurking at the back of the pantry are donated. Either via school or the local church and I feel slightly redeemed in the knowledge that I've palmed off some Spam to a pensioner. They probably won't even eat it.

Halloween is still looming. We went to America once over the October half-term and they really go nuts for Halloween. We stayed in Florida and couldn't move for cobwebs and spiders (and that was just our hotel room). The theme parks really go to town. They open late and have these scare fests. Where punters can walk about while maniacal staff in terrifying costumes leap out in the dark. And that's fun?

We went on one of those immersive simulator rides – The Phantom of the Tomb it was called, it was in the lobby of a resort hotel in the theme park. We were greeted by an actor playing the part of an archaeologist, adventurer type. He gave us all some scripted dramatic spiel about 'how we should beware because the Phantom of the Tomb had been awakened after thousands of years and we all needed to investigate his empty crypt'. Really? I thought that's a bit of a flimsy storyline. Not much depth or substance. I mean why was the Phantom of the Tomb in Orlando? Was he on holiday?

The archaeologist ushered about thirty of us into a large

service elevator with a sliding cage door we could all see through. An image was projected on to the surrounding walls, then the elevator began to vibrate violently, and we appeared to plummet downwards at an exhilarating rate. I must admit it was a clever effect. Other people in the elevator screamed with terror. We didn't, we're British, any kind of emotion was immediately suppressed.

The actor playing the archaeologist really hammed it up shouting his lines – 'EVERYBODY HOLD ON! THE PHANTOM IS DOING THIS, HE KNOWS WE'RE ENTERING HIS TOMB!' He tried to stop the elevator, frantically pushing prop buttons. Then he pulled out a walkie-talkie – 'WE'RE FALLING! SOMEBODY HELP US PLEASE!!!' Then there was an almighty judder as the lift stopped (I threw up a little in my mouth) and then we were all plunged into darkness, cue more screams.

It was very impressive. The ride was over. Everybody started to file out of the elevator and through a side exit, but I spied an opportunity to have some fun.

'Excuse me, how do we get back up?'

'Pardon sir, you just exit through the side door,' the archaeologist said, gesturing towards the exit.

'But we're still underground.'

'Pardon sir.'

'The elevator dropped; we're thousands of feet underground, how do we get back up?'

'Sir, that was part of the simulator ride.'

'Eh?'

'That was part of the ride, sir.'

'Look, son, I know we dropped. People were screaming, could you not hear them? I felt it, I saw it with my own eyes.'

'Sir, that was a visual effect. Footage was projected on screens from outside the elevator.'

But I was having none of it.

'I know what I saw, man. We're still MILES underground. How do we get back to the hotel reception?'

'Sir, we've not moved anywhere. That was all part of the illusion.'

'Illusion? You were on your walkie-talkie shouting for HELP!'

'That was also part of the illusion, sir.'

'Look, I'm getting a bit claustrophobic now, son,' I said, loosening the top button on my polo shirt. By now Susan and the children were yanking on my arm. Mumbling lines like 'Leave it, Dad,' but I was having too much fun.

'How do we get back up to the hotel?'

'Sir, we're still in the hotel lobby.'

'BOLLOCKS, WE DROPPED.'

Somehow the actor remained professional. Insisting we follow him. He lifted a black curtain revealing a green exit sign.

'I'm not going down there. Not while this Phantom's loose.'

Then he pushed open the exit door, daylight shone in, and we could see the hotel lobby. I acted all astonished. 'Oh my God. How's that even possible?' My eyes wide, a beaming smile. I even hugged him.

# OCTOBER

'Thank the Lord we're safe,' I said. 'It's a miracle. Hey, we've got to go on that again.'

My family weren't keen. Neither was the archaeologist.

# November

Before the pumpkins have rotted and the Halloween decorations have been stored away the fireworks are erupting. Who are those annoying arseholes who set them off too early? I've said that same thing every year forever. 'It's not even Bonfire Night.'

Every 5th of November we celebrate an attempted terrorist attack on the Houses of Parliament. I'm never sure, are we celebrating Guy Fawkes being thwarted or that he may have been successful? Either way, Bonfire Night or Guy Fawkes Night signifies that autumn is now in full throttle. The clocks are fully back, and boy can't we tell? It's now dark ridiculously early. It feels like the day is over so early. We're ready for bed by the end of *The One Show*. The weather takes a turn. Colder, more rain. Cold rain. The only consolation is the gorgeous autumnal colours that decorate the skyline. Shades of orange, gold, crimson and brown embellish the pathways.

# NOVEMBER

(I'm really glad I downloaded a thesaurus app.)

I've fond memories of rehearsing a Greek tragedy when I was at Salford University. One weekend in November the cast had to help paint the stage set. As it was high autumn some of us walked leaves onto the stage on the bottom of our shoes. The director arrived, saw the leaves randomly strewn across the stage and yelled 'WHO'S WALKED LEAVES IN?' Timidly we glanced at each other. 'Er … we all must have,' I responded. We anticipated an impending hurricane to follow, as the director was prone to going off the deep end and losing his rag while he flipped his lid. Once, during the panto rehearsals he threw a music stand at Widow Twankey when she dropped her washing.

Surprisingly in this instance he remained calm. Quietly surveying the stage for what seemed like an eternity before declaring, 'I like the leaves … I think we should cover the whole set with leaves. Let's bring the outside inside.' He then had us all outside forever bagging up leaves off the ground. We'd brought them back into the theatre (well, it was actually a lecture theatre), where we proceeded to chuck them around the set. I thought it was all a tad pretentious, but hey, who was I to criticise the theatrical mind?

In the show my character had to perform a huge eight-page monologue. Well, I say show, it was a theatrical production. It wasn't Mike Yarwood and The Nolans at the Blackpool Opera House, now that was a show (and a bloody good one too). I spent weeks learning the monologue at every possible opportunity. Working my shift as an usher at the cinema. At home with my mum. I even recorded the monologue on to a tape cassette so I could listen to it on my Walkman while I travelled to university, and while I slept. Hoping it might sink into my subconscious.

During rehearsals I'd tried the monologue in my normal accent but heard a few titters from the rest of the cast. The Lancashire accent didn't bode well for a Greek tragedy, so after a chat with the director we agreed a Northern Irish accent might work. It's always been an easy accent for me to slip into, especially with my mum being Irish. I realised there probably isn't an abundance of Greek Irish men, but our flamboyant director had already decided to relocate our version of *Electra* by Sophocles to sixties gangland London so my having a Northern Irish accent was completely incongruous.

*Electra* was my first serious role, and it wasn't easy. I felt deprived playing it straight. I'd always felt more comfortable with humour. But as disconcerted as I was, I respected the situation, learnt my monologue, of which I was immensely proud and tried my absolute best over the four nights we performed the production. Well, until the final performance when I couldn't suppress my comedic desires any longer.

The very last scene of *Electra* is harrowing. Agamemnon has killed his mother Clytaemnestra, stabbing her as she sat on her throne. My character watches the tragedy unfold. I had to glare at Agamemnon and the rest of the courtiers with complete contempt. Then slowly walk down a set of stage steps, gazing at the audience in disbelief and exit through a set of fire doors into the car park. The director insisted all this be performed in complete silence. Leaving the audience captivated.

At the end of the final performance, I did all the above. I watched Agamemnon stab his mother to death. I stared at the courtiers with contempt, gazed at the audience, but then I felt compelled in that final moment to perform what can only be described as 'an Eric Morecambe double take' before exiting through the fire doors. This evoked a big laugh from the audience, as I knew it would. The director was fuming. 'You couldn't resist, could you, you had to get one laugh, always the joker.' He wasn't wrong but bloody hell it felt good.

It was Bonfire Night yesterday and I've never seen it so foggy, it was a right pea souper. I appreciate fog is standard for 'bommy night' but driving home from the firework shop I couldn't even see the car in front. Then when I'd eventually figured out where my fog lights were (they don't get used much in Bolton) I was home.

For years I've got my fireworks from Bashir's Big Bangs of Bolton. It's not one of those pop-up firework shops that disappear after a fortnight. Bashir's been at it for years and stocks hundreds of fireworks. He's a proper virtuoso. He even goes to the trouble of filming each and every firework going off in his back garden. I bet his neighbours love him. This allows the customer the unique opportunity to view footage of their fireworks on a monitor which sits on his counter.

Usually, I buy one big firework that gives a massive display. You could say that I'm burning money, literally, but I really don't care. It's an annual treat and it always gets a round of applause from the neighbours. Fireworks have some ridiculous names and the one I bought was no exception. I had a choice between a few: Collateral Damage, Dr Apocalypse, Hiroshima Sunset, Heat Stroke, Red November, The Whistling Gypsy, A Breach of the Peace, Neighbour's Nemesis, The Town Bully, Oppenheimer's Fury and Hasta La Vista. I went with the last one.

On Bonfire Night I placed Hasta La Vista right in the centre of the garden, lit it, then fell flat on my face as I ran up the garden. Much to the amusement of my family who were watching from the vestibule. With hindsight, slippers were probably not the best footwear when lighting fireworks. With mud up the arse of my tracky bottoms I clambered to the house just as the firework detonated behind me. It was like a scene from *Platoon*.

SIDENOTE: Did you ever make firework pictures at school? I'd draw all kinds of whizzes, bangs and fizzes in different coloured crayons. Then paint over them with black water-based paint, which somehow magically sidestepped the wax and hey presto a spectacular bonfire picture. Despite this fine work I still only got that single GCSE in Art.

Another good tip is to get a cheap pencil sharpener. Sharpen some different coloured crayons. Gather up the shavings, and sprinkle them randomly in the centre of a pre-folded piece of white paper. Then delicately fold the paper closed and run a warm iron over the folded paper for a few seconds. The iron will melt the crayons and when you open it up, voila, you've got a stunning butterfly picture. I think I might bring back *Take Hart*.

The tradition on Bonfire Night is to start with some sparklers. I love the intoxicating smell you get from sparklers. It transports me straight back to my childhood. My parents would light the sparklers by jamming them in between the bars on the gas fire. I'm pretty sure that wasn't part of the firework code. Suddenly sparks would flicker and quickly the sparkler would be handed to R Julie or myself. Then cautiously we'd carry them out into the backyard. Refraining from waving them around until my mum said we could. Then we'd rotate them like maniacs, wrists going berserk, a trace of glowing swirls, trying desperately to write your name before it disappeared. Five minutes later we were both brave enough to wave a lit sparkler in each hand. My mum was a bag of nerves, poised with a bucket of sand.

I blame those public information films they used to show. Talk about disturbing. Especially the one where the little girl picks up a sparkler and burns her hand. There's an authoritative voiceover – 'Make sure your child doesn't start November 6th like this.' Then the girl sheepishly raises her bandaged hand to camera. I mean, you'd have to be a bit thick to pick up a sparkler just after it's gone out. Fire, hot, burn. That's page one, textbook stuff.

Public information films left an indelible mark on anybody who saw them. Cleverly segued between kids' programmes, they had the capacity to scare the shit out of you and leave you traumatised for the rest of your life. Personally, I think society would benefit from public information films if they showed them today. Especially the green cross code films. I'm sick of absent-minded kids wandering into the road. Looking neither left nor right. Air pods in their ears, iPhone in one hand, strawberry vape in the other. I'm slamming on the brakes, while they don't even glance up.

Stop, look right, look left. Not a chance these days.

The green cross code man would give them a thick ear, knock their air pods out.

Anyway, those public information films would definitely be deemed too scary for today's society. But ironically it was the fear they instilled that caused them to work so well. They certainly made my generation think twice about getting in cars with strangers, flying kites near electricity pylons or swimming in lakes. Especially when the grim reaper's watching you from the shore. Do you remember that one? Donald Pleasance provided the chilling voice of the grim reaper.

There was another horrific one when a boy ran down a beach towards a discarded piece of glass and the film paused just as he was about to put his foot down on it.

There were also the classics, like Charlie Says, Tufty Rabbit, they even had one with Rolf Harris begging kids to 'learn to swim' (I'd have swum away from him as fast as I possibly could). Jimmy Savile telling us to 'clunk, click, every trip' when we got in a car. On reflection he'd have been better advising on not getting into cars with strangers. The fucking hypocrite.

\* \* \*

Where was I? Oh yeah, I'd just slipped in the mud after light-ing Hasta La Vista in our front garden. We stood and watched the bursts exploding in the sky. In anticipation my mum turned her hearing aids down. Then her friend Shirley rang right in the middle of the display. 'Have you heard that noise, Shirley? It's like Beirut.'

I had my fingers in my ears because I hate loud bangs. I'd have been shit in the war. I'm in my fifties and still terrified at balloons popping. Probably caused by a distant memory of my dad popping balloons in my face when I was a toddler. He thought it was funny, but it's left me with a phobia. I can't even stand being near balloons, so I'm not much fun at parties. I've just googled that phobia too. Globophobia – is an extreme and irrational fear of balloons popping. Christ, with that and my bathmophobia, being up a hill with a balloon sounds like my worst nightmare.

Every year my dad would buy a box of fireworks from our newsagents on his way home from work. I'd been excited for weeks and recall the delight when the fireworks would appear behind the display glass under the counter. I'd stare at the different coloured packaging. Catherine Wheels, bangers. Air-bomb repeaters, rockets and mini-rockets which were my favourite. I'd always hold a mini-rocket back which I'd always set off on Christmas Eve when we walked over to church for confession. I've no idea why or how this tradition came about but I kept it up for years. My mum hated it. I'd smuggle the mini-rocket under my coat along with a box of matches. I'd hang back as we walked up Roland Road then light the rocket. It'd shoot up into the sky, with a high-pitched squeal followed by an inevitable bollocking from my mum. At least I had something to confess when I got to church.

Our newsagent always sold Standard Fireworks which were the ones my dad would always buy. I'd never realised how humorous the name Standard Fireworks was until I mentioned them to my children in passing.

'So, they were just standard fireworks?'

'No, that was their name, but yes, I suppose they were.'

Bog standard fireworks. Maybe they should have added the word 'bog' before the standard on the box.

Always adhering to the letter of the firework code (otherwise my mum would lose her mind) my dad would decant the contents of the Standard Fireworks into a tin. Usually, a biscuit tin. McVitie's to be precise. That was our firework tin for years. My mum's still got the same tin today; she uses it for her sewing kit. Nobody in their right mind throws away an empty tin. It can have a plethora of uses. Medical supplies, family photos, toy cars, felt tips, Pokémon cards etc.

It's hard to beat the unbridled joy of opening a biscuit selection tin. Lifting the lid. Gazing at the options in front of you. Gently tearing the polythene. If you're a pig like me, you'll eat your favourite from the top layer, then craftily reach your hand underneath to the second layer for some more of the same. Then sneakily put the top layer back in place and nobody's any the wiser. Well, not until they get to the second layer and find half of the biscuits have gone. Which is quite common in our house.

Along with the McVitie's tin, my dad was also prepared with a bucket of sand and a torch. That was usually in my bedroom. I had hours of fun with the family torch. Shadow puppets on the ceiling. Shining it under the duvet or just covering the beam with my fingers so red shone through. I told everyone it was my blood.

So, we'd be gathered inside the kitchen watching my dad through the window preparing his pyrotechnic presentation. He'd pick a random firework out of his tin. Hold it at arm's length. Squinting his eyes in trepidation. At the first sign of sparks, he'd leg it up the backyard as fast as he could. Giving us the thumbs up. We'd smile in anticipation. Some of the fireworks wouldn't even ignite. If they didn't my dad would cautiously walk back over and give the firework a swift kick with the tip of his slip-on shoe. If it did ignite, he'd run like buggery, and we'd all laugh.

A box of Standard Fireworks always came with a Roman Candle and a Traffic Lights firework that was supposed to replicate the colours of, you'll never guess, a traffic light. But it'd just turn pink, slightly green, and then burned bright white before promptly fizzling out. Then there was the Catherine Wheel. That required a bit more attention. My dad would hammer it onto a plank of wood. Cockily he once hammered two Catherine Wheels to the end of his wooden ladders fastened to the wall but that gamble quickly backfired when the two Catherine Wheels collided with each other, burst into flames, and set fire to his ladders. Quick-thinking, my mum raced out with a bowl of dishwater and doused the flames.

# NOVEMBER

Miss Wild next door wasn't too happy with the palaver. Smoke pouring over her wall. Well, it was Bonfire Night. Everywhere smelled of smoke. Anyway, maybe it was karma: a few months before my dad had been doing his crossword at the kitchen table when he saw smoke pouring out of Miss Wild's back pantry and over our wall.

We had to stifle our laughs when he told us this story as he had a penchant for embellishing the truth. 'Quickly I ran outside and leapt the back wall like a panther.' (My dad suffered from osteoporosis, so there wouldn't have been much leaping going on.)

'I didn't have a key so had to kick Miss Wild's back door in, then when I got inside I realised it wasn't smoke, it was condensation. The windows and walls were sopping wet, and all I could hear was a whistling sound. I saw a kettle, it was boiled dry, so I grabbed a cloth and ripped it off the hob. It was a struggle as it practically welded to the cooker ring. I went looking for Miss Wild. She was in her back room watching telly, oblivious to everything. "AMY!" I shouted, "AMY!" but she's bloody deaf. She turned to me, looked at the kettle in my hand and said, "Oh I'll have two sugars if you're making a brew, Michael."' We laughed and laughed.

Collecting bommy wood was always a rousing lead up to Bonfire Night. I still can't figure out why we called it bommy wood and not bonny wood, surely that would have made more sense? Along with all the other local kids we'd scour the neighbourhood for wood. Skips, derelict houses, building sites, the local orphanage.

# NOVEMBER

There's one tradition that's fallen out of favour – penny for the guy. That was a bizarre tradition in retrospect. Getting some old clothes or a pillowcase, then stuffing them so they vaguely resemble a person. We'd wheel it around the streets in a pram asking for people to give us money. It was a bit like crowd funding. Simon Darcey's dad collapsed on Bonfire Night. He lay in the street for hours, people kept stepping over him, they thought he was a guy. When somebody finally got an ambulance, it was too late, he was gone. Then to add insult to injury there was only £1.20 in his hat. Not much for a man's life.

On the 5th of November there'd be bonfires everywhere. Back streets, spare land, you'd find one every hundred yards and you could hear sirens all night long. The fire brigade racing up and down main roads. It must have been hard for them. So dangerous when you think back. The hazardous cocktail of kids, fireworks and flames. Particularly when people built bonfires directly underneath phone lines and electric cables or too close to somebody's house.

Like Shaun Pepper, he constructed a bonfire in the front garden of his house, and he was warned. We lived opposite Shaun's house at the bottom of Bloomfield Road. After my dad's 'standard' firework display, we decamped into the front room to watch *3-2-1* when I noticed blue lights flashing on our chimney breast. Intrigued, I pulled back the curtains to see two fire engines at the bottom of the hill and a small crowd gathered. Something was clearly ablaze. A brilliant glow was illuminating the sky above Shaun Pepper's house. It was gripping stuff, and it easily wiped the floor with Ted Rogers and Dusty Bin.

Without hesitation, we started badgering my dad to go and see what was happening.

'Bugger off, I'm not going down there.' But we begged and pleaded until he was left with no choice but to put on his slippers and wander down the hill. We watched his silhouette slowly disappear into the pulsating blue lights. Orange and yellow embers floated high above the rooftops.

Ten minutes later my dad ambled back up the hill. His face was ashen, and he looked shaken after seeing a body removed from one of the burning houses. It turned out to be Shaun Pepper's elderly neighbour. She'd fallen asleep with her electric fire on full. I'd assumed it was Shaun's precarious bonfire, but apparently he never got a chance to light it.

Shaun and his sister Vicky reeked like a bonfire for the next few months. I called round his house after school, and it still stunk of smoke damage. Shaun wanted to show me a pair of his neighbour's glasses that he'd somehow salvaged from the inferno. Lord knows how he'd got them. They had some of her hair caught in the screw in the corner frame. Gross. Coincidentally, Shaun popped up on *Four in a Bed* last week running a B&B in Conwy. He came fourth after they found pubes on his bathmat.

We only ever had one bonfire. I stumbled upon a massive steel container on the tip. It was rectangular in shape and weighed a ton. I had to get my grandad to give me a lift to get it back home. We wheeled it through the streets on a couple of skateboards. The 'tip' as we called it was actually a strip of spare land where a social club once stood called The Aquarius. It burnt down. I heard it was 'allegedly' for insurance purposes and used the idea for *Phoenix Nights*. It'd happened many years previous but the burnt-out club ruins remained, overgrown with weeds and wild grass. People took to dumping all kinds of crap there in between the unkempt mounds and peaks. I used to play army with my grandad after school on the tip. Well, I'd roll around making shooting noises, while my grandad pretended to fire at me with a stick. I completely adored him and was devastated when he died in 1990. Much too young at sixty-eight.

My grandad had a huge influence on me. He had a happy personality, always placid and content. Forever cracking jokes and forever in my memory he's smiling. I rarely ever saw him angry or fed up. My parents worked long hours so my grandad would watch me after school and during the holidays.

He taught me how to play snap, draughts and daft songs like:

> *'The Yellow Rose of Texas and the man from*
> *   Laramie*
> *invited Davy Crockett to have a cup of tea.*
> *The tea was very tasty, so he had another cup,*
> *then poor old Davy Crockett had to do the*
> *   washing up.'*

Another one was 'Peter Kay is no good, chop him up for fire-wood.' Silly nonsense that made me chuckle as he sat in the armchair with a big grin on his face.

He'd make absurd statements like 'Why wear a watch when you can look at a clock through somebody's front room window?' and one of my favourites: 'If it takes a week to walk a fortnight, how many apples are in a barrel of grapes?' He'd buy chips from a chippy, then walk further up the street, call at another chippy and cheekily add some more salt and vinegar.

He kept me off school once and we spent all day at the pictures. There was a double bill at the Odeon: *The Pink Panther Strikes Again* and *The Spy Who Loved Me*. A bit of a weird combination but that's what they did in the seventies. They'd have these five-hour double bills where you could stay all day, it was fantastic, but it felt a bit risky being off school for the whole day. He told me not to tell my mum and I never have. She'll probably find out if she reads this.

We asked my grandad and nana to look after our goldfish when we went on holiday to Butlin's, but he accidentally left the fishbowl sitting on the oil heater and boiled the fish.

There was another side to my grandad that he never talked about. The time he served as a soldier in World War II. I never got to know where he was stationed or his rank, but I treasure a handsome portrait of him looking smart in his uniform. I worked out that he would have been in his late teens when he was conscripted. I know after the war he worked on the steam trains as a stoker. Then in coal mines. Breathing in all the dust down the pits took its toll and like a lot of miners he developed lung disease over the years which tragically led to a heart attack in his fifties. He was advised to take early retirement. Reluctantly he agreed. He would have been roughly the same age as I am now. It must have been tough, and his pride would have been knocked as he'd always grafted. I knew he found it hard doing nothing, so he filled his days looking after me and getting out and about. He had a dog, a wire-haired fox terrier called Benji who he adored. They were best buddies, and they'd go walking for miles. Benji got out once and my grandad was heartbroken. Everybody in the neighbourhood was out searching for hours. Luckily, we found him, he was up on the tip, trying to mount a poodle. Benji was on heat. We had to throw some cold water on them just to get them apart. I felt bad for Benji, he just wanted his oats.

Anyway, I've drifted again. Where was I? Oh yes, I'd found a steel container on the tip and just wheeled it home with my grandad. He drilled holes in the steel container, he said they would allow any wood in the bonfire to burn better. I was just chuffed we were having our first family bommy. We even invited my uncle Frank and his family round. What a treat. We'd been round to their house for many a bonfire. They had a semi-detached with a garden, which felt like Beverly Hills to us.

We sat the steel container on a couple of bricks, and it blazed away in our backyard. The sound of fireworks erupting above as we all stood freezing, eating black peas and jacket potatoes my mum roasted inside the bonfire, wrapped in foil. We also had some Parkin loaf and bonfire toffee. Then we went to bed stinking of smoke, but all that's the British tradition of Bonfire Night.

The memory of that bonfire remains close to my heart. It was Saturday 5 November 1983. The same day my dad came home with 'Uptown Girl' – Billy Joel, which he'd spontaneously bought for me as a gift. Wow! It was number one in the charts. I'd never felt so trendy. The record was a twelve-inch EP, it also had three other Billy Joel songs, 'My Life', 'Just the Way You Are' and 'It's Still Rock and Roll to Me'. It was like a mini greatest hits and I played it non-stop. This completely spontaneous gesture from my dad meant the world to me and bonded us over Billy Joel. I remained a massive fan and went to see Billy Joel live many times. And now all these years later I'm proud to call Billy Joel a friend. How the hell did that happen? A subconscious yearning of the heart? What I do know is the good fortune of my career has allowed me the opportunity to meet many of my heroes, including Billy Joel. When he played seven nights in the UK in 2007, I decided to go to every show. Why not? That's what fans do.

Over the course of those shows I slowly got to know Billy Joel. Unbelievable. We met each other backstage a few times and spent some time together. Sadly, my dad had passed away by this point, he'd have loved that opportunity.

The last night of Billy Joel's tour was at Croke Park in Dublin. We caught up before the show when he said, 'Wouldn't it be funny if we played the overture at the start of the show, but when my piano rises up from beneath the stage, they see you instead of me. What do you think?'

What?! I was still reeling from talking to Billy Joel, let alone him suggesting this utter madness. This would be his first live show in Dublin for over fifteen years and he wanted to open with a prank?! Next thing I knew I was climbing over the rigging underneath the huge stage production to reach Billy Joel's grand piano; nervously I sat at his piano stool. Listening to his familiar opening theme, 'The Natural' by Randy Newman which he plays before every performance.

The piano started to rise, I could hear the throng of eighty-five thousand people in the stadium, cheering, clapping, whistling. Surprisingly the deafening noise didn't subside, even when the enormous screens revealed that it was me sat at Billy Joel's piano. With tears in my eyes, I soaked in every second. Then Billy Joel appeared behind me laughing, we embraced. My dad would never have believed it. How had I gone from playing my twelve-inch of 'Uptown Girl' to this?

Each November brings Armistice Day. Where ceremonies commemorate the military service men and women of the two world wars and the conflicts since. It's a moving and crucial ritual and I've always made time to visit the cenotaph on Remembrance Sunday.

Suited and booted my dad and grandad used to take me when I was a boy, and now I take my children. I think it's important that we never forget the people who laid down their lives for us.

# NOVEMBER

When I was a boy, I'd wear my poppy with pride as we walked into the town hall square.

It was always emotional seeing crowds gather each year. The dwindling number of ex-service men and women. I was always impressed by the parades that marched past the cenotaph. It was a spectacle to behold. The music, and the pivotal moment at eleven o'clock when the 'Last Post' is played by a lone bugle, followed by the moving two-minute silence. Tanks would fire and I'd jump out of my skin. I still do. An old man leaned over to me and whispered, 'That bang frightens the young'un's every year.' I thought, 'Yeah and some of the adults too. I suffer from globophobia, buddy.'

Sadly, the respect had somewhat waned this year. When we had the two-minute silence somebody received a text message. 'Beep, Beep.' Then a woman right in front of me was vaping. And somebody brought a bloody puppy. Barking and yapping all through the service. Rude fuckers.

Strange how your mind can play tricks on you. I woke on Remembrance Sunday this year and in those first few minutes of disorientation I recalled what the day ahead was and thought I'll take my dad and grandad to the cenotaph. Then suddenly I remembered they'd both died, and my heart hit the floor.

OK, let's get things back on a more joyful note. One of my fondest all-time memories from the month of November is a wedding I attended in 1991. The scene was a picture postcard of autumnal colours as you'd expect, but surprisingly framed by some unseasonal snow that had fallen the previous day. The clear sky was pale blue, and glorious sunshine lit the snow which had crystallised overnight. The light shimmered on the frosted snow which rested along stone walls and branches in the rural churchyard. I was especially delighted with the weather as not only had I been invited as a guest but also to film the day's events.

After I completed my BTEC in Performing Arts, I chose to tenuously remain in some kind of showbiz by filming wedding videos. Completely determined, I even planned to set up my own wedding filming business. Even going as far as to book an appointment with a career advisor to structure a business plan. There was a slight flaw in my plan. I didn't own a video camera. But undeterred I enrolled on a video camera course on Thursday afternoons back at Bolton College. After a few weeks I was allowed to borrow a camera for the weekend, hence the opportunity to film my first wedding video.

Loaded up with a brand-new three-hour VHS tape and a couple of microphones from Tandy I spent the day capturing many heartfelt moments between the bride and groom.

Surrounded by their family and friends. The ceremony, the speeches, the happy couple's first dance. That's when a fight kicked off. The groom's ex was leathered and threw a punch. Without wasting any time, I yanked the camera off the tripod and waded straight in to capture the action.

I got some belting shots. A bridesmaid drop-kicking the groom's ex. The landlord leaping over the bar with a cricket bat. I showed the happy couple a slow-motion montage with

'Endless Love' playing over the footage, but they failed to appreciate my work. Ah well. It wouldn't have been a wedding without a fight. Fortunately, everybody got distracted when the quick-thinking DJ announced the buffet was open. Nothing gets in the way of food. The big lights were flicked on and a queue was swiftly formed, snaking the full length of the function suite.

There was another slight kick-off when a greedy pig tried to jump the queue by subtly chatting to someone they vaguely knew in line. 'Hey, there's a queue here dickhead,' came a voice. Thwarted and embarrassed, the pig reluctantly made their way to the back of the room. There were also a few frowns when a woman was spotted queuing with two paper plates. Guilt stricken, she felt obliged to tell everybody that she was getting buffet for somebody else. Probably her lazy husband sat on his arse – 'Oh, you're going to the buffet, could you get me some?'

The bride and groom asked if I could film the buffet. Weird but I obliged, filming moving shots of ham sandwiches, vol-au-vents, quiche, chicken legs, pork pies and those cock-tail sticks with cheese cubes on the end. When I watched the footage back, you'd have sworn it was stuck on a loop as the buffet was basically the same food repeated across four trestle tables. This was the basic buffet menu for every function I'd ever attended. Remarkable how it's never really changed.

After the buffet the big lights went off and the disco commenced. I got the chance to film some classic wedding footage. Like the walking to the dancefloor dance. People can't help themselves when they hear a certain song. That night it was 'Dancing Queen' and the guests rose from their seats as if they were entranced. Some still in mid-conversation as they made their way to the dancefloor. What made me laugh was seeing people starting to dance while they walked. Moving their bodies to music, accentuating their limbs the closer they got to the dancefloor. It's hilarious to watch.

I caught a couple of women arguing in the corner. So, I zoomed in, only to discover they weren't rowing, they were frantically mouthing the lyrics of 'I Will Survive' to each other. I filmed dads dancing half-pissed with their ties fastened around their heads aimlessly thrashing on air guitars to 'Livin' On A Prayer'. A bit of rock 'n' roll went down a storm when the DJ played 'Swing the Mood' – Jive Bunny; there was a couple front and centre in seconds, precision jiving to perfection. But both had such serious faces it was hard to tell if they were enjoying themselves or not.

An enthusiastic crowd gathered around a young, drunk groomsman as he tried to breakdance. He still had the moves (in his mind) as he body-popped, moonwalked, then launched himself onto the dancefloor for a quick caterpillar. He topped this off with a head spin before twatting the bride on the shins. Another skirmish followed but it was quickly quelled by the announcement of desserts.

Another queue formed as sweet-toothed guests hankered for a slice of apple pie, Black Forest gateau or Sara Lee cheese-cake. Washed down with either fresh pouring cream or Tip Top. I also got some shots of the spectacular tiered wedding cake on display at the end of the desserts table. But nobody was allowed to touch that until the end of the night, when it was delicately sliced and individually wrapped in paper napkins by some aunties. Who both proudly sauntered around the room dishing out portions on big silver trays.

The DJ, Vinyl Ritchie – I shit you not – had his girlfriend with him for some reason. Probably so he wouldn't cop off with someone. She was sat on a table at the back of the stage with a face like a smacked arse. Watching his every move. Throwing daggers at every female who drunkenly requested a song.

DJs who cater for events such as weddings, etc., can have a wavering career. On one hand they curate a selection of music that, if chosen wisely, can lift an audience to a euphoric state. On the flipside they spend their weekends driving and lugging heavy equipment up and down fire escapes. They also get a lot of abuse. Guests hounding them with requests for songs that will definitely clear the dancefloor. Then the person who requested it doesn't even get up and dance.

That night Vinyl Ritchie ended with two steadfast songs that have probably ended every wedding I've ever been to. 'You'll Never Walk Alone' – Gerry & The Pacemakers, and 'Hi Ho Silver Lining' – Jeff Beck. In fact, up to 1988 I think it was illegal to end a wedding reception without playing both those songs back-to-back. Those songs were Ronseal, and everybody had to get up whether they liked them or not. And I mean EVERYBODY. Even if you'd refused to move from your seat all night. Even if you'd sat in silence, in a corner, riddled with social anxiety. You had to get up when those songs played because it was manners. It was your gratitude of thanks for being invited out for the night.

You'd hear the opening bars and couldn't hide as some auntie mouthed the words 'YOU UP, NOW' from across the room, followed by a look that could curdle milk. You simply had no choice but to gather in a big circle in the centre of the dancefloor with all the other guests and the bride and groom in the middle.

Sweaty hands intertwined. Bodies swaying forwards and backwards to the music. On the chorus some joker pulled everybody into the centre of the circle for a rogue hokey-cokey move. Desperately trying to catch the eye of the 'happy couple'. That could unnerve the bride and groom. Especially when the groom's ex jogged into the middle and shouted, 'That should have been me, you bitch.' Another scuffle developed but Vinyl saved the night yet again by hastily mixing into 'New York, New York' – Frank Sinatra.

The fracas dissipated as the swaying circle transitioned into an ensemble of high kicks. I filmed the occasional stiletto hitting the ceiling as a muffled announcement came over the microphone, 'Taxi for Hargreaves, taxi for Hargreaves'.

'New York, New York' reached its final crescendo as the big lights came on again. Staff carrying bin bags attempted to clear tables of glasses and paper plates. But the guests dug their heels in. With pints lined up on, and under, the table. Doormen tried to get punters to leave – 'Do your drinking while you're talking and you're talking while you're walking.'

But it was a Mexican stand-off, and the diehards weren't going anywhere. They'd already started a sing-along.

It was the end of a long day. Tired, I packed up the camera and tripod from college as Vinyl Ritchie packed up his DJ equipment and I watched his heavily pregnant girlfriend carrying an amp out to his van.

Three weeks later I presented the finished wedding video to the bride and groom in a souvenir plastic video case masquerading as a hardback book. They were thrilled. It's a shame I didn't get paid, but it was my wedding gift to them both.

Do you remember those plastic video cases that looked like books? My dad had his full video collection in them. All lined up in the front room. His friends would say, 'Hey Mick, you're doing a lot of reading?' 'Oh, they're not books, lads,' he'd say with mischievous pride as he lifted one from the shelf, opened it and revealed a VHS tape secreted inside.

My business venture dream of filming wedding videos fell by the wayside. I filmed three in total but as I said earlier it was a struggle having to borrow the video camera from college.

I'll end this chapter on a story about a mate of mine who filmed a wedding with one of the first video cameras that ever came out. Before then there'd just been silent cine cameras and Super 8.

The day after the wedding everybody gathered at the bride's house to watch the footage. My mate wired his new camera up to the TV, pressed play then had a panic attack when he heard sound. Birds tweeting, the sound of traffic and suddenly he realised his new-fangled video camera had a microphone. 'Shit!'

They watched the wedding car pull up at the church. The bride stepping out and then they heard my mate's private commentary. 'Look at the state of that dress, she looks like a fucking meringue.' Fortunately, by that point he'd had the foresight to slip out of the bride's house before a riot ensued.

# December

And so we reach the last month of the year and the final chapter of this book, December. Which as you know falls greatly into the shadow of Christmas, a magical time which I think we should have every year.

Everyone has a different moment when they feel Christmas begins. For some, it's on 1 December with a new advent calendar. You can buy them with all sorts of things inside – lavish gifts, toys, chocolates. I'd have loved chocolate in my advent calendar growing up. All I had was the joy of opening a cardboard door every day to find a picture of a donkey or a bell and on 25 December there'd be a slightly bigger cardboard door but with a picture of the baby Jesus behind it. Fair enough, it was his birthday, but I'd much have preferred a Malteser or a Rolo.

For others, Christmas begins when the decorations go up or when they finish for the holidays. For me, it's the first time I see the Coca-Cola advert on telly. As soon as I see Father Christmas winking on the back of that truck, Christmas has officially started.

Now obviously if you're a shopworker Christmas begins in the middle of August when you start putting tinsel out next to the sun cream. That must be so surreal.

Then shops start playing the festive music. It's the same album every year – '*Now that's what I call too bloody early!*'

I think it's a conspiracy. Noddy Holder, Shakin' Stevens and Cliff Richard infiltrate every supermarket and Poundshop in Britain with their Christmas songs. Then take the rest of the year off counting their royalties. I wouldn't be surprised to find out Mariah Carey's got shares in Home Bargains.

At school, Christmas would always start with rehearsals for the nativity. We had one every year as the nuns lacked imagination when it came to theatrics. To be fair, they did try to jazz things up one year by having the three wise men arrive on BMX bikes but there was too much banging on stage, and you couldn't have Mary giving birth with three lads bunny hopping behind her. And the gifts they brought for baby Jesus. Gold, frankincense and KerPlunk!

I was always in the choir. I had the occasional solo on 'Silent Night' or 'Little Donkey' but I really wanted to be up on stage with all the other shepherds with tea towels round their heads. Then luckily Stuart Regan got suspended for sniffing Magic Markers and I was hastily offered the role of innkeeper. I had one line. I had to tell Mary and Joseph 'there was no room at the inn' but I offered them an en suite with a full English breakfast. The nuns weren't amused but the audience loved it.

Every December my dad would take me to children's parties at various social clubs around Bolton. The Rumworth Labour Club was one. My dad would be sinking pints and potting snooker balls in the games room with my uncle Frank, while I was dumped next door playing musical statues with two hundred hyperactive kids.

Geriatric committee members would struggle to control the bedlam. The kids would be throwing pasties, jelly and ice cream, while some pensioner tried showing cartoons on a projector. Those parties were carnage. I'd find bits of jelly stuck in my hair for days after. I looked like I'd head-butted a trifle.

The committee would try to distract the kids by getting them to sing 'Jingle Bells' as loud as they could till Father Christmas arrived. But it was never the real Father Christmas; it was one of the committee members wearing a tatty old costume that they kept in a box under the stage. I knew it wasn't the real Father Christmas even when I was six. I used to check all committee members' shoes so I'd know which one was playing Father Christmas. Any matching shoes would be the giveaway, Father Christmas would never wear beige slip-ons. Well, not while he was working.

One year disabled Colin from the committee had his turn at playing Father Christmas and I'll never forget him rolling out from behind the fire door with his wheelchair badly disguised as a sleigh. Everyone knew it was Colin. I didn't even need to check his shoes. The kids loved it, though; not only did we get to sit on Santa's knee, but we also got to do doughnuts in the car park after.

We all had to queue to meet Father Christmas and get a present from him. You'd always get something decent. One year I got a car transporter and some felt tips. Plus you always got a chocolate selection box. It was well worth the price of the ticket. My dad loved a bargain, so he kept putting my name down for Christmas parties even when I was too old to go. He'd just go down the club and collect my present and he'd still be doing it now if someone from the committee hadn't found out I was married with kids.

After the Labour club party I'd be over the road at the Connie Club. Their parties were always a bit more posh. Their Father Christmas had a real beard. The food was better, all free-range, and the presents were fantastic. One year I got some chocolate money and sixteen acres of land.

The committee had acts performing. Well, I say acts, we had the same magician three years in a row. The Great Bambini – but there was nothing great about him. He did the same card trick every year with a duck wearing a blindfold. The duck was a puppet, by the way; I don't want the RSPB kicking off. No ducks were hurt, although they might have been if they'd watched the act … it was crap.

I bumped into The Great Bambini in the toilets once and said, 'You're not doing the duck routine again, are you?' He gave me a filthy look, then he zipped his flies and stormed out. The dirty pig didn't even wash his hands. Great Bambini wasn't the Great Hygienei so I wouldn't be picking a card from his duck's mouth, not for all the fish in Fleetwood.

The next year, he pushed the boat out and started his act with all this theatrical fog drifting across the stage. We were all very impressed until some kids sat at the front started choking and then a committee member noticed that two bins in the backstreet had been set alight by yobbos. The fire brigade had to come out and we all got evacuated; it turned out to be the best Christmas party we ever had.

You know people say Christmas is about family. It's not, it's about sitting on the bonnet of a Ford Capri watching the emergency services hosing down melting wheelie bins.

Another sign that Christmas is approaching is when you start to see decorations go up in people's houses. And on the outside too. First there's a few lights, then the next time you pass the whole house is plastered in coloured lights from top to bottom. I get a migraine just looking at it. It must be like living in a fruit machine. Ah well, if it makes them happy. Mind you, they'll not be happy when they get their leccy bill.

Some people can't wait to put their decorations up, they have them up in November, October even! They may as well have Father Christmas riding a broomstick wearing a witch's hat … with a sparkler in his mouth.

Every year we get our decorations down from the attic. Unpack the boxes. How the fairy lights get so tangled up I'll never know. It's only been twelve months since we last had the decs up, but I can never remember where everything goes.

We have one artificial pre-lit tree. It's supposed to be easier, but you've still got all the different connectors to link together before the lights will turn on.

'Plug section C into section D.' That's great but you've got to find them first and they're hidden deep in the tree somewhere. So, we're reaching inside scratching our arms on the plastic pine needles. Agony!

We dress the tree playing Christmas songs in the background, bickering over what decorations go where. 'It's big balls to the bottom.' Everyone knows that.

For years we had a real tree. I loved the smell, but it was always a gamble whether it'd last until Christmas or dry up. Shedding pine needles everywhere. We'd all be walking around on tiptoes. Someone could fart six feet across the room and a thousand pine needles would drop to the floor. And they clog up your Dyson. One year our tree was completely bald by Christmas Eve – just tinsel and lights. So that's why we got a plastic one.

The house gets cleaned ready for the big day. My nan wanted her carpets cleaned so I hired a Rug Doctor. She said, 'What time is he coming?' I said, 'It's a machine, it's not a fella.' She thought it was an actual doctor – white coat and a stethoscope. Listening to the bugs in her shag pile.

The next thing you know Christmas cards start to arrive. Every year we'd get those 'mystery cards' from people we didn't know. They'll be signed something like 'All the best, Linda, Graham and kids'. Who the hell are 'Linda, Graham and kids'? We never did find out and we never send them a card back. You'd think they'd have got the message by now, wouldn't you?

Whoever Linda, Graham and kids are, their card will end up on our Christmas card washing line in the front room. This would be a piece of string hanging from one side of the chimney breast to the other. Each card delicately held in place with tiny red and green pegs. Then someone would open the front door, and a gust of wind would blow all the cards back to front and topsy turvy. 'QUICK! SHUT THE DOOR!!' but it's too late. So we'd be up straightening them all again, and again and again.

They've got Christmas cards for everyone now. My sister even sends us one from her cat! She's clearly written it with her left hand, so it looks like the cat's done it. I never know if I'm supposed to write it one back. Because I'm one of those rare people who still writes Christmas cards every year. I know it's a dying art but I feel obliged. It's not pleasurable. Sitting on the couch for hours with an old dog-eared address book and glue tongue from licking all the envelopes. It's a big job, but I get them all written and posted. Then what are the first Christmas cards we receive in the post? They're from people I missed off my bloody list. Never fails, so now I've got to write even more cards, extra cards. It's a never-ending cycle. I bet Linda, Graham and kids never have that problem …

I've got fond memories of sending Christmas cards in primary school. The thrill of posting them through a gigantic cardboard post-box that sat in reception. Stinking of PVA glue and covered in glitter.

# DECEMBER

Each year a lucky child would get picked to play postman, and then they'd go round each class delivering cards. I remember getting a card from my first real crush at school, Charlotte Fox (and trust me she was). I slept with her, well I slept with her card under my pillow. I used to kiss it every night before I went to sleep … and the card. Careful!

So the weeks fly by and before you know it we reach those final frantic days where people always ask each other, 'Are you ready for it?' 'Nearly. I've just got to get some bits.' What the hell are bits? Bits of what? Bits of tinsel, bits of food, bits of drink? Drill bits? I'm amazed no one has opened a shop that sells 'bits for Christmas', they'd be raking it in. Hand over fist.

People start panic buying, and the supermarket shelves are empty, why? It's one day! But we shop like 25 December is the last day on Earth. It's not even the last day of December. All the shops are back open on Boxing Day. Surely we can't eat that much. WE CAN'T, that's why we've still got loads left at New Year.

I've never really been a fan of New Year. It's cold and dark, everyone's skint, everyone thinks they're overweight. I don't know what there is to celebrate. People will ask, 'What are you doing for New Year's Eve?' and it's always the same reply, 'Oh, we're just having a quiet one. We're just going to stay in this year. Just us.'

Things change. Gone are the days of wandering around pubs in the freezing cold. In the town hall square at midnight watching drunk girls trying to stroke a police horse. Trying to sing 'I Will Survive', using the horse's tail as a microphone.

No, now we just stay in eating the left-over dregs from Christmas Day, dark chocolates and stale Pringles. All the broken Pringles left in the bottom of the tube, I just drink them back in one gulp. Tragic. Sat reading those shite New Year text messages that start arriving in the middle of the afternoon – '*As the sun sets on the end of this year and before the phone lines get too busy, may we wish all the very best, with a champagne glass so fizzy*' – followed by a line of party emojis.

Telly's always crap but you feel obliged to stay up until midnight – watching Jools Holland's *Hootenanny*. And that was filmed in October. My mum was shocked. 'No way, Peter, this is definitely live.'

'Oh yeah, course it's live, Mum. Sir Tom Jones, Stormzy and Lulu have all given up New Year's Eve with their families so they can sing on BBC2.' It's Jools Holland I feel sorry for, filming a New Year's Eve show in October; his body clock must be all over the place. I bet he's opening Easter eggs in January.

Last New Year we threw the towel in and went to bed early. Then we got woken up by all the fireworks at midnight. It was like the bloody Blitz. I love fireworks as you know, but proper ones, not some scally setting bangers off outside Greggs! I like the New Year fireworks on the telly. They're always hosted by a presenter you've never seen before who's drawn the short straw. You know they really wanted Davina

McCall or Claudia Winkleman but they've ended up with some bloke from BBC Radio Wales. Stood freezing his knackers off on the Embankment, trying to get tourists to sing 'Auld Lang Syne'.

No, I do like the fireworks in London. Seeing them all firing into the sky. All the glorious colours shooting and spattering, in the shadow of Big Ben. Rockets exploding off the London Eye. 'I hope there's nobody's still on it.' I say that every year.

I remember the year we said farewell to Her Majesty the Queen and a formation of drones created a picture of her face in the sky. She'd have loved that. I bet it was one of the last things she requested on her death bed.

There are always shots of people's emotional faces as they reflect on the year gone by and tingle with excitement at the year ahead. Then the magic was suddenly broken by my mum saying, 'How much does ALL this cost? It looks well bad having them having these fireworks and the NHS is in such a mess.'

'Bloody hell, Mum, you'll be saying it isn't LIVE next!'

We never used to have fireworks on New Year's Eve. It all started back at the Millennium, when club and pub owners got greedy and started charging treble for ticket prices. You'd go in free the rest of the year; suddenly they stuck a bouncer on the door and tried charging a tenner. So, people rebelled and had their own celebrations. They had house parties and bought fireworks. Or in our case ONE MASSIVE FIREWORK, which cost a small fortune. We all chipped in for this giant rocket from Bashir's Big Bangs of Bolton. But we couldn't decide which one to get. There were so many. It was a toss-up between Rear Entry, Gangbang, Black Op's, Grounds for Divorce, Royal Funeral, Scottish House Party, Thatcher's Cabinet, Barely Legal, ASBO and The Mother-in-law.

We went with The Mother-in-law in the end, because it was clearly the best name and Bashir threw in some sparklers for free.

So, we had this New Year's party at my in-laws. It was fancy dress. I'm not so keen on fancy dress. It's a lot of effort. I used to be up for it at one time but now if I get invited I just go in my own clothes and say I'm a werewolf but there's no full moon.

On Millennium Eve I dressed up as Gary Glitter; it cost me a fortune in foil. Now because I don't drink it means I end up being a taxi driver for everybody.

'Don't worry, Peter'll give you a lift home.'

'Will I?'

It's a nightmare. Especially when you've got drunk relatives trying to cram more people in.

'Just one more, Peter.'

'I can't. I've got seven in now. It's only a hatchback.'

'Come on, please, she's going that way.'

'What way?'

Before I know it, they're grabbing her legs and hitching her up into the car.

'Get her ankles! Shove her in ... (slam the door) ... she's in, she's alright.'

'Her dress is caught in the door.'

But I'm driving off. Bugger her dress. So now I've got my wife's cousin's sister squashed in the back. Spreadeagled on the back seat. One foot on the back shelf, the other twatting the back of my head every time we go over a speed bump.

Her stiletto jammed in my cheek. She's unconscious.

'Does anybody know where she lives?'

'I know it's near a bus stop.'

'Which one?'

'Where do you live, Michelle love?'

'Straight on.'

I can see her in my mirror, she's not even got her eyes open.

'We're at traffic lights now. Is it left or right, Michelle?'

'Straight on.'

'You sure? Big roundabout, which way?'

'Straight on, straight on.'

'Well, we're going to have to stop cause we're in Blackpool.'

'Straight on.'

'What, into the sea?'

Then I still ended up picking up some relatives from another party, a husband and wife in fancy dress, as a nun and priest. She was blind drunk, and they ended up having a row in the back of my Peugeot. When we stopped at the traffic lights, I'll never forget the looks from other motorists as they glanced over to see a nun and priest effing and blinding on the back seat and Gary Glitter driving. Then we had to pull over because she needed the toilet. I don't know if you've ever seen a drunk nun having a wee in a lay-by. It's a messy habit I can tell you!

Anyway, I've drifted over to New Year's, and we've not even had Christmas yet. Where was I? Oh, I was talking about the build-up to Christmas which for me is the best time. Counting the days, the hours. The thrill of it all. That excitement starts in childhood and never leaves. But I want to shine a light on the big man himself, Father Christmas. He's an oddity, that fella. And never mind Type 2 diabetes, he's easily got to be Type 5, all those cookies he eats on Christmas Eve.

Apparently, he sees you when you're sleeping, and he knows when you're awake. I mean, how creepy is that? Especially for children. Don't talk to strangers, kids, just write to one every year, telling him what you want and where you live?! Mental.

Talk about confusing, and frightening, some weird bloke rocking up in the middle of the night when they're asleep, landing a sleigh on the roof ... with eight reindeer, then he breaks in via the chimney. And that's all acceptable? It's terrifying. Kids are cowering under their duvets. They need toys just to calm them down.

When I was at school I wrote a story called The Night Father Christmas Got Arrested. He comes down the chimney but he's had a few by now, all those glasses of sherry around the world, and he's staggering around rat-arsed. He slips on a mince pie, trips and knocks himself out. Hearing the noise the family wake up, go downstairs and find Father Christmas spark out down under the tree. The mum calls the police while the dad ties him up with some fairy lights and sits on his sack. Painful.

Sadly I never got time to finish the end of the story but I did get a gold star from Miss Price for creative writing.

My worry is how we keep the magic of Father Christmas alive without our lies backfiring? It's an insane carry-on. Children aren't stupid and inevitably there'll come a point when they start asking questions, because there's always some big mouth at school who'll go around telling everyone that 'it's really the parents that do it all'.

Parents go mad when they hear this. 'HE SAID WHAT?? Do you think me and your mum have got the time and the money to organise presents? I suppose *you* think the whole world is telling this lie?' BUT THEY ARE. The whole world is in on this humungous ginormous lie, and this isn't a little white lie, oh no, it's a big jolly Red and White one. And this lie is passed down through the generations. It's astonishing, what a conspiracy, it's right up there with the fake moon landings … or the Earth being round. What? Really? Nobody told me.

But is it all really worth all the stress just to keep the children happy? YES! Of course it is. Absolutely and completely. But it's exhausting. Children have so many questions, especially on Christmas Eve when you're trying to get them to sleep.

'How does he get in?'

'Chimney.'

'What if there's no chimney?'

'He's got a magic key.'

'What if you've got locks?'

'He's got magic dust.'

'What does that do?'

'It magics him inside.'

'Are you telling the truth?'

# DECEMBER

'YOU CAN'T HANDLE THE TRUTH. NOW GET TO SLEEP CAUSE ME AND YOUR MUM ARE GONNA BE UP FOR ANOTHER FOUR HOURS SORTING BLOODY PRESENTS.'

Shrewd parents exploit the concept of Father Christmas to their own advantage. A couple I know (who will remain anonymous, for my own safety) told their four-year-old that if she saw the alarm sensor flashing red in the corner of the room it meant that Father Christmas was watching and checking she was behaving. Now that's harsh. Ingenious but harsh. It worked for a couple of years until the parents caught their daughter showing the toy section in the Argos catalogue to the alarm sensor.

Christmas Eve was when I found out Father Christmas wasn't real. I'll never forget it. I couldn't sleep, too excited. Then I heard shouting in the street below. I climbed up onto my window ledge and saw my mum and dad arguing. They were both struggling to carry black bin bags, then one of the bags split and all these toys spilled out on the pavement. A Rubik's Cube, some LEGO, a game of Mousetrap. I'll never forget the sight of seeing my dad chasing after a Girl's World head as it rolled into the gutter.

I'd had my suspicions, but this confirmed it. I got back in bed, devastated. Bloody Mousetrap?! I hadn't even asked for that. With tears in my eyes I eventually nodded off to sleep. Only slightly consoled by the fact I'd be getting all those presents I'd seen in just a few hours. My sister curious why her Girl's World had gravel in its hair.

It really is unfair that Father Christmas takes all the credit when parents are up till all hours, sorting, sticking, wrapping, assembling toys, with a Korean instruction manual in one hand and a screwdriver in the other. That's why they're always asleep on Christmas Day in the afternoon, they're knackered from being up all night. Kids wants to dive straight into their presents, they don't want to be sat there while you search the house for batteries.

And parents, PLEASE heed this warning: don't forget to buy batteries or you'll be down the local garage Christmas morning, paying three times over the odds for a pack of triple A's ... or worse nicking them out of the remote control OR worser still nicking them out the smoke alarm like my mum used to.

Finally all the presents are carefully stacked in neat piles under the tree. Funny, when children are young their pile of toys is generally massive, it looks impressive, but as they get older their presents gets smaller and smaller but the prices go through the roof. An Amazon gift card and a couple of Xbox games cost a fortune and can never compete with the size of a Hot Wheels garage in a box as big as a washing machine.

Christmas morning we'd all stagger downstairs, yawning from two hours' kip.

My dad would always ask, 'Has he been?', wiping sleep from his eyes.

Some families are up at ridiculous o'clock. It's weird, you can never get your kids up for school, but they'll soon get up when there's presents for them.

# DECEMBER

There'd always be a flurry of excitement when we'd discover a half-eaten carrot or the foil from a mince pie. Evidence that he's been!! Then the thrill of going into the front room. The heart pounding with excitement. What has he brought me? How good have I been? Then five minutes later the room looks like a bomb's hit it. Debris everywhere. Paper, cardboard, plastic and that familiar plea from parents, 'Don't open that now or you'll lose all the pieces,' but the children never listen.

Among the LPs my parents owned was *The Jim Reeves Christmas Album*. It was the only festive record we had and every year before I went up to bed on Christmas Eve I'd place the vinyl on the turntable, cue the needle to the first song on side one, then I'd turn the power off. This meant that as we entered the room on Christmas morning all I had to do was flick the power on the wall and the room would instantly fill with the sound of Jim Reeves singing 'Jingle Bells' as we opened our presents. It's a tradition I've continued, only the record player has been replaced by a Bluetooth speaker and *The Jim Reeves Christmas Album* is now on my iPhone. Jim wouldn't have believed it.

Almost all my memories of opening presents on Christmas morning blend into one. There were a few gifts that stand out from my childhood. A red Trumpton fire engine that said 'Pugh, Pugh, Barney McGrew, Cuthbert, Dibble and Grub' when you pushed a black button. Some face paints, a Terry's Chocolate Orange (apparently one of your five a day), a vending machine that took 2ps and rewarded you with tiny Dairy Milks. I'd eaten all of them before breakfast.

A small transistor radio which I was shocked to receive and at the time slightly disappointed as it hadn't been on my carefully crafted Christmas list that I'd posted at the end of November. My look of disenchantment must have been obvious, and my dad called me an ungrateful sod. But I couldn't understand why. He wasn't responsible for Father Christmas's delivery. Well, that's what I still believed. Ironically that transistor radio turned out to be one of the best Christmas presents ever and I treasured it. My dad knew what I'd like all along.

In 1980 Father Christmas brought me a Race 'n' Chase. A mediocre version of Scalextric with a slight spin on *The Dukes of Hazard* (which was popular at the time). The premise was a police car in hot pursuit of a villain in a white and yellow sports car. Yee-ha! Sadly, there weren't many hot pursuits. It was so badly designed you could neither 'race' nor 'chase' because the cars only occasionally worked in fits and starts. Push too hard on the control and the cars would fly off the track. What a swizz. There was more action in the artwork on the lid of the box.

Like most of these toys they always looked amazing on the TV ad but crap on our front room carpet. Toy adverts were never honest. They always showed toys in context of some fabulous scenery. Never the reality of coffee table legs or your dad's slippers as he snoozes in his armchair. Why? Because they wouldn't sell any.

The joy of Christmas morning was always thwarted by having to go to church. Why did Jesus have to ruin it? I'd never been so jealous of the atheists.

# DECEMBER

We just wanted to play with our toys but instead we had to change into our best Christmas clothes and go to mass. 'Just five more minutes playing, Mum, please?'

I didn't really mind mass; the Christmas service was always special. Seeing the cheery faces of the parishioners, also in their best Christmas clothes. The church looked beautiful, in particular the nativity scene in the alcove near the christening font. The carols were always joyous. Bill Chadwick, who did the collection, lived for flicking on all the interior lights for the final chorus of 'Oh Come All Ye Faithful'.

Sally Fitton played the organ and every year when I went up for Holy Communion I'd lean over her shoulder and deliberately push down some random keys. This caused a racket that echoed through the church. Everybody looked around as Sally blushed with embarrassment as she tried to keep playing. Some years Sally would see me coming and attempt to block me with her elbows. Shouldering her body left and right. I'd pretend to give up. Walk past, then quickly jog back when she wasn't looking and push some keys down over her shoulder. Very childish.

After mass we'd head straight back home to play with my toys and for one of my highlights, the full Christmas Day breakfast. Oh yes! I couldn't wait to smell the glorious aroma of bacon and sausage under the grill. While it was cooking we'd watch Noel Edmonds dishing out his Christmas presents.

Such a heartbreaking programme; we'd be in floods of tears every year. Sometimes my mum would get so distracted watching Noel she'd burn the breakfast but nobody would realise because she'd nicked all the batteries out the smoke alarm – they were inside a Care Bear.

Grazing would continue after breakfast as my mum placed bowls of Roses and Quality Street around the house. What a treat. (Also bowls of nuts but they'd still be sat there in February.) Christmas Day is pure decadence. Like I've said, I don't drink but come Christmas morning I'm pouring Baileys on my cornflakes.

I'd be too full for Christmas dinner which we always had at three o'clock on the dot just as the Queen was starting her speech. That was our family tradition. It's not the same with King Charles; mind you, seeing his podgy fingers always reminds me to stick the pigs in blankets on.

My dad and grandparents would roll in from the pub just in time. All merry, stinking of booze and cigarette smoke. Then they'd insist on standing up for the national anthem.

I was too distracted, poised down at the video recorder, ready to tape the big James Bond film which was always on after the Queen's speech.

Then we'd eat Christmas dinner, sat on our emergency chairs. All at varying heights. Pulling crackers was a nightmare. One up here, one down there. I lost count of the Christmas dinners I spent staring into my grandad's groin. That put me right off my turkey, I can tell you. 'Pass the potatoes, Peter.' 'Hang on, I'll just get a step ladder!'

Emergency chairs were a common sight on Christmas Day. They still are. People use anything, deckchairs, high stools, even the odd pouffe. One year my mum sat on a bean bag with her chin just touching the table, while my auntie was perched on a space hopper. She had terrible indigestion but it was great for her core.

Christmas dinner was the only time we were allowed to have some proper Coca-Cola. Now that was a festive treat. I'd dash around to Tony's off-licence.

He never seemed to shut shop, and he sold everything, and I mean EVERYTHING and anything. If you needed Tampax and a quarter of Lemon bonbons, Tony was your man. A bottle of bleach and a shoehorn at half four in the morning? Go and see Tony. The man was a marvel.

Christmas dinner wouldn't have been the same without a big bottle of coke. It was a joy just to get some respite from the crap cola my mum used to buy the rest of the year. Three litres for 40p, and always warm because it was too big to fit in the fridge, so it lived down the side of the cupboard. No, Christmas dinner wouldn't have been the same washed down with a warm glass of Rola Cola.

Christmas is about sharing, so we used to invite Miss Wild round for Christmas dinner. She was the lovely old lady who lived on her own next door. She could be a bit dotty. I remember when we had a power cut once and my mum went round to see if she was OK. 'Are you alright, Amy? We've had a power cut.'

She said, 'I thought we'd had a power cut but then the bus went past with its lights on.'

'Yeah, they plug the buses in now and run a wire around town.'

My mum could be quite sarcastic.

One Christmas Miss Wild got her false teeth stuck on a toffee penny. They're lethal. She was mortified. My dad had to wedge her dentures into the vice on his Black+Decker work bench and prise the toffee off with a chisel.

After dinner, we'd do what everybody else in Britain did and slob out in front of the TV. Uncomfortably full (no, not Pink Floyd). Stuffed with all the trimmings, plenty of chocolate, and guilt. Promising ourselves we'll make a fresh start on a diet again in January. Then ten minutes later, 'Would anybody like some dessert?'

(Pause) 'Go on, I'll have a look.' Then an hour after – 'Anybody for cheese and biscuits?' Perhaps a few grapes on the side for sophistication. You can't stop eating. It's pure gluttony. And you can't do much for the rest of the day because you can't physically move. We'd sit and watch *The Snowman* AGAIN! It was on four times last Christmas.

*The Snowman* is a firm favourite. *The Snow Dog* too. Sometimes they show a weird version of *The Snowman* where David Bowie appears at the beginning introducing the story. Apparently, that was added in at the last minute just so Americans would buy it.

It's bizarre that David Bowie is in the attic, reminiscing as if he's the little boy in the story. (Though I do struggle with the thought of that little boy growing up, dressing like Ziggy Stardust, or rolling around naked on a beach, while having sex and singing 'China Girl'.)

You all must know the story of *The Snowman*. A small boy (let's call him Ziggy) builds a snowman that somehow magically comes to life. Then Ziggy sneaks the Snowman into his house. Where they go upstairs to the parents' bedroom for a bit of cross-dressing (the parents must be deaf, they don't even stir). The next thing the Snowman is pulling Ziggy up the garden, where he lifts him completely off the ground and up into the sky. Cue 'Walking in the Air'. It's a heart-warming moment that never fails to move me (or maybe it's just indigestion).

They both fly to the North Pole to visit the big man himself, Father Christmas. He dishes out presents and then some international snowmen arrive (including a Chinese snowman sporting a triangular bamboo hat and two slanted lines for eyes. That's not aged well). There's much merriment, and a bit of dancing before the Snowman flies them both back home. They have a big hug and say goodnight, and when Ziggy wakes in the morning the Snowman's melted. It's bloody devastating! The credits roll as Ziggy stands in the garden sobbing.

Only in Britain would we have an ending like that. It's probably cost this country millions in child therapy. Kids plagued with abandonment issues for the rest of their lives. While some kids probably can't even pick up a snowball without bursting into tears.

Meanwhile, I look around the front room and nobody's watching telly. They're on their phones, sending 'Merry Christmas' texts filled with festive emojis. Some are sat cross-legged on the floor building LEGO, searching for 'that' missing piece or trying to fathom the instructions to a new board game. Because it wouldn't be Christmas Day without a family argument over a board game. It's the worst time to play. Everybody's ratty and tired.

Parents nod off as soon as they sit down. Spark out on the couch with a lopsided paper hat and biscuit crumbs down their jumpers. And then before you know it Christmas Day is over and we enter a strange shapeless wilderness. The no-man's-land that exists between Christmas and New Year. Crimbo limbo. When time has no meaning, every day feels like a Sunday and nobody knows which wheelie bin to put out ... or when. We just copy the neighbour. The Binfluencer at number 12, and if they get it wrong everyone's knackered.

Then just when you think you've finally reached New Year's Eve you suddenly realise it's only 30 December and you've got another flaming day to go.

Speaking of New Year I forgot to finish off telling you my big firework story, the big rocket we bought on Millenium Eve, the Mother-in-law.

So it was almost midnight, 11.59 to be precise, and we'd planted the Mother-in-law in a bucket of sand outside. We all gathered at the kitchen door. I was still dressed as Gary Glitter, and the nun and the priest were still rowing. The fuse was lit, and we started the countdown but we were so frightened of the explosion we all ran back inside. The Mother-in-law shot off into the sky, so powerful it lifted the bucket of sand up with it. Ten of us got wedged in the kitchen door trying to have a look. We heard a huge explosion but all we managed to see were a few coloured sparks petering out in the sky. What a waste. Then there was an almighty crash as the bucket of sand smashed through the neighbour's conservatory roof. Happy New Year!

So that's Christmas over, everybody's worn out, yet somehow we manage to eat another roast dinner on New Year's Day ... and the last of the dark chocolates at the bottom of the tin. The diet definitely starts Monday (which I'll end up saying every Monday for the rest of the year).

Then it's the worst bit of Christmas for me, the decorations coming down. I have to do it in stages because I can't cope. It's too much. I grieve for Christmas! I have to go cold turkey. Huddled in the corner of the front room with a blanket wrapped around me. The Christmas card washing line is taken down and tiny coloured pegs are all packed away. Cards go in the recycling, except for the special homemade ones we want to keep. Then finally the Christmas tree is taken down and the space it leaves is enormous.

We always say, 'Doesn't it look empty? Didn't we have something else there?'

The walls are as bare as an elephant's arse. All the boxes of festive decorations slowly go back up into the attic one by one. The fairy lights are coiled back in a ball (they'll be a nightmare to untangle next Christmas) and when everything's finally back in its place I whisper a familiar family prayer to the heavens. 'Keep us safe and hold us dear, until Christmas comes again next year.'